Crochet
for Babies™

the Needlecraft Shop

Crochet for Babies™

EDITOR	Bobbie Matela
ART DIRECTOR	Brad Snow
PUBLISHING SERVICES DIRECTOR	Brenda Gallmeyer
ASSOCIATE EDITOR	Mary Ann Frits
ASSISTANT ART DIRECTOR	Nick Pierce
COPY SUPERVISOR	Michelle Beck
COPY EDITORS	Mary O'Donnell, Judy Weatherford
TECHNICAL ARTIST	Connie Rand
GRAPHIC ARTS SUPERVISOR	Ronda Bechinski
GRAPHIC ARTIST	Amy S. Lin
PRODUCTION ASSISTANTS	Marj Morgan, Judy Neuenschwander
PHOTOGRAPHY SUPERVISOR	Tammy Christian
PHOTOGRAPHY	Don Clark, Matthew Owen, Jackie Schaffel
PHOTO STYLISTS	Tammy Nussbaum, Tammy Smith
CHIEF EXECUTIVE OFFICER	David McKee
BOOK MARKETING DIRECTOR	Dwight Seward

FIRST PRINTING 2007
LIBRARY OF CONGRESS NUMBER 2006928387
HARDCOVER ISBN 978-1-57367-259-7
SOFTCOVER ISBN 978-1-57367-261-0
Printed in China

1 2 3 4 5 6 7 8 9

Welcome!

Babies are the perfect excuse for keeping our crochet hooks in motion. While we anticipate the birth of the next new child, we feel excited, but the wait can have its anxious moments. Spending the time creating unique sweaters, blankets and other special crochet finery makes the time go by more quickly, may calm nerves, and with the designs in this sparkling collection, will express your love.

You'll find clever ideas especially for newborns in the Hello, Little One chapter and wonderful gift blankets in the Wrapped in Love chapter.

If you know it's a girl, check out Sugar n' Spice Baby Girls. Or if a boy is in your future, see the unique styles for Bouncing Baby Boys.

Find two heavenly outfits to dress your little angel in a Cherub Christening.

For ages 2 to 4 active babes, look to our Toddler Town for fashionable options.

With warm thoughts,

Bobbie Matela

Contents

Hello, Little One

Wrapped In Love

Sugar & Spice Baby Girls

Cherub Christening

Toddler Town

Bouncing Baby Boys

Hello, Little One

While waiting for baby, make
these booties, hats, sweaters,
homecoming outfits and more.

Pleasant Dreams

Design by Anita Closic

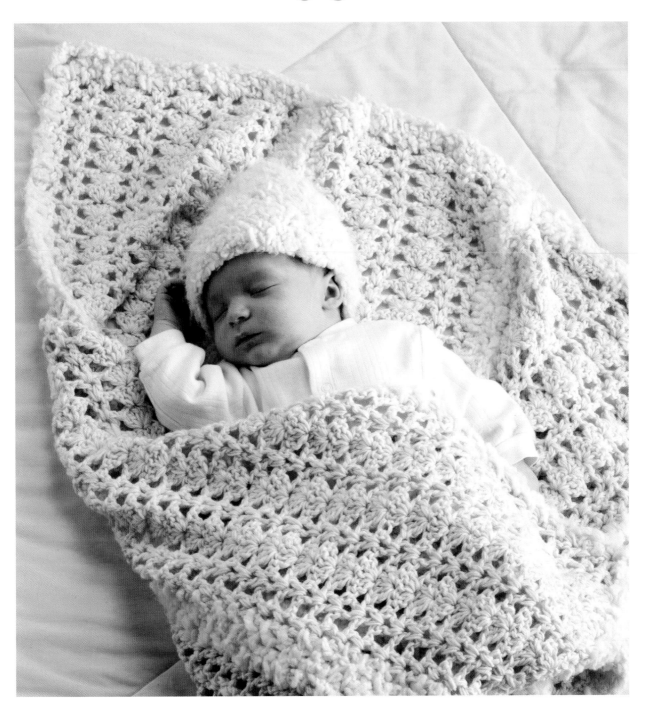

FINISHED SIZES
Afghan: approximately 32 x 30 inches

Hat: 18 inches in circumference

MATERIALS
- Plymouth Dreambaby DK light (light worsted) weight yarn (1¾ oz/183 yds/50g per ball): 10 balls #204 baby variegated (A)
- Plymouth Heaven super bulky (super chunky) weight yarn (1¾ oz/55 yds/50g per ball): 4 balls #114 variegated (B)
- Sizes H/8/5mm, I/9/5.5mm and L/11/8mm crochet hooks or size needed to obtain gauge
- Tapestry needle

GAUGE
Size H hook and 2 strands of A:
1 shell = 1½ inches

Take time to check gauge.

SPECIAL STITCHES
V-stitch (V-st): In st indicated work (dc, ch 1, dc).
Shell: In st indicated work 5 dc.

Instructions

AFGHAN
END PANEL
MAKE 2.
Foundation row (RS): With H hook and 2 strands of A held tog, ch 29; dc in 5th ch from hook (*beg 4 sk chs count as a dc and a ch-1 sp*), ch 1, sk next 2 chs, in next ch work **V-st** (*see Special Stitches*); *ch 1, sk next 2 chs, in next ch work **shell** (*see Special Stitches*); sk next 2 chs, V-st in next ch; rep from * twice; ch 1, sk next 2 chs, V-st in last ch, turn.

Row 1: Ch 4 (*counts as a dc and a ch-1 sp on this and following rows*), dc in next ch-1 sp, ch 1, V-st in ch 1 sp of next V-st; ch 1; * shell in 3rd dc of next shell; V-st in ch-1 sp of next V-st; rep from * twice; ch 1, V-st in sp formed by beg 4 sk chs, turn.

Row 2: Ch 4, dc in next ch-1 sp, ch 1, V-st in ch 1 sp of next V-st; ch 1; * shell in 3rd dc of next shell; V-st in ch-1 sp of next V-st; rep from * twice; ch 1, V-st in sp formed by turning ch-4, turn.

Rows 3–54: Rep row 2.

Fasten off.

BORDER
Hold piece with RS facing you

and last row worked at top; with L hook, join B with sl st in first st in upper right-hand corner; ch 1, sc evenly around sides; join in first sc.

Fasten off and weave in all ends.

CENTER PANEL
Foundation row (WS): With H hook and 2 strands of A held tog, ch 24; dc in 5th ch from hook *(beg 4 sk chs count as a dc and a ch-1 sp)*, ch 1, sk next 2 chs, V-st in next ch, ch 1; *sk next 2 chs, shell in next ch, ch 1, sk next 2 chs, V-st in next ch; rep from * once; sk next 2 chs, V-st in last ch, turn.

Row 1 (RS): Ch 4 *(counts as a dc and a ch-1 sp on this and following rows)*, dc in next ch-1 sp, ch 1, V-st in ch 1 sp of next V-st; ch 1; * shell in 3rd dc of next shell; V-st in ch-1 sp of next V-st; rep from * once; ch 1, V-st in sp formed by beg 4 sk chs, turn.

Row 2: Ch 4, dc in next ch-1 sp, ch 1, V-st in ch 1 sp of next V-st; ch 1; * shell in 3rd dc of next shell; V-st in ch-1 sp of next V-st; rep from * once; ch 1, V-st in sp formed by turning ch-4, turn.

Rows 3–54: Rep row 2.

Fasten off.

BORDER
Work same as Border for Panel.

ASSEMBLY
Hold 1 long side of 1 End Panel and corresponding long side of 1 Center Panel with WS tog; with L hook and working through

both thicknesses at same time, join B with sl st in first st in upper right-hand corner; ch 1, sc in same st and in each st across side. Fasten off. Rep with other End Panel, joining long side of End Panel with unworked long side of Center.

TOP BORDER
Hold afghan with 1 short end at top; with L hook, join B in first st in upper right-hand corner; sc evenly across side. Fasten off. Rep on opposite short end.

Weave in all ends.

HAT
Row 1 (RS): With I hook and B, ch 21; sc in 2nd ch from hook and in each rem ch, turn. *(20 sc)*

Row 2: Ch 1, sc in each sc, turn.

Rep row 2 until piece measures 4 inches.

Next row: Ch 1, **sc dec** *(see Stitch Guide)* in first 2 sc; [sc dec in next 2 sc] 9 times, turn. *(10 sc)*

Next row: Ch 1, sc in first sc, [sc dec] twice; sc in next sc, [sc dec] twice. *(6 sc)*

Fasten off, leaving long end for sewing. Weave in other end.

FINISHING
With tapestry needle, weave long end through sc of last row. Gather sts and secure end. With B, sew side seam.

Soft Shells Layette

Design by Karen Whooley

SKILL LEVEL
■■■□ INTERMEDIATE

FINISHED SIZES
Instructions for Sweater, Hat and Booties fit sizes 3– 6 months; changes for 9–12 months and 18–24 months are in [ ].

FINISHED GARMENT MEASUREMENTS
Chest: 17 [18, 20] inches

Hat:15 [17, 19]-inch circumference

Booties: 4 [5, 6] inches long

Afghan: approximately 33 x 38 inches

MATERIALS
• Light (light worsted) weight yarn:
   21 [25, 28] oz (1,890 [2,250, 2,520] yds, 595 [709, 794]g) white/pink/purple variegated
• Sizes G/6/4mm and H/8/5mm crochet hooks or sizes needed to obtain gauge
• Tapestry needle
• Stitch markers
• 3 [3, 4] ⅞-inch matching buttons
• Sewing needle and matching thread

GAUGE
Size G hook: 14 dc = 4 inches
Size H hook: 12 sc = 4 inches

Take time to check gauge.

SPECIAL STITCH
Shell: 5 dc in st indicated.

Instructions

SWEATER
BODY
Row 1: Starting at neck edge with H hook, ch 40 [44, 48]; sc in 2nd ch from hook and in each rem ch, turn. *(39 [43, 47] sc)*

Row 2: Ch 1, sc in first 6 [7, 8] sc, 2 sc in each of next 2 sc; sc in next 3 sc, 2 sc in each of next 2 sc; sc in next 13 [15, 17] sc, 2 sc in each of next 2 sc; sc in next 3 sc, 2 sc in each of next 2 sc; sc in last 6 [7, 8] sc, turn. *(47 [51, 55] sc)*

Row 3: Ch 1, sc in each sc, turn.

Row 4: Ch 1, sc in first 7 [8, 9] sc, 2 sc in each of next 2 sc; sc in next 5 sc, 2 sc in each of next 2 sc; sc in next 15 [17, 19] sc, 2 sc in each of next 2 sc; sc in next 5 sc, 2 sc in each of next 2 sc; sc in last 7 [8, 9] sc, turn. *(55 [59, 63] sc)*

Row 5: Rep row 3.

Row 6: Ch 1, sc in first 8 [9, 10] sc, 2 sc in each of next 2 sc; sc in next 7 sc, 2 sc in each of next 2 sc; sc in next 17 [19, 21] sc, 2 sc in each of next 2 sc; sc in next 7 sc, 2 sc in each of next 2 sc; sc in last 8 sc, turn. *(63 [67, 71] sc)*

Row 7: Rep row 3.

Row 8: Ch 1, sc in first 9 [10, 11] sc, 2 sc in each of next 2 sc; sc in next 9 sc, 2 sc in each of next 2 sc; sc in next 19 [21, 23] sc, 2 sc in each of next 2 sc; sc in next 9 sc, 2 sc in each of next 2 sc; sc in last 9 [10, 11] sc, turn. *(71 [75, 79] sc)*

Row 9: Rep row 3.

Row 10: Ch 1, sc in first 10 [11, 12] sc, 2 sc in each of next 2 sc; sc in next 11 sc, 2 sc in each of next 2 sc; sc in next 21 [23, 25] sc, 2 sc in each of next 2 sc; sc in next 11 sc, 2 sc in each of next 2 sc; sc in last 10 [11, 12] sc, turn. *(79 [83, 87] sc)*

Row 11: Rep row 3.

Row 12: Ch 1, sc in first 11 [12, 13] sc, 2 sc in each of next 2 sc; sc in next 13 sc, 2 sc in each of next 2 sc; sc in next 23 [25, 27] sc, 2 sc in each of next 2 sc; sc in next 13 sc, 2 sc in each of next 2 sc; sc in last 11 [12, 13] sc, turn. *(87 [91, 95] sc)*

Row 13: Rep row 3.

Row 14: Ch 1, sc in first 12 [13, 14] sc, 2 sc in each of next 2 sc; sc in next 15 sc, 2 sc in each of next 2 sc; sc in next 25 [27, 29] sc, 2 sc in each of next 2 sc; sc in next 15 sc, 2 sc in each of next 2 sc; sc in last 12 [13, 14] sc, turn. *(95 [99, 103] sc)*

Row 15: Rep row 3.

Row 16: Ch 1, sc in first 13 [14, 15] sc, 2 sc in each of next 2 sc; sc in next 17 sc, 2 sc in each of next 2 sc; sc in next 27 [29, 31] sc, 2 sc in each of next 2 sc; sc in next 17 sc, 2 sc in each of next 2 sc; sc in

last 13 [14, 15] sc, turn. (103 [107, 111] sc)

Row 17: Rep row 3.

For Size 3-6 Months Only
Continue with For All Sizes.

For Size 9-12 Months Only
Row 18: Ch 1, sc in first 15 sc, 2 sc in each of next 2 sc; sc in next 19 sc, 2 sc in each of next 2 sc; sc in next 31 sc, 2 sc in each of next 2 sc; sc in next 19 sc, 2 sc in each of next 2 sc; sc in last 15 sc, turn. (115 sc)

Row 19: Rep row 3.

Continue with For All Sizes.

For Size 18-24 Months Only
Row 18: Sc in first 16 sc, 2 sc in each of next 2 sc; sc in next 19 sc, 2 sc in each of next 2 sc; sc in next 33 sc, 2 sc in each of next 2 sc; sc in next 19 sc, 2 sc in each of next 2 sc; sc in last 16 sc, turn. (119 sc)

Row 19: Rep row 3.

Row 20: Ch 1, sc in first 17 sc, 2 sc in each of next 2 sc; sc in next 21 sc, 2 sc in each of next 2 sc; sc in next 35 sc, 2 sc in each of next 2 sc; sc in next 21 sc, 2 sc in each of next 2 sc; sc in last 17 sc, turn. (127 sc)

Row 21: Rep row 3.

Continue with For All Sizes.

For All Sizes
Row 18 [20, 22]: Ch 1, sc in first 15 [17, 19] sc, ch 5 [6, 7]—*underarm made;* sk next 21 [23, 25] sc, sc in next 31 [35, 39] sc, ch 5 [6, 7]—*underarm made;* sk next 21 [23, 25] sc, sc in last 15 [17, 19] sc, turn.

Row 19 [21, 23]: Ch 1, sc in each sc and in each ch, turn. (71 [81, 91] sc)

Row 20 [22, 24]: Ch 3 (counts as a dc on this and following rows), 2 dc in first sc; *sk next 4 sc, in next sc work **shell** (see Special Stitch); rep from * to last 5 sc; sk next 4 sc, 3 dc in last sc, turn. (13 [15, 17] shells)

Row 21 [23, 25]: Ch 3, dc in each dc and in 3rd ch of turning ch-3, turn.

Row 22 [24, 26]: Ch 3, 2 dc in first dc; *sk next 4 dc, shell in next dc; rep from * to last 4 dc and turning ch-3; sk last 4 dc, 3 dc in 3rd ch of turning ch-3; turn.

Rows 23–28 [25–32, 27–36]: [Work rows 21 and 22 [23 and 24, 25 and 26]] 3 [4, 5] times.

Fasten off and weave in ends.

SLEEVE
MAKE 2.
Rnd 1: Hold Body with RS facing you; join yarn with sl st in 3rd [3rd, 4th] ch of 1 underarm; ch 3,

4 dc in same sc; working around armhole opening, sk next 4 sts; *shell in next st; sk next 4 sts; rep from * around; join with sl st in 3rd ch of beg ch-3, turn. *(6 [7, 8] shells)*

Rnd 2: Ch 3, dc in each dc; join with sl st in 3rd ch of beg ch-3; turn. *(30 [35, 40] dc)*

Rnd 3: Sl st in next 2 dc; ch 3, 4 dc in same dc as last sl st made; *sk next 4 dc, shell in next dc; rep from * around; join with sl st in 3rd ch of beg ch-3.

Rnds 4–9 [4–11, 4–13]: [Work rnds 2 and 3] 3 [4, 5] times.

Fasten off and weave in ends.

Work 2nd Sleeve in same manner in rem armhole.

BUTTONHOLE PLACKET & NECK EDGING
Row 1 (RS): Hold Body with RS facing you, right-front edge at top; with G hook, join yarn with

sl st in sp formed by edge st of last row of Body; ch 1, 2 sc in same sp; working across front edge in sps formed by edge sts of rows, 2 sc in each of next 8 [12, 16] rows; sc in sps between sc rows to next corner; 3 sc in corner—*corner made;* working across neck edge in unused lps of beg ch, sc in each lp; 3 sc in next corner—*corner made;* working across left edge, sc in sps between sc rows; working in sps formed by edge sts of rem 19 [13, 17] rows, 2 sc in each sp, turn. *(115 [147, 163] sc)*

Row 2: Ch 1, sc in each sc to 2nd sc of next corner; 3 sc in 2nd sc; sc in each sc to next corner; 3 sc in 2nd sc; *ch 2—*buttonhole made;* sk next sc, sc in next 4 sc; rep from * 2 [2, 3] times; sc in rem sc, turn.

Row 3: Ch 1, sc in each sc and in

each ch-2 sp and 3 sc in 2nd sc of each corner.

Fasten off and weave in ends.

FINISHING
With sewing needle and matching thread, sew buttons opposite buttonholes.

HAT
Rnd 1: With G hook, ch 4; 9 dc in 4th ch from hook *(beg 3 sk chs count as a dc);* join with sl st in 3rd ch of beg 3 sk chs. *(10 dc)*

Rnd 2: Ch 3 *(counts as a dc on this and following rnds)*, dc in same ch as joining; 2 dc in each rem dc; join with sl st in 3rd ch of beg ch-3. *(20 dc)*

Rnd 3: Ch 3, 2 dc in next dc; *dc in next dc, 2 dc in next dc; rep from * around; join with sl st in 3rd ch of beg ch-3. *(30 dc)*

Rnd 4: Ch 3, dc in next dc, 2 dc in next dc; *dc in next 2 dc, 2 dc in next dc; rep from * around; join with sl st in 3rd ch of beg ch-3. *(40 dc)*

Rnd 5: Ch 3, dc in next 2 dc, 2 dc in next dc; *dc in next 3 dc, 2 dc in next dc; rep from * around; join

with sl st in 3rd ch of beg ch-3. *(50 dc)*

For Size 3-6 Months Only
Continue with For All Sizes.

For Size 9-12 Months Only
Rnd 6: Ch 3, dc in next 3 dc, 2 dc in next dc; *dc in next 4 dc, 2 dc in next dc; rep from * around; join with sl st in 3rd ch of beg ch-3. *(60 dc)*

Continue with For All Sizes.

For Size 18-24 Months Only
Rnd 6: Ch 3, dc in next 3 dc, 2 dc in next dc; *dc in next 4 dc, 2 dc in next dc; rep from * around; join with sl st in 3rd ch of beg ch-3. *(60 dc)*

Rnd 7: Ch 3, dc in next 4 dc, 2 dc in next dc; *dc in next 5 dc, 2 dc in next dc; rep from * around; join with sl st in 3rd ch of beg ch-3. *(70 dc)*

Continue with For All Sizes.

For All Sizes
Rnd 6 [7, 8]: Ch 3, 4 dc in same ch as joining—*beg shell made;* *sk next 4 dc, shell in next dc; rep from * around; join with sl st in 3rd ch of beg ch-3, turn. *(10 [12, 14] shells)*

Rnd 7 [8, 9]: Ch 3, dc in each dc;

join with sl st in 3rd ch of beg ch-3, turn. *(50 [60, 70] dc)*

Rnd 8 [9, 10]: Sl st in next 2 dc; ch 3, 4 dc in same dc as last sl st made; sk next 4 dc; *shell in next dc; sk next 4 dc; rep from * around; join with sl st in 3rd ch of beg ch-3.

Fasten off and weave in ends.

BOOTIE
MAKE 2.
Row 1: With H hook, ch 6; sc in 2nd ch from hook and in each rem ch, turn. *(5 sc)*

Row 2: Ch 1, sc in each sc, turn.

Rows 3 & 4: Rep row 2.

Row 5: Ch 1, sc in each sc; ch 17 [21, 25]; join with sc in first sc.

Note: *Mark 9th [11th, 13th] ch for cuff placement. Rem of Bootie is worked in rnds.*

Rnd 1: Ch 1, working along next side, sc in sps between rows; working across next side in unused lps of beg ch, sc in each lp; working across next side, sc in sps between rows; sc in side of last sc row and in next 17 [21, 25] chs; join with sl st in **back lp** *(see Stitch Guide)* of last sc on row 5. *(32 [36, 40] sc)*

Rnd 2: Ch 1, working in back lps only, sc in same lp as joining and in each rem sc; join with sl st in first sc.

Rnd 3: Ch 1, sc in same sc and in each rem sc; join with sl st in first sc.

Rnd(s) 4 [4, 4–6]: Rep rnd 3.

Rnd 5 [5, 7]: Ch 1, sc in same sc and in each rem sc; join with sl st in back lp of first sc.

Rnd 6 [6, 8]: Ch 1, working in

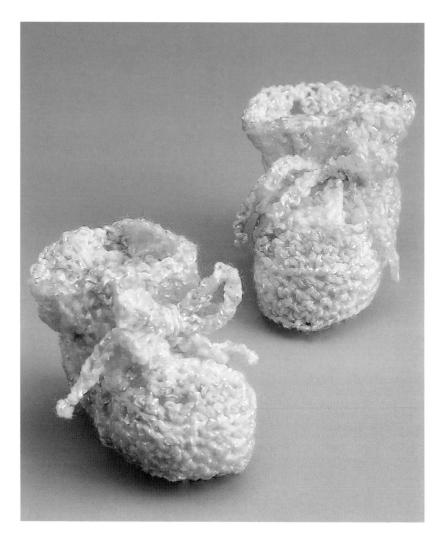

back lps only, sc in same lp as joining and in next 3 sc; **sc dec** *(see Stitch Guide)* in next 2 sc; sc in next 4 sc, sc dec in next 2 sc; sc in next 8 [10, 12] sc; *sc dec in next 2 sc, sc in next 4 [5, 6] sc; rep from * once; join with sl st in first sc. *(28 [32, 36] sc)*

Rnd 7 [7, 9]: Ch 1, sc in same sc and in next 3 sc; sc dec; sc in next 3 sc, sc dec; sc in next 7 [9, 11] sc; *sc dec, sc in next 3 [4, 5] sc; rep from * once; join with sl st in first sc; ch 1; sc in same st as joining and in first 5 sc of rnd, sl st in next sc.

Fasten off, leaving a 6-inch end for sewing.

ASSEMBLY
With tapestry needle and long end, sew bottom seam.

CUFF
Rnd 1: Hold piece with RS facing you; join yarn with sl st in unused lp of marked ch; ch 4 *(counts as a dc and a ch-1 sp)*, dc in same lp; ch 1; working in rem unused lps of ch-17 and rem sts; *sk next st, dc in next st, ch 1; rep from * around; join with sl st to 3rd ch of beg ch. *(12 [14, 16] dc)*

For Sizes 3-6 Months & 9–12 Months Only
Rnd 2: Ch 1, 2 [3] sc in first ch-1 sp; sc in each dc and in each rem ch-1 sp; join with sl st in first sc. *(24 [29] sc)*

Continue with For All Sizes.

For Size 18-24 Months Only
Rnd 2: Ch 1, 2 sc in next ch-1 sp; *sc in next dc, sc in next ch-1 sp; rep from * to last dc and ch-1 sp; sc in last dc, 2 sc in last ch-1 sp; join with sl st in first sc. *(34 sc)*

Continue with For All Sizes.

For All Sizes
Rnd 3: Ch 3, 4 dc in same sc; *sk 4 sc, shell in next sc; rep from * to last 3 sc; sk last 3 sc; join with sl st in 3rd ch of beg ch-3.

Fasten off and weave in ends.

TIE
MAKE 2.
Ch 90 [100, 110]. Fasten off and weave in ends.

FINISHING
Weave 1 Tie through ch-1 sps on rnd 1 of Cuff. Tie in bow. Rep on other Cuff with rem Tie. Tie knots at ends of Ties to secure.

AFGHAN
Row 1 (WS): With H hook, ch 104; 2 dc in 4th ch from hook *(beg 3 sk chs count as a dc)*, *sk next 4 chs, in next ch work **shell** *(see Special Stitches)*; rep from * to last 5 chs; sk next 4 chs, 3 dc in last ch, turn. *(19 shells)*

Row 2 (RS): Ch 3 *(counts as a dc on this and following rows)*, dc in each rem dc and in 3rd ch of beg 3 sk chs, turn. *(101 dc)*

Row 3: Ch 3, 2 dc in first dc; sk next 4 dc, shell in next dc; rep from * to last 4 dc and turning ch-3; sk last 4 dc, 3 dc in 3rd ch of beg ch-3, turn.

Rows 4–51: [Work rows 2 and 3] 24 times.

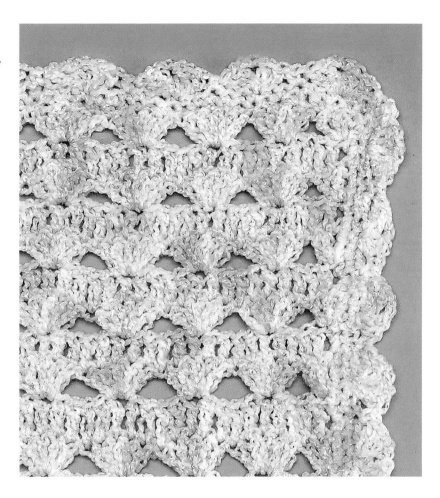

EDGING
Rnd 1: Ch 1, 3 sc in first dc—*corner made;* sc in next 97 dc, 3 sc in next dc—*corner made;* working across next side in ends of rows, work 146 sc evenly spaced; working across next side in unused lps of beg ch, 3 sc in first lp—*corner made;* sc in next 97 lps, 3 sc in last lp—*corner made;* working across next side in ends of rows, work 146 sc evenly spaced; join with sl st in first sc. *(498 sc)*

Rnd 2: Ch 1, sc in same sc; *3 sc in next sc—*corner made;* sc in next 99 sc, 3 sc in next sc—*corner made;* sc in next 148 sc, 3 sc in next sc—*corner made;* sc in next 99 sc, 3 sc in next sc—*corner made;* sc in next 147 sc; join with sl st in first sc. *(506 sc)*

Rnd 3: Sl st in next 2 sc, ch 1, [sc in next sc, sk next 2 sc, shell in next sc; sk next 2 sc] 17 times; sc in next 3 sc, sk next 2 sc, shell in next sc; sk next 2 sc, [sc in next sc, sk next 2 sc, shell in next sc, sk next 2 sc] 24 times; sc in next 3 sc, sk next 2 sc, shell in next sc; sk next 2 sc, [sc in next sc, sk next 2 sc, shell in next sc, sk next 2 sc] 16 times; sc in next 3 sc, sk next 2 sc, shell in next sc; sk next 2 sc, [sc in next sc, sk next 2 sc, shell in next sc, sk next 2 sc] 24 times; sc in next 2 sc; join with sl st in first sc.

Fasten off and weave in ends.

Pretty Floral Overalls

Design by Tamara Gonzales

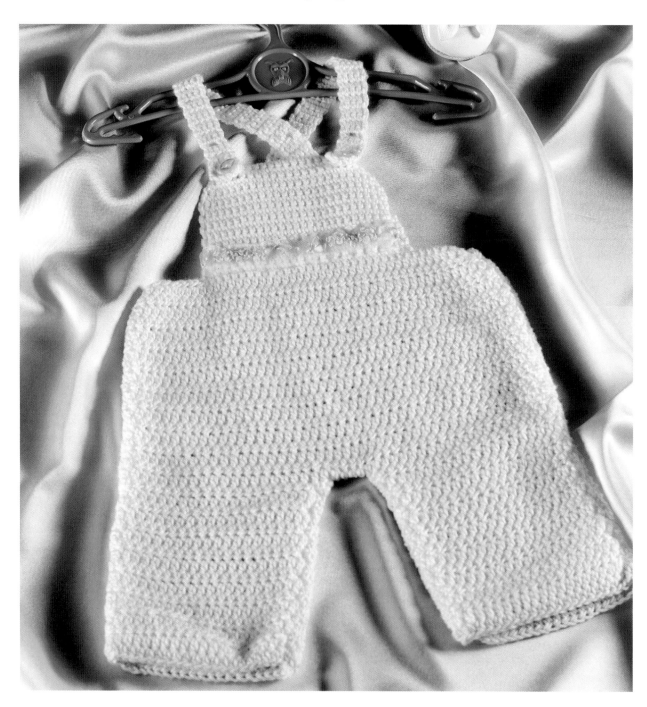

FINISHED SIZES
Instructions given fit child's size 3 months, 6–12 months and 18–24 months. Hook size determines garment finished size. Information for larger sizes is in [ ].

FINISHED GARMENT MEASUREMENTS
Waist: 15 [18, 22] inches

MATERIALS
- DMC Senso Microfiber size 3 crochet cotton (178 yds):
  3 [3, 4] balls #1101 white *(A)*
  2 yds #1104 pink *(B)*
- Size 1/2.25mm steel crochet hook or size needed to obtain gauge (for size 3 months)
- Size 00/2.70mm steel crochet hook or size needed to obtain gauge (for size 6–12 months)
- Size F/5/3.75mm crochet hook or size needed to obtain gauge (for size 18–24 months)
- Tapestry needle
- 2 white ½-inch buttons
- 5½ [6, 6½] inches white lace trim
- Sewing needle and matching thread

GAUGE
Size 1 hook: 6 hdc = 1 inch
Size 0 hook: 5 hdc = 1 inch
Size 00 hook: 4 hdc = 1 inch

Take time to check gauge.

Instructions

Note: Overalls are worked with hook specified for desired size.

FRONT
Row 1 (RS): Beg at top with A, ch 19; sc in 2nd ch from hook and in each rem ch, turn. *(18 sc)*

Row 2: Ch 1, 2 sc in first sc; sc in next 16 sc, 2 sc in last sc, turn. *(20 sc)*

Row 3: Ch 1, 2 sc in first sc, sc in each sc to last sc; 2 sc in last sc, turn. *(22 sc)*

Row 4: Rep row 3. *(24 sc)*

Row 5: Ch 1, sc in each sc, turn.

Row 6: Rep row 3. *(26 sc)*

Rows 7–20 [7–23, 7–20]: Rep row 5.

Row 21 [24, 21]: Ch 11, sc in 2nd ch from hook, in next 9 chs, and in each sc; hdc in end of last sc just made, [hdc in end of hdc just made] 9 times, turn. *(46 sts)*

For Sizes 3 Months & 6–12 Months Only
Row 22 [25]: Ch 2 *(counts as a hdc on this and following rows)*, hdc in each rem st, turn. *(46 hdc)*

Row 23 [26]: Ch 2, hdc in first hdc and in each rem hdc to turning ch-2; 2 hdc in 2nd ch of turning ch-2, turn. *(48 hdc)*

Row 24 [27]: Ch 2, hdc in first hdc and in each rem hdc to turning ch-2; 2 hdc in 2nd ch of turning ch-2, turn. *(50 hdc)*

Row 25 [28]: Ch 2, hdc in each rem hdc and in 2nd ch of turning ch-2, turn.

Rows 26–40 [29–40]: Rep row 25 [28].

RIGHT LEG
Row 41: Ch 2, sk first hdc, hdc in next 22 sts, turn, leaving rem sts unworked. *(23 hdc)*

Row 42: Ch 2, sk first hdc, hdc in each rem hdc, turn.

Rows 43–56: Rep row 42. Fasten off.

LEFT LEG
Row 1: Sk next 4 sts on row 41 from Right Leg; join A with sl st in next st; ch 2, hdc in next 22 sts, turn. *(23 hdc)*

Row 2: Ch 2, sk first hdc, hdc in each rem hdc, turn.

Rows 3–16: Rep row 2. Fasten off.

Continue with Back.

For Size 18–24 Months Only
Row 22: Ch 1, sc in each st, turn. *(46 sc)*

Row 23: Ch 1, 2 sc in first sc; sc in each rem sc to last sc; 2 sc in last sc, turn. *(48 sc)*

Row 24: Rep row 22. *(50 sc)*

Row 25: Ch 1, sc in each sc, turn.

Rows 26–50: Rep row 25.

RIGHT LEG
Row 51: Ch 1, sc in next 23 sts, turn. *(23 sc)*

Row 52: Ch 1, sc in each sc, turn.

Rows 53–84: Rep row 2. Fasten off.

LEFT LEG
Row 1: Sk next 4 sts on row 50 from Right Leg; join A with sl st in next st; ch 1, sc in same st and in next 22 sts, turn. *(23 sc)*

Row 2: Ch 1, sc in each sc, turn.

Rows 3–34: Rep row 2. Fasten off.

Continue with Back.

BACK
Row 1: With A, ch 19; sc in 2nd ch from hook and in each rem sc, turn. *(18 sc)*

Row 2: Ch 1, 2 sc in first sc; sc in next 16 sc, 2 sc in last sc, turn. *(20 sc)*

Row 3: Ch 1, 2 sc in first sc, sc in each sc to last sc; 2 sc in last sc, turn. *(22 sc)*

Row 4: Rep row 3. *(24 sc)*

Row 5: Ch 1, sc in each sc, turn.

Row 6: Rep row 3. *(26 sc)*

Rows 7–12 [7–15, 7–12]: Rep row 5.

Row 13 [16, 13]: Ch 11, sc in 2nd ch from hook, in next 9 chs, and in each sc; hdc in end of last sc just made, [hdc in end of hdc just made] 9 times, turn. *(46 sts)*

For Sizes 3 Months & 6–12 Months Only
Row 14 [17]: Ch 2 *(counts as a hdc on this and following rows)*, hdc in each rem st, turn. *(46 hdc)*

Row 15 [18]: Ch 2, hdc in first hdc and in each rem hdc to turning ch-2; 2 hdc in 2nd ch of turning ch-2, turn. *(48 hdc)*

Row 16 [19]: Ch 2, hdc in first hdc and in each rem hdc to turning ch-2; 2 hdc in 2nd ch of turning ch-2, turn. *(50 hdc)*

Row 17 [20]: Ch 2, hdc in each

rem hdc and in 2nd ch of turning ch-2, turn.

Rows 18–32 [21–32]: Rep row 17 [20].

RIGHT LEG
Row 33: Ch 2, sk first hdc, hdc in next 22 sts, turn, leaving rem sts unworked. *(23 hdc)*

Row 34: Ch 2, sk first hdc, hdc in each rem hdc, turn.

Rows 35–49: Rep row 34. Fasten off.

LEFT LEG
Row 1: Sk next 4 sts on row 32 from Right Leg; join A with sl st in next st; ch 2, hdc in next 22 sts, turn. *(23 hdc)*

Row 2: Ch 2, sk first hdc, hdc in each rem hdc, turn.

Rows 3–17: Rep row 2. Fasten off.

Continue with Strap.

For Size 18–24 Months Only
Row 14: Ch 1, sc in each st, turn. *(46 sc)*

Row 15: Ch 1, 2 sc in first sc; sc in each rem sc to last sc; 2 sc in last sc, turn. *(48 sc)*

Row 16: Rep row 15. *(50 sc)*

Row 17: Ch 1, sc in each sc, turn.

Rows 18–42: Rep row 17.

RIGHT LEG
Row 19: Ch 1, sc in next 23 sts, turn. *(23 sc)*

Row 20: Ch 1, sc in each sc, turn.

Rows 21–52: Rep row 20. Fasten off.

LEFT LEG
Row 1: Sk next 4 sts on row 18 from Right Leg; join A with sl st in

next st; ch 1, sc in same st and in next 22 sts, turn. *(23 sc)*

Row 2: Ch 1, sc in each sc, turn.

Rows 3–35: Rep row 2. Fasten off.

Continue with Strap.

STRAP
MAKE 2.
Row 1: With A, ch 5; sc in 2nd ch from hook and in each rem ch, turn. *(4 sc)*

Row 2: Ch 1, sc in each sc, turn.

Row 3: Ch 1, sc in first sc, ch 2—*buttonhole made*; sk next 2 sc, sc in last sc, turn.

Row 4: Ch 1, sc in first sc, 2 sc in next ch 2 sp; sc in last sc, turn.

Rows 5–7: Rep row 2.

Rows 8 & 9: Rep rows 3 and 4.

Rep row 2 until strap measures 9 [10, 11] inches from beg.

Fasten off and weave in ends.

ASSEMBLY
Hold RS of Front and Back tog. Sew side seams and crotch seams. Sew Straps to Back, leaving buttonhole edge unsewn. Criss-cross Straps in back and tack at crossing. Sew buttons to Front. Referring to photo for placement, sew ribbon trim to Front.

LEG EDGING
Hold 1 Leg with opening at top; join B in 1 seam; ch 1, sc in same sp and in each st around; join with sl st in first sc.

Fasten off and weave in ends.

Rep on rem Leg.

Ruffled Dress-Up Set

Design by Peggy Longshore

SKILL LEVEL

INTERMEDIATE

FINISHED SIZES
Instructions for Dress, Panties, Beret and Booties fit 3–6 months or 6–12 months, according to size of hook used.

FINISHED GARMENT MEASUREMENTS
Chest: 32½ [34] inches

Beret: 15 [16]-inch circumference

Booties: 9 [9½] inches long

Afghan: approximately 34 inches in diameter

MATERIALS

- Bernat Baby Coordinates light (light worsted) weight yarn (6 oz/471 yds/170g per ball): 4 skeins #01001 pink
- Size H/8/5mm crochet hook or size needed to obtain gauge (for size 3–6 months and afghan)
- Size I/9/5.5mm crochet hook or size needed to obtain gauge (for size 9–12 months)
- Tapestry needle
- 6 light pink 1-inch organza flowers with white pearl centers
- Sewing needle and matching thread
- Liquid seam sealant (optional)

GAUGE
Size H hook: 7 dc = 2 inches
Size I hook: 10 dc = 3 inches

Take time to check gauge.

SPECIAL STITCH
Cluster (cl): Keeping last lp of each dc on hook, dc in 3 sts indicated; yo and draw through all 4 lps on hook.

Instructions

Note: Dress, Panties, Beret and Booties are worked with hook specified for desired size.

DRESS
Row 1 (RS): Starting at neckline, ch 32; dc in 4th ch from hook *(beg 3 sk chs count as a dc)*; *ch 1, ch 1, dc in next 2 chs; rep from * across, turn. *(30 dc)*

Row 2: Ch 3 *(counts as a dc on this and following rows)*, dc in next dc; *2 dc in next ch-1 sp; dc in next 2 dc; rep from * last ch-1 sp; 2 dc in last ch-1 sp; dc in next dc and in 3rd ch of beg 3 sk chs, turn. *(58 dc)*

Row 3: Ch 3, dc in next dc; *ch 1, dc in next 2 dc; rep from * to last dc and turning ch; ch 1, dc in last dc and in 3rd ch of turning ch-3, turn. *(58 dc)*

Row 4: Ch 3, dc in next dc; *2 dc in next ch-1 sp; dc in next 2 dc; rep from * to last ch-1 sp; 2 dc in last ch-1 sp; dc in next dc and in 3rd ch of turning ch-3, turn. *(114 dc)*

Row 5: Ch 3, dc in each dc and in 3rd ch of turning ch-3, turn.

Row 6: Rep row 5.

Row 7: Ch 3, dc in next dc; *ch 1, dc in next 2 dc; rep from * to last dc and turning ch-3; ch 1, dc in last dc and in 3rd ch of turning ch-3, turn. *(114 dc)*

Row 8: Ch 3, dc in next dc, 2 dc in next ch-1 sp; [dc in next 2 dc, 2 dc in next ch-1 sp] 7 times; sk next 12 ch-1 sps—*armhole opening made;* 2 dc in next ch-1 sp; [dc in next 2 dc, 2 dc in next ch-1 sp] 15 times; sk next 12 ch-1 sps—*armhole opening made;* [2 dc in next ch-1 sp, dc in next 2 dc] 7 times; 2 dc in next ch-1 sp; dc in next dc and in 3rd ch of turning ch-3, turn. *(126 dc)*

Note: *Rem dress is worked in rnds.*

Rnd 1: Ch 3, dc in each dc and in 3rd ch of turning ch-3; join with sl st in 3rd ch of turning ch-3.

Rnd 2: Ch 3, dc in each dc; join with sl st in 3rd ch of beg ch-3.

Rnds 3 & 4: Rep rnd 2.

Rnd 5: Ch 3, dc in next dc, ch 1; *dc in next 2 dc, ch 1; rep from * around; join with sl st in 3rd ch of beg ch-3. *(126 dc)*

Rnd 6: Ch 3, dc in next dc, 2 dc in next ch-1 sp; *dc in next 2 dc; 2 dc in next ch-1 sp; rep from * around; join with sl st in 3rd ch of beg ch-3. *(252 dc)*

Rnds 7–12: Rep rnd 2.

Rnd 13: Ch 1, sc in same ch as joining and in next dc, ch 3, sk next dc; *sc in next 2 dc, ch 3, sk next dc; rep from * around; join with sl st in first sc. *(168 sc)*

Rnd 14: Sl st in next sc and in next ch-3 sp; ch 1, in same sp and in each rem ch-3 sp work (sc, 3 dc, sc); join with sl st in first sc.

Fasten off and weave in ends.

SLEEVE
MAKE 2.

Rnd 1 (RS): Hold piece with RS facing you; join yarn with sl st around **post** *(see Stitch Guide)* of dc of row 8 at bottom of 1 armhole opening; ch 3, dc around post of same dc; working in sk sts of row 7, dc in next 2 dc, [2 dc in next ch 1 sp, dc in next 2 dc] 12 times; 2 dc around post of next dc on row 8; join with sl st in 3rd ch of beg ch 3. *(54 dc)*

Rnd 2: Ch 3, dc in each dc; join with sl st in 3rd ch of beg ch-3.

Rnds 3 & 4: Rep rnd 2.

Rnd 5: Ch 3, **dc dec** *(see Stitch Guide)* in next 2 dc; *dc in next dc, dc dec in next 2 dc; rep from * around; join with sl st in 3rd ch of beg ch-3. *(36 dc)*

Rnd 6: Ch 1, sc in same ch as joining and in next 2 dc, sk next dc; *sc in next 3 dc, sk next dc; rep from * around; join with sl st in first sc. *(27 sc)*

Rnd 7: Ch 1, sc in same sc and in each rem sc; join with sl st in first sc.

Rnds 8 & 9: Rep rnd 7.

Rnd 10: Ch 1, sc in same sc and in next sc, ch 3, sk next sc, [sc in next 2 sc, ch 3, sk next sc] 8 times; join with sl st in first sc. *(18 sc)*

Rnd 11: Sl st in next sc and in next ch-3 sp, ch 1, in same sp and in each rem ch-3 sp work (sc, 3 dc, sc); join with sl st in first sc.

Fasten off and weave in ends.

SLEEVE TIE
MAKE 2.
Ch 60. Fasten off and weave in ends.

NECK TRIM & TIES
Hold Dress with RS facing you and beg ch at top; ch 25, working in unused lps of beg ch, sc in each unused lp; ch 25. Fasten off.

BODICE RUFFLES & TIES
FIRST RUFFLE
Row 1 (RS): Hold Dress with RS facing you and neckline at bottom; ch 25, sc around post of beg ch-3 of row 1 and around post of next dc; *ch 3, sc around post of next 2 dc on row 1; rep from * across; ch 25. Fasten off.

Row 2: Join yarn with sl st in first ch-3 sp of row 1; ch 1, in same sp and in each rem ch-3 sp work (sc, 3 dc, sc). Fasten off.

2ND RUFFLE
Row 1 (RS): Hold Dress with RS facing you and neckline at bottom; ch 25, sc around post of beg ch-3 of row 3 and next dc; *ch 3, sc around post of next 2 dc on row 3; rep from * across; ch 25. Fasten off.

Row 2: Rep row 2 of First Ruffle.

3RD RUFFLE
Row 1 (RS): Hold Dress with RS facing you and neckline at bottom; ch 25, sc around post of beg ch-3 of row 7 and next dc; *ch 3, sc around post of next 2 dc on row 7; rep from * across; ch 25. Fasten off.

Row 2: Rep row 2 of First Ruffle.

SKIRT RUFFLE
Rnd 1 (RS): Hold Dress with RS facing you and neckline at bottom; make slip knot on hook and join with sc around post of beg ch-3 of rnd 13; sc around post of next dc, ch 3; *sc around next 2 dc, ch 3; rep from * around; join with sl st in first sc.

Rnd 2: Sl st in next sc and in next ch-3 sp, ch 1, in same sp and in each rem ch-3 sp work (sc, 3 dc, sc); join with sl st in first sc.

Fasten off and weave in ends.

FINISHING
Step 1: If desired, apply seam sealant to ends of each Sleeve Tie. Weave 1 Sleeve Tie through ch-3 sps on rnd 10 of 1 Sleeve. Tie in bow at top of Sleeve. Rep on rem Sleeve with 2nd Sleeve Tie.

Step 2: If desired, apply seam sealant to ends of Neck and Bodice Ties.

Step 3: With sewing needle and matching thread, sew 1 flower to center front of Dress above 2nd ruffle.

PANTIES
Row 1 (RS): Ch 60, dc in 4th ch from hook *(beg 3 sk chs count as a dc)* and in each rem ch; join with sl st in 3rd ch of beg ch-3. *(58 dc)*

Rnd 2: Ch 3 *(counts as a dc on this and following rnds),* dc in each rem dc; join with sl st in 3rd ch of beg ch-3.

Rnds 3–10: Rep rnd 2.

FIRST LEG
Rnd 11: Ch 12, sk same ch as joining and next 28 dc, sl st in next dc, ch 3 *(counts as a dc),* dc in 28 dc and in same ch as beg ch-12 made; dc in next 12 chs of beg

ch-12; join with sl st in 3rd ch of next ch-3. *(42 dc)*

Rnd 12: Ch 3, **dc dec** *(see Stitch Guide)* in next 2 dc; *dc in next dc, dc dec in next 2 dc; rep from * around; join with sl st in 3rd ch of beg ch-3. *(28 dc)*

Rnd 13: Ch 1, sc in same ch as joining and in each dc to last 2 dc; **sc dec** *(see Stitch Guide)* in last 2 dc; join with sl st in first sc. *(27 sc)*

Rnd 14: Ch 1, sc in same sc and in each rem sc; join with sl st in first sc.

Rnds 15 & 16: Rep rnd 14.

Rnd 17: Ch 1, sc in same sc and in next sc, ch 3, sk next sc; *sc in next 2 sc, ch 3, sk next sc; rep from * around; join with sl st in first sc. *(18 sc)*

Rnd 18: Sl st in next sc and in next ch-3 sp, ch 1, in same sp and in each rem ch-3 sp work (sc, 3 dc, sc); join with sl st in first sc.

Fasten off and weave in ends.

2ND LEG
Rnd 1: Hold piece with RS facing you; join yarn with sl st in first unused lp of beg ch-12 of rnd 1 of First Leg; ch 3, sc in next 11 unused lps, dc in same dc on rnd 10 as ch-12 made, in next 29 dc and in same dc as sl st of rnd 1 of

First Leg made; join with sl st in 3rd ch of beg ch-3. *(42 dc)*

Rnds 2–8: Rep rnds 12–18 of First Leg.

TIE
MAKE 2.
Ch 60. Fasten off and weave in ends.

WAIST TRIM & TIES
Hold Panties with RS facing you and beg ch at top; ch 25; working in unused lps of beg ch, sc in first unused lp, *sk next lp, sc in next 2 lps; rep from* across; ch 25. Fasten off.

FINISHING
Step 1: If desired, apply seam sealant to ends of each Tie. Weave 1 Tie through ch-3 sps on rnd 17 of 1 Leg. Tie in bow at front of Leg. Rep on rem Leg with 2nd Tie.

Step 2: If desired, apply seam sealant to ends of Waist Ties.

Step 3: With sewing needle and matching thread, sew 1 flower to Rnd 5 on center back of Panties.

BERET
Rnd 1 (RS): Ch 4; 9 dc in 4th ch from hook *(beg 3 sk chs count as a dc);* join with sl st in 3rd ch of beg ch-3. *(10 dc)*

Rnd 2: Ch 3 *(counts as a dc on this and following rnds),* dc in same ch; ch 1; *2 dc in next dc; ch 1; rep from * around; join with sl st in 3rd ch of beg ch-3. *(20 dc)*

Rnd 3: Ch 3, dc in next dc, 2 dc in next ch-1 sp; *dc in next 2 dc, 2 dc in next ch-1 sp; rep from * around; join with sl st in 3rd ch of beg ch-3. *(40 dc)*

Rnd 4: Ch 3, dc in next dc, ch 1; *dc in next 2 dc, ch 1; rep from * around; join with sl st in 3rd ch of beg ch-3. *(40 dc)*

Rnd 5: Ch 3, dc in next dc, 2 dc in ch-1 sp; *dc in next 2 dc, 2 dc in next ch-1 sp; rep from * around; join with sl st in 3rd ch of beg ch-3. *(80 dc)*

Rnd 6: Ch 3, dc in each dc; join with sl st in 3rd ch of beg ch-3.

Rnd 7: Ch 3, dc in each dc to last dc; 2 dc in last dc; join with sl st in 3rd ch of beg ch-3. *(81 dc)*

Rnd 8: Ch 3, working in **back lps** *(see Stitch Guide)* only, dc in each dc; join with sl st in 3rd ch of beg ch-3.

Rnd 9: Ch 3, dc in each dc; join with sl st in 3rd ch of beg ch-3.

Rnd 10: Ch 3, **dc dec** *(see Stitch Guide)* in next 2 dc; *dc in next dc, dc dec; rep from * around; join with sl st in 3rd ch of beg ch-3. *(54 dc)*

Rnd 11: Ch 1, sc in same ch as joining and in next 4 dc, sk next dc; *sc in next 5 dc, sk next dc; rep from * around; join with sl st in first sc. *(45 sc)*

Rnd 12: Ch 1, sc in same sc and in each rem sc; join with sl st in first sc.

Rnds 13 & 14: Rep rnd 12.

Rnd 15: Ch 1, sc in same sc and in next sc, ch 3, sk next sc; *sc

in next 2 sc, ch 3, sk next sc; rep from * around; join with sl st in first sc. *(30 sc)*

Rnd 16: Sl st in next sc and in next ch-3 sp; ch 1, in same sp and in each rem ch-3 sp work (sc, 3 dc, sc); join with sl st in first sc.

Fasten off and weave in ends.

RUFFLE TRIM
Rnd 1 (RS): Hold piece with RS facing you; make slip knot on hook and join with sc around **post** *(see Stitch Guide)* of beg ch-3 of rnd 2; sc around post of next dc, ch 3; *sc around post of next 2 dc, ch 3; rep from * around; join with sl st in first sc.

Rnd 2: Sl st in next sc and in next ch-3 sp, ch 1, in same sp and in each rem ch-3 sp work (sc, 3 dc, sc); join with sl st in first sc.

Fasten off and weave in ends.

TIE
Ch 90. Fasten off and weave in ends.

FINISHING
Step 1: If desired, apply seam sealant to ends of Tie. Weave Tie through ch-3 sps on rnd 15. Tie in bow at 1 side.

Step 2: With sewing needle and matching thread, sew 1 flower to center top of Beret.

BOOTIE
MAKE 2.
Rnd 1 (RS): Ch 10; 3 dc in 4th ch from hook *(beg 3 sk chs count as a dc)* and in next 5 chs, 7 dc in last ch; working on opposite side in unused lps of beg ch, dc in next 5 lps, 3 dc in last lp; join with sl st in 3rd ch of beg 3 sk chs. *(24 dc)*

Rnd 2: Ch 1, sc in ch as joining; 2 sc in next dc; sc in next dc, 2 sc in next dc; sc in next 5 dc, 2 sc in next dc; [sc in next dc, 2 sc in next dc] 3 times; sc in next 5 dc, 2 sc in next dc; sc in next dc, 2 sc in last dc; join with sl st in **back lp** *(see Stitch Guide)* of first sc. *(32 sc)*

Rnd 3: Ch 3 *(counts as a dc on this and following rnds)*, working in back lps only, dc in each rem sc; join with sl st in 3rd ch of beg ch-3.

Rnd 4: Ch 3, dc in next 7 dc, dc dec in next 2 dc; **cl** *(see Special Stitch)* in next 3 dc; [cl in next 3 dc] 3 times; **dc dec** *(see Stitch Guide)* in next 2 dc; dc in next 8 dc; join with sl st in 3rd ch of beg ch-3. *(22 dc)*

Rnd 5: Ch 1, sc first 7 dc, [dc dec] 4 times; sc in next 7 sc; join with sl st in first sc. *(18 sts)*

Rnd 6: Ch 1, sc in same sc and in each rem st; join with sl st in back lp of first sc.

Rnd 7: Ch 1, sc in same lp as joining and in back lp of each rem sc; join with sl st in first sc. Turn.

Rnd 8: Ch 1, working in unused lps of rnd 7, sc in first 2 lps, ch 3; *sc in next 2 lps, ch 3; rep from * around; join with sl st in first sc.

Rnd 9: Sl st in next sc and in next ch-3 sp, ch 1, in same sp and in each rem ch-3 sp work (sc, 3 dc, sc); join with sl st in first sc.

Fasten off and weave in ends.

TIE
MAKE 2.
Ch 65. Fasten off and weave in ends.

FINISHING
Step 1: If desired, apply seam sealant to ends of Ties. Weave 1 Tie through ch-3 sps on rnd 7 of each Bootie. Tie in bow on outside edge of each Bootie.

Step 2: With sewing needle and matching thread, sew 1 flower to toe of each Bootie.

AFGHAN
Rnd 1 (RS): With H hook, ch 4; 9 dc in 4th ch from hook *(beg 3 sk chs count as a dc)*; join with sl st in 3rd ch of beg ch-3. *(10 dc)*

Rnd 2: Ch 3 *(counts as a dc on this and following rnds)*, dc in same ch; ch 1; *2 dc in next dc; ch 1; rep from * around; join with sl st in 3rd ch of beg ch-3. *(20 dc)*

Rnd 3: Ch 3, dc in next dc, 2 dc in next ch-1 sp; *dc in next 2 dc, 2 dc in next ch-1 sp; rep from * around; join with sl st in 3rd ch of beg ch-3. *(40 dc)*

Rnd 4: Ch 3, dc in next dc, ch 1; *dc in next 2 dc, ch 1; rep from * around; join with sl st in 3rd ch of beg ch-3. *(40 dc)*

Rnd 5: Ch 3, dc in next dc, 2 dc in next ch-1 sp; *dc in next 2 dc, 2 dc in next ch-1 sp; rep from * around; join with sl st in 3rd ch of beg ch-3. *(80 dc)*

Rnd 6: Ch 3, dc in each dc; join with sl st in 3rd ch of beg ch-3.

Rnd 7: Rep rnd 6.

Rnd 8: Ch 3, dc in next dc, ch 1; *dc in next 2 dc, ch 1; rep from * around; join with sl st in 3rd ch of beg ch-3. *(80 dc)*

Rnd 9: Ch 3, dc in each dc and in each ch-1 sp; join with sl st in 3rd ch of beg ch-3. *(120 dc)*

Rnds 10–13: Rep rnd 6.

Rnd 14: Ch 3, dc in next dc, ch 1; *dc in next 2 dc, ch 1; rep from * around; join with sl st in 3rd ch of beg ch-3. *(120 dc)*

Rnd 15: Ch 3, dc in each dc and in each ch-1 sp; join with sl st in 3rd ch of beg ch-3. *(180 dc)*

Rnds 16–21: Rep rnd 6.

Rnd 22: Ch 3, dc in next dc, ch 1; *dc in next 2 dc, ch 1; rep from * around; join with sl st in 3rd ch of beg ch-3. *(180 dc)*

Rnd 23: Ch 3, dc in each dc and in each ch-1 sp; join with sl st in 3rd ch of beg ch-3. *(270 dc)*

Rnds 24–31: Rep rnd 6.

Rnd 32: Ch 1, sc in same ch as joining and in next dc, ch 3, sk next dc; *sc in next 2 dc, ch 3, sk next dc; rep from * around; join with sl st in first sc. *(180 sc)*

Rnd 33: Sl st in next sc and in next ch-3 sp, ch 1, in same sp and in each rem ch-3 sp work (sc, 3 dc, sc); join with sl st in first sc.

Fasten off and weave in ends.

FIRST RUFFLE
Rnd 1 (RS): Hold Afghan with RS facing you; with H hook, make slip knot on hook and join with sc around **post** *(see Stitch Guide)* of beg ch-3 of rnd 2; sc around post of next dc; *ch 3, sc around post of next 2 dc; rep from * around; join with sl st in first sc.

Rnd 2: Sl st in next sc and in next ch-3 sp, ch 1, in same sp and in each rem ch-3 sp work (sc, 3 dc, sc); join with sl st in first sc.

Fasten off and weave in ends.

2ND RUFFLE
Work same as First Ruffle on rnd 4.

3RD RUFFLE
Work same as First Ruffle on rnd 8.

4TH RUFFLE
Work same as First Ruffle on rnd 14.

FINISHING
With sewing needle and matching thread, sew 1 flower to the center of row 1.

Out-With-Baby Bag

Design by Cindy Adams

SKILL LEVEL
INTERMEDIATE

FINISHED SIZES

Approximately 22½ inches long x 10½ inches wide x 18¼ inches high before felting, excluding handles

Approximately 13½ inches long x 7 inches wide x 11 inches high after felting (size will vary depending on amount of felting), excluding handles

MATERIALS

- Patons Classic Merino Wool medium (worsted) weight yarn (3½ oz/223 yds/100g per ball):
  - 2 balls #77734 too teal (A)
  - 1 ball #00204 old gold (B)
  - 1 ball #00238 paprika (C)
  - 1 ball #00201 winter white (D)
  - 1 ball #00209 old rose (E)
- Size J/10/6mm crochet hook or size needed to obtain gauge
- Tapestry needle
- Small amount of gold embroidery floss
- 13½ x 7-inch piece of plastic canvas or cardboard

GAUGE

9 sc = 4 inches

SPECIAL STITCH

Cluster (cl): In row below working row, draw up lp in sc below sc just worked and in next 2 sc, without skipping any sc on working row, insert hook in next sc on working row, draw lp through sc and 3 lps on hook, yo and draw through rem 2 lps on hook.

PATTERN NOTE

To change color, work last stitch until 2 loops remain on hook; with new color, yarn over and draw through 2 loops on hook. Cut old color.

Instructions

BOTTOM

Row 1 (RS): With A, ch 51; sc in 2nd ch from hook and in each rem ch, turn. *(50 sc)*

Row 2: Ch 1, sc in each sc, turn.

Rep row 2 until piece measures 10½ inches from beg, ending with a RS row. At end of last row, do not turn.

SIDES

Row 1: Working across next side in ends of rows, work 23 sc evenly spaced; working across next side in unused lps of beg ch, sc in each lp; working across next side in ends of rows, work 23 sc evenly spaced, turn. *(146 sc)*

Row 2: Ch 1, sc in each sc, turn.

Row 3: Rep row 2.

Row 4: Rep row 2, changing to B in last sc. Cut A, leaving 12-inch end for sewing.

Row 5: Ch 1, sc in first 2 sc; *cl (see Special Stitch); on working row, sc in next 4 sc; rep from * to last 4 sc; cl; sc in last 3 sc, turn.

Row 6: Ch 1, sc in each st, turn.

Row 7: Rep row 2.

Row 8: Rep row 2, changing to C in last sc; cut B.

Rows 9–12: Rep rows 5–8, changing to D in last sc of row 8; cut C.

Rows 13–16: Rep rows 5–8, changing to E in last sc of row 8; cut D.

Rows 17–20: Rep rows 5–8, changing to A in last sc of row 8; cut E.

Rows 21–24: Rep rows 5–8,

changing to B in last sc of row 8; cut A.

Rows 25–28: Rep rows 5–8, changing to C in last sc of row 8; cut B.

Rows 29–32: Rep rows 5–8, changing to D in last sc of row 8; cut C.

Rows 33–36: Rep rows 5–8, changing to E in last sc of row 8; cut D.

Rows 37–39: Rep rows 5–7.

Rows 40–42: With A, rep row 2.

Fasten off and weave in all ends, except long end left for sewing.

ASSEMBLY
With tapestry needle and long end, sew side seam.

HANDLE
MAKE 2.
Row 1 (RS): With A, loosely ch 76; sc in 2nd ch from hook and in each rem ch, turn. *(75 sc)*

Row 2: Ch 1, sc in each sc, turn.

Rows 3 & 4: Rep row 2.

Fasten off and weave in ends.

LARGE FLOWER
MAKE 5.
Note: *Use colors as desired for each flower.*

Rnd 1: With first color, ch 4; join with sl st to form ring; ch 5 *(counts as a sc and ch-3 sp)*, [sc in ring, ch 3] 4 times; join with sl st in 2nd ch of beg ch-5. *(5 ch-3 sps)*

Rnd 2: In each ch-3 sp work (sc, hdc, 3 dc, hdc, sc)—*petal made;* join with sl st in first sc. Fasten off.

Rnd 3: Join 2nd color with sl st in first sc of any petal; sc in same sc;

ch 4; [sk next 6 sts, sc in next sc, ch 4] 4 times; join with sl st in first sc.

Rnd 4: In each ch-4 sp work (sc, hdc, dc, 3 tr, dc, hdc, sc)—*large petal made;* join with sl st in first sc.

Fasten off and weave in all ends.

SMALL FLOWER
MAKE 4.
Note: *Use colors as desired for each flower.*

Rnds 1 & 2: Rep rnds 1 and 2 of Large Flower.

Rnd 3: Join 2nd color with sl st in first sc of any petal; sc in same sc; ch 3, [sk next 6 sts, sc in next sc, ch 3] 4 times; join with sl st in first sc.

Rnd 4: In each ch-3 sp work (sc, hdc, 4 dc, hdc, sc); join with sl st in first sc.

Fasten off and weave in all ends.

FELTING
Felt Bag, Handles and Flowers separately as follows: Place pieces in washing machine along with 1 tablespoon of detergent and a pair of jeans or other laundry. (Remember, do not wash felting with other clothing that releases its own fibers.) Set washing machine on smallest load using hot water. Start machine and check progress after 10 minutes. Check progress more frequently after pieces start to felt. Reset machine if needed to continue agitation cycle. As pieces become more felted, you may need to pull them into shape. When pieces have felted to desired sizes,

rinse them by hand in warm water. Remove excess water either by rolling in a towel and squeezing, or in the spin cycle of your washing machine. Block pieces into shape, and let air dry. It may be helpful to stuff Bag with a towel to help it hold its shape while drying.

FINISHING
With embroidery floss, sew Handle to each short end of bag using blanket st.

With embroidery floss, sew Flowers randomly around top of bag with 6 French Knots (see Fig. 1) in center of each Flower.

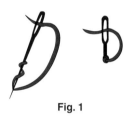

Fig. 1

Visiting Granny Hat

Design by Bonnie Pierce

SKILL LEVEL

INTERMEDIATE

FINISHED SIZES

Instructions given fit infant sizes 3–6 and 9–12 months; size is determined by hook size.

FINISHED GARMENT MEASUREMENTS

Circumference: approximately 16 [18] inches

MATERIALS

• Red Heart Super Saver medium (worsted) weight yarn (7 oz/364 yds/198g per skein):
   4 yds #311 white *(A)*
   4 yds #358 lavender *(B)*
   4 yds #347 light periwinkle *(C)*
• Size G/6/4mm or H/8/5mm

crochet hook or sizes needed to obtain gauge for desired size
• Tapestry needle
Note: *Yarn amounts are sufficient for either size.*

GAUGE

Size G hook: rnds 1 and 2 = 2 inches
Size H hook: rnds 1 and 2 = 2½ inches

Take time to check gauge.

SPECIAL STITCH

Roll stitch (roll st): Yo 15 times loosely and evenly, insert hook in sp indicated, yo, draw up lp even with 15 lps on hook, yo and draw through all 17 lps.

Instructions

TOP

Rnd 1 (RS): With desired hook and A, ch 5; in 5th ch from hook work [dc, ch 1] 5 times; join with sl st in 3rd ch of beg ch-5. *(6 dc)*

Fasten off.

Rnd 2: Join B with sl st in any ch-1 sp; ch 3 *(counts as a dc on this and following rnds),* 3 dc in same sp; ch 1, in each rem ch-1 sp work (4 dc, ch 1); join with sl st in 3rd ch of beg ch-3. *(24 dc)*

Fasten off.

Rnd 3: Join C with sl st in any ch-1 sp; ch 3, 4 dc in same sp; ch 2, in each rem ch-1 sp work (4 dc, ch 2); join with sl st in 3rd ch of beg ch-3. Fasten off.

Rnd 4: Join A with sl st in any ch-2 sp; ch 3, in same sp work (2 dc, ch 1, 3 dc); *ch 1, sk next 2 dc, in next dc work [dc, ch 1] twice; in next ch-2 sp work (3 dc, ch 1, 3 dc); rep from * 4 times; ch 1, sk next 2 dc, in next dc work [dc, ch 1] twice; join with sl st in 3rd ch of beg ch-3. Fasten off.

Rnd 5: Join B with sl st in any ch-1 sp; ch 4 *(counts as a hdc and a ch-2 sp),* in each rem ch-1 sp work (hdc, ch 2); join with sl st in 2nd ch of beg ch-4. *(24 hdc)*

Rnd 6: Sl st in next ch-2 sp, ch 1, 2 sc in same sp and in each rem ch-

2 sp; join with sl st in first sc. *(48 sc)*

Fasten off.

SIDES
Row 1 (RS): Hold Top with RS facing you; with desired hook, join C with sl st in any sc of rnd 6; ch 15; sc in 2nd ch from hook and in next 13 chs, sl st in next 2 sc on rnd 6, turn.

Row 2: Working in **back lps** *(see Stitch Guide)* only, sc in each sc, turn.

Row 3: Ch 1, working in back lps only, sc in each sc, sl st in next 2 sc on rnd 6, turn.

Rows 4–47: [Work rows 2 and 3] 22 times.

Row 48: Rep row 2.

Joining row: Turn piece inside out; bring beg ch-15 behind working row; working in unused lps of beg ch and in back lps of corresponding sc on row 48 at same time, sl st in each st.

Fasten off and weave in all ends.

EDGING
Hold piece with RS facing you; with desired hook, join A with sl st in ch-1 sp at end of any row of Sides; ch 3, **roll st** *(see Special Stitch)* in same sp; in each rem ch-1 sp work (sl st, ch 3, roll st); join with sl st in base of beg ch-3.

Fasten off and weave in ends.

Fancy Footwear

Designs by Sheila Leslie

Daisy Baby Booties

SKILL LEVEL
EASY

FINISHED SIZE
Approximately 4 inches from heel to toe

MATERIALS
• Bernat Softee Baby light (DK) weight yarn (5 oz/455 yds/140g per ball):
8 yds #02003 lemon *(A)*

8 yds #02000 white *(B)*
8 yds #02004 mint *(C)*
• Size F/5/3.75mm crochet hook or size needed to obtain gauge
• Tapestry needle
• Stitch markers

GAUGE
5 sc = 1 inch

Take time to check gauge.

SPECIAL STITCH
Front post double crochet (fpdc): Yo, insert hook from front to back to front around **post** *(see Stitch Guide)* of st indicated, draw

lp through, [yo, draw through 2 lps on hook] twice.

Instructions

**BOOTIE
MAKE 2.**

SOLE
Note: *Sole is worked in continuous rnds. Do not join unless specified; mark beg of rnds.*

Rnd 1 (RS): With B, ch 14; sc in 2nd ch from hook and in next 7 chs, hdc in next 4 chs, 5 hdc in last

ch; working on opposite side in unused lps of beg ch, hdc in next 5 lps, sc in next 7 lps, 3 sc in last lp. *(32 sts)*

Rnd 2: 2 sc in next sc; sc in next 8 sts, hdc in next 5 sts, 2 hdc in each of next 3 sts; hdc in next 5 sts, sc in next 8 sts, 2 sc in each of next 2 sts. *(38 sts)*

Rnd 3: 2 sc in next sc; sc in next 10 sts, hdc in next 5 sts, [2 hdc in next st, hdc in next st] 3 times; hdc in next 5 sts, sc in next 7 sts, [2 sc in next st, sc in next st] twice. *(44 sts)*

Rnd 4: 2 sc in first sc; sc in next 15 sts, [2 sc in next st, sc in next st] 4 times; sc in next 11 sts, 2 sc in next st; sc in next 4 sts; join with sl st in first sc. *(50 sc)*

Fasten off and weave in ends.

INSTEP
Row 1 (RS): With C, ch 8; sc in 2nd ch from hook and in each rem ch, turn. *(7 sc)*

Row 2: Ch 1, sc in each sc, turn.

Rows 3–8: Rep row 2.

Row 9: Ch 1, **sc dec** *(see Stitch Guide)* in first 2 sc; sc in next 3 sc, sc dec in last 2 sc. *(5 sc)*

Fasten off and weave in ends.

SIDES
Note: Sides are worked in continuous rnds. Do not join unless specified; mark beg of rnds.

Rnd 1 (RS): With A make slip knot on hook and join with sc in side of row 1 of Instep; working in ends of rows, work 8 sc across side of Instep; working across last row of Instep, 2 sc in first sc; sc in next 3 sc, 2 sc in last sc; working across next side of Instep, work 9 sc across side; ch 25.

Rnd 2: Working in **back lps** *(see Stitch Guide)* only, sc in next 25 sc, sc in next 25 chs. *(50 sc)*

Rnd 3: Sc in each sc.

Rnds 4 & 5: Rep rnd 3.

Fasten off and weave in ends.

ASSEMBLY
Hold WS of Sole facing WS of Sides, carefully matching sts; with A and beg at heel end, sl st Sole and Sides tog in back lps only of corresponding sts.

SOCK
Rnd 1 (RS): Starting at heel end and working in unused lps of beg ch of Sides, with B make slip knot on hook and join with sc in 13th lp before Instep; sc in next 11 lps, sc dec in next lp and first unused lp of beg ch of Instep; sc in next 5 lps, sc dec in last lp of Instep and in next unused lp of beg ch-25 of Sides, sc in next 11 lps. *(30 sc)*

Rnd 2: Sc in next 11 sc, sc dec; sc in next 5 sc, sc dec; sc in next 10 sc. *(28 sc)*

Rnd 3: Sl st in next sc, ch 3 *(counts as a dc)*, dc in each sc; join in 3rd ch of beg ch-3; change to A by drawing lp through; drop B to WS.

Rnd 4: Ch 1, **fpdc** *(see Special Stitch)* around beg ch-3 and around each rem dc; insert hook in first fpdc, change to B by drawing lp through st and lp on hook; drop A to WS.

Rnd 5: Ch 1, fpdc around each st; insert hook in first fpdc, change to A by drawing lp through st and lp on hook; drop B to WS.

Rnd 6: Ch 1, fpdc around each st; insert hook in first fpdc, change to B by drawing lp through st and lp on hook; drop A to WS.

Rnds 7 & 8: Rep rnds 5 and 6.

Rnd 9: Ch 1, fpdc around each st; join with sl st in first fpdc.

Fasten off and weave in all ends.

DAISY
MAKE 2.
Rnd 1 (RS): Starting at center with A, ch 2; 4 sc in 2nd ch from hook. Do not join. *(4 sc)*

Rnd 2: 2 sc in each sc; join with sl st in first sc. *(8 sc)*

Fasten off.

Rnd 3: Working in **front lps** *(see Stitch Guide)* only, join B with sl st in any sc; ch 2, in same sc work (hdc, ch 2, sl st)—*beg petal made*; in each rem sc work (sl st, ch 2, hdc, ch 2, sl st)—*petal made*. *(8 petals)*

Rnd 4: Working behind petals in unused lps of rnd 2, in first lp work (sl st, ch 3, dc, ch 3, sl st); in each rem unused lp work (sl st, ch 3, dc, ch 3, sl st).

Fasten off and weave in all ends.

FINISHING
With tapestry needle and B, tack 1 Daisy to Instep of each Bootie.

Rose Baby Booties

SKILL LEVEL
EASY

FINISHED SIZE
Approximately 4 inches from heel to toe

MATERIALS
- Bernat Softee Baby light (DK) weight yarn (5 oz/455 yds/140g per ball):
  8 yds #02001 pink *(A)*
  8 yds #02000 white *(B)*
  8 yds #30301 baby pink marl *(C)*
- Size F/5/3.75mm crochet hook or size needed to obtain gauge
- Tapestry needle
- Stitch markers

GAUGE
5 sc = 1 inch

Take time to check gauge.

SPECIAL STITCH
Front post double crochet (fpdc): Yo, insert hook from front to back to front around **post** *(see Stitch Guide)* of st indicated, draw lp through, [yo, draw through 2 lps on hook] twice.

Instructions

BOOTIE
MAKE 2.

SOLE
Note: *Sole is worked in continuous rnds. Do not join unless specified; mark beg of rnds.*

Rnd 1 (RS): With B, ch 14; sc in 2nd ch from hook and in next 7 chs, hdc in next 4 chs, 5 hdc in last ch; working on opposite side in unused lps of beg ch, hdc in next 5 lps, sc in next 7 lps, 3 sc in last lp. *(32 sts)*

Rnd 2: 2 sc in next sc; sc in next 8 sts, hdc in next 5 sts, 2 hdc in each of next 3 sts; hdc in next 5 sts, sc in next 8 sts, 2 sc in each of next 2 sts. *(38 sts)*

Rnd 3: 2 sc in next sc; sc in next 10 sts, hdc in next 5 sts, [2 hdc in next st, hdc in next st] 3 times; hdc in next 5 sts, sc in next 7 sts, [2 sc in next st, sc in next st] twice. *(44 sts)*

Rnd 4: 2 sc in first sc; sc in next 15 sts, [2 sc in next st, sc in next st] 4 times; sc in next 11 sts, 2 sc in next st; sc in next 4 sts; join with sl st in first sc. *(50 sc)*

Fasten off and weave in ends.

INSTEP
Row 1 (RS): With A, ch 8; sc in 2nd ch from hook and in each rem ch, turn. *(7 sc)*

Row 2: Ch 1, sc in each sc, turn

Rows 3–8: Rep row 2.

Row 9: Ch 1, **sc dec** *(see Stitch Guide)* in first 2 sc; sc in next 3 sc, sc dec in last 2 sc. *(5 sc)*

Fasten off and weave in ends.

SIDES

Note: *Sides are worked in continuous rnds. Do not join unless specified; mark beg of rnds.*

Rnd 1 (RS): With A make slip knot on hook and join with sc in side of row 1 of Instep; working in ends of rows, work 8 sc across side of Instep; working across last row of Instep, 2 sc in first sc; sc in next 3 sc, 2 sc in last sc; working across next side of Instep, work 9 sc across side; ch 25.

Rnd 2: Working in **back lps** (see Stitch Guide) only, sc in next 25 sc, sc in next 25 chs. (50 sc)

Rnd 3: Sc in each sc.

Rnds 4 & 5: Rep rnd 3.

Fasten off and weave in ends.

ASSEMBLY
Hold WS of Sole facing WS of Sides, carefully matching sts; with A and beg at heel end, sl st Sole and Sides tog in back lps only of corresponding sts.

SOCK
Rnd 1 (RS): Starting at heel end and working in unused lps of beg ch of Sides, with B make slip knot on hook and join with sc in 13th lp before Instep; sc in next 11 lps, sc dec in next lp and first unused lp of beg ch of Instep; sc in next 5 lps, sc dec in last lp of Instep and in next unused lp of beg ch-25 of Sides, sc in next 11 lps. (30 sc)

Rnd 2: Sc in next 11 sc, sc dec; sc in next 5 sc, sc dec; sc in next 10 sc. (28 sc)

Rnd 3: Sl st in next sc, ch 3 (counts as a dc), dc in each sc; join in 3rd ch of beg ch-3; change to A by drawing lp through; drop B to WS.

Rnd 4: Ch 1, **fpdc** (see Special Stitch) around beg ch-3 and around each rem dc; insert hook in first fpdc, change to B by drawing lp through st and lp on hook; drop A to WS.

Rnd 5: Ch 1, fpdc around each st; insert hook in first fpdc, change to A by drawing lp through st and lp on hook; drop B to WS.

Rnd 6: Ch 1, fpdc around each st; insert hook in first fpdc, change to B by drawing lp through st and lp on hook; drop A to WS.

Rnds 7 & 8: Rep rnds 5 and 6.

Rnd 9: Ch 1, fpdc around each st; join with sl st in first fpdc.

Fasten off and weave in all ends.

ROSE
MAKE 2.
Rnd 1: With C, ch 2; 6 sc in 2nd ch from hook; join with sl st in **front lp** (see Stitch Guide) of first sc.

Rnd 2: Ch 1, in same lp as joining work (sc, hdc, dc, hdc, sc, sl st)—*beg petal made;* in working in front lps only, in each rem sc work (sl st, sc, hdc, dc, hdc, sc, sl st)—*petal made.* (6 petals)

Rnd 3: Working behind petals in unused lps of rnd 1, [sl st in next lp, ch 3] 6 times; join with sl st in first sl st. (6 ch-3 sps)

Rnd 4: Sl st in next ch-3 sp, ch 1, in same sp and in each rem ch-3 sp work (sc, hdc, 2 dc, hdc, sc); join in first sc.

Fasten off and weave in ends.

FINISHING
With tapestry needle and C, tack 1 Rose to Instep of each Bootie.

Mary Jane Booties

SKILL LEVEL

EASY

FINISHED SIZE
Approximately 4 inches from heel to toe

MATERIALS
• Bernat Softee Baby light (DK) weight yarn (5 oz/455 yds/140g per ball):

 3
 LIGHT

  8 yds #30185 soft lilac (A)
  8 yds #02000 white (B)
• Sizes B/1/2.25 and F/5/3.75mm crochet hooks or size needed to obtain gauge
• Tapestry needle
• Stitch marker

GAUGE
Size F hook: 5 sc = 1 inch

Take time to check gauge.

SPECIAL STITCH
Front post double crochet (fpdc): Yo, insert hook from front to back to front around **post** (see Stitch Guide) of st indicated, draw lp through, [yo, draw through 2 lps on hook] twice.

Instructions

BOOTIE
MAKE 2.

SOLE
Note: *Sole is worked in continuous rnds. Do not join unless specified; mark beg of rnds.*

Rnd 1 (RS): With F hook and B, ch 14; sc in 2nd ch from hook and in next 7 chs, hdc in next 4 chs, 5 hdc in last ch; working on opposite side in unused lps of beg ch, hdc in next 5 lps, sc in next 7 lps, 3 sc in last lp. *(32 sts)*

Rnd 2: 2 sc in next sc; sc in next 8 sts, hdc in next 5 sts, 2 hdc in each of next 3 sts; hdc in next 5 sts, sc in next 8 sts, 2 sc in each of next 2 sts. *(38 sts)*

Rnd 3: 2 sc in next sc; sc in next 10 sts, hdc in next 5 sts, [2 hdc in next st, hdc in next st] 3 times; hdc in next 5 sts, sc in next 7 sts, [2 sc in next st, sc in next st] twice. *(44 sts)*

Rnd 4: 2 sc in first sc; sc in next 15 sts, [2 sc in next st, sc in next st] 4 times; sc in next 11 sts, 2 sc in next st; sc in next 4 sts; join with sl st in first sc. *(50 sc)*

Fasten off and weave in ends.

INSTEP
Row 1 (RS): With size F hook and B, ch 8; sc in 2nd ch from hook and in each rem ch, turn. *(7 sc)*

Row 2: Ch 1, sc in each sc, turn.

Rows 3–5: Rep row 2.

Fasten off.

Row 6: Hold piece with RS facing you; with A make slip knot on hook and join with sc in first sc; sc in each rem sc, turn.

Rows 7 & 8: Rep row 2.

Row 9: Ch 1, **sc dec** *(see Stitch Guide)* in first 2 sc; sc in next 3 sc, sc dec in last 2 sc. *(5 sc)*

Fasten off and weave in ends.

SIDES
Note: *Sides are worked in continuous rnds. Do not join unless specified; mark beg of rnds.*

Rnd 1 (RS): With A make slip knot on hook and join with sc in side of row 1 of Instep; working in ends of rows, work 8 sc across side of Instep; working across last row of Instep, 2 sc in first sc; sc in next 3 sc, 2 sc in last sc; working across next side of Instep, work 9 sc across side; ch 25.

Rnd 2: Working in **back lps** *(see Stitch Guide)* only, sc in next 25 sc, sc in next 25 chs. *(50 sc)*

Rnd 3: Sc in each sc.

Rnds 4 & 5: Rep rnd 3.

Fasten off and weave in ends.

ASSEMBLY
Hold WS of Sole facing WS of Sides, carefully matching sts; with A and beg at heel end, sl st Sole and Sides tog in back lps only of corresponding sts.

SOCK
Rnd 1 (RS): Starting at heel end and working in unused lps of beg ch of Sides, with B make slip knot on hook and join with sc in 13th lp before Instep; sc in next 11 lps, sc dec in next lp and first unused lp of beg ch of Instep; sc in next 5 lps, sc dec in last lp of Instep and in next unused lp of beg ch-25 of Sides, sc in next 11 lps. *(30 sc)*

Rnd 2: Sc in next 11 sc, sc dec; sc in next 5 sc, sc dec; sc in next 10 sc. *(28 sc)*

Rnd 3: Sl st in back lp of next sc, ch 3 *(counts as a dc)*, working in back lps only, dc in each sc; join in 3rd ch of beg ch-3.

Rnd 4: Ch 1, **fpdc** *(see Special Stitch)* around beg ch-3 and around each rem dc; join with sl st in first fpdc.

Rnd 5: Ch 1, fpdc around each st; join with sl st in first fpdc.

Rnds 6–9: Rep rnd 5.

Fasten off.

RUFFLE
Hold piece with RS facing you and rnd 9 at bottom; starting at center back in unused lps of rnd 2, join B in first unused lp; ch 3, *sl st in next lp, ch 3; rep from * around; join with sl st in joining sl st.

Fasten off and weave in all ends.

STRAP
Join A with sl st in first unused lp of rnd 2 at 1 side of Bootie; ch 10, sl st in corresponding unused lp on opposite side of Bootie, ch 4,

sl st in same lp as last sl st made; working across strap, sl st in next 10 chs and in same lp as joining ls st made. Fasten off. Rep on rem Bootie, beg and ending Strap on opposite of Bootie.

BOW
MAKE 2.
Row 1: With B hook and A, ch 3; sc in 2nd ch from hook and in next ch, turn. *(2 sc)*

Row 2: Ch 1, sc in each sc, turn.

Row 3: Ch 1, 2 sc in each sc, turn. *(4 sc)*

Row 4: Ch 1, sc in each sc, sl st in same sc as last sc made. Fasten off.

Row 5: Hold piece with beg ch

at top; with B hook and A make slip knot on hook and join with sc in first unused lp of beg ch; sc in next unused lp, turn. *(2 sc)*

Rows 6–8: Rep rows 2–4.

TIE
With B hook and A, ch 7; sl st in 2nd ch from hook and in each rem ch. Fasten off, leaving 12-inch end for sewing.

FINISHING
Wrap 1 Tie around middle of 1 Bow, sewing ends of Tie tog at back of Bow. Tack 1 Bow to first A row of each Instep.

Running Shoes

SKILL LEVEL ■■□□ EASY

FINISHED SIZE
Approximately 4 inches from heel to toe

MATERIALS
• Bernat Softee Baby light (DK) weight yarn (5 oz/455 yds/140g per ball):
    8 yds #02002 pale blue *(A)*
    8 yds #02000 white *(B)*
• Red Heart Sport fine (sport) weight yarn (2½ oz/240 yds/70g per skein):
    small amount #846 skipper blue *(C)*
• Sizes E/4/3.5mm and F/5/3.75mm crochet hooks or size needed to obtain gauge
• Tapestry needle
• Stitch markers

GAUGE
Size F hook: 5 sc = 1 inch

Take time to check gauge.

Instructions

BOOTIE
MAKE 2.

SOLE
Note: *Sole is worked in continuous rnds. Do not join unless specified; mark beg of rnds.*

Rnd 1 (RS): With F hook and B, ch 14; sc in 2nd ch from hook and in next 7 chs, hdc in next 4 chs, 5 hdc in last ch; working on opposite side in unused lps of beg ch, hdc in next 5 lps, sc in next 7 lps, 3 sc in last lp. *(32 sts)*

Rnd 2: 2 sc in next sc; sc in next 8 sts, hdc in next 5 sts, 2 hdc in each of next 3 sts; hdc in next 5 sts, sc in next 8 sts, 2 sc in each of next 2 sts. *(38 sts)*

Rnd 3: 2 sc in next sc; sc in next 10 sts, hdc in next 5 sts, [2 hdc in next st, hdc in next st] 3 times; hdc in next 5 sts, sc in next 7 sts, [2 sc in next st, sc in next st] twice. *(44 sts)*

Rnd 4: 2 sc in first sc; sc in next 15 sts, [2 sc in next st, sc in next st] 4 times; sc in next 11 sts, 2 sc in next st; sc in next 4 sts; join with sl st in first sc. *(50 sc)*

Fasten off and weave in ends.

INSTEP
Row 1 (RS): With F hook and A, ch 8; sc in 2nd ch from hook and in each rem ch, turn. *(7 sc)*

Row 2: Ch 1, sc in each sc, turn.

Rows 3–8: Rep row 2.

Row 9: Ch 1, **sc dec** *(see Stitch Guide)* in first 2 sc; sc in next 3 sc, sc dec in last 2 sc. *(5 sc)*

Fasten off.

SIDES

Note: *Sides are worked in continuous rnds. Do not join unless specified; mark beg of rnds.*

Rnd 1 (RS): With F hook and A make slip knot on hook and join with sc in side of row 1 of Instep; working in ends of rows, [sc in next 4 rows, ch 3] twice; working across last row of Instep, 2 sc in first sc; sc in next 3 sc, 2 sc in last sc; ch 3, working across next side of Instep in ends of rows, [sc in next 4 rows, ch 3] twice; sc in last sc, ch 25.

Rnd 2: Pushing ch-3 lps toward center and working in **back lps** *(see Stitch Guide)* only, sc in next 25 sc, sc in next 25 chs. *(50 sc)*

Rnd 3: Sc in each sc.

Rnds 4 & 5: Rep rnd 3.

Fasten off.

ASSEMBLY

Hold WS of Sole facing WS of Sides, carefully matching sts; with F hook and C and beg at heel end, sc Sole and Sides tog in back lps only of corresponding sts.

SOCK

Rnd 1 (RS): Starting at heel end and working in unused lps of beg ch of Sides, with F hook and B make slip knot on hook and join with sc in 13th lp before Instep; sc in next 11 lps, sc dec in next lp and first unused lp of beg ch of Instep; sc in next 5 lps, sc dec in last lp of Instep and in next unused lp of beg ch-25 of Sides, sc in next 11 lps. *(30 sc)*

Rnd 2: Sc in next 11 sc, sc dec; sc in next 5 sc, sc dec; sc in next 10 sc. *(28 sc)*

Rnd 3: Sl st in next sc, ch 3 *(counts as a dc)*, dc in each sc; join with sl st in 3rd ch of beg ch-3.

Rnd 4: Ch 1, **fpdc** *(see Special Stiches)* around beg ch-3 and around each rem dc; join with sl st in first fpdc.

Rnd 5: Ch 1, fpdc around each st; insert hook in first fpdc, change to A by drawing lp through st and lp on hook; drop B to WS.

Rnd 6: Ch 1, fpdc around each st; insert hook in first fpdc, change to B by drawing lp through st and lp on hook; drop A to WS.

Rnd 7: Ch 1, fpdc around each st; insert hook in first fpdc, change to C by drawing lp through st and lp on hook; drop B to WS.

Rnd 8: Ch 1, fpdc around each st; insert hook in first fpdc, change to B by drawing lp through st and lp on hook; drop C to WS.

Rnd 9: Ch 1, fpdc around each st; join with sl st in first fpdc.

Fasten off all colors and weave in all ends.

TRIM
MAKE 8.
With E hook and C, ch 6.

Fasten off and weave in ends.

TIE
MAKE 2.
With E hook and B, ch 115.

Fasten off and weave in ends.

FINISHING
Step 1: Referring to photo for placement, sew 1 Trim to side of shoe at lp closest to Instep, from rnd 2 of Side and angled back down to joining of Sole and Sides. Sew 2nd Trim about ½ inch from first Trim, closer to toe end. Rep on other side. Rep on other shoe with rem 4 Trims.

Step 2: Lace 1 Tie through lps made on rnd 1 of Sides on 1 Bootie. Tie in bow. Rep on other Bootie.

Cozy Sacque for Preemie

Design by Cassandra Hennen

SKILL LEVEL
■■□□ EASY

FINISHED SIZE
Preemie

FINISHED GARMENTS MEASUREMENTS
Chest: approximately 15 inches

Hat: approximately 15 inches in circumference

MATERIALS
- Red Heart Super Saver medium (worsted) weight yarn (5 oz/278 yds/141g per skein): 1 skein #994 banana berry print
- Size H/8/5mm crochet hook or size needed to obtain gauge
- Tapestry needle
- 2 yellow ½-inch buttons
- ¾ yd ⅜-inch-wide green picot-edged ribbon
- Sewing needle and matching thread

GAUGE
7 sc = 2 inches

Take time to check gauge.

Instructions

SACQUE
BODY
Row 1 (RS): Ch 23; sc in 2nd ch from hook and in next 2 chs, 3 sc in next ch; sc in next 3 chs, 3 sc in next ch; sc in next 6 chs, 3 sc in next ch; sc in next 3 chs, 3 sc in next ch; sc in last 3 chs, turn. *(30 sc)*

Row 2: Ch 1, sc in first 4 sc, 3 sc in next sc; sc in next 5 sc, 3 sc in next sc; sc in next 8 sc, 3 sc in next sc; sc in next 5 sc, 3 sc in next sc; sc in last 4 sc, turn. *(38 sc)*

Row 3: Ch 1, sc in first 5 sc, 3 sc in next sc; sc in next 7 sc, 3 sc in next sc; sc in next 10 sc, 3 sc in next sc; sc in next 7 sc, 3 sc in next sc; sc in last 5 sc, turn. *(46 sc)*

Row 4: Ch 1, sc in first 6 sc, 3 sc in next sc; sc in next 9 sc, 3 sc in next sc; sc in next 12 sc, 3 sc in next sc; sc in next 9 sc, 3 sc in next sc; sc in last 6 sc, turn. *(54 sc)*

Row 5: Ch 1, sc in first 8 sc, ch 5, sk next 11 sc, sc in next 16 sc, ch 5, sk next 11 sc, sc in last 8 sc, ch 1, turn.

Row 6: Ch 1, sc in each st and ch, turn. *(42 sc)*

Row 7: Ch 1, sc in each sc, turn.

Rows 8 & 9: Rep row 7.

Row 10: Ch 1, sc in each sc, turn.

Row 11: Ch 2, 2 hdc in first sc; hdc in next sc; *2 hdc in next sc; hdc in next sc; rep from * across, turn. *(63 sc)*

Row 12: Ch 2, hdc in each hdc, turn.

Row 13: Rep row 12.

Note: *Remainder of piece is worked in joined rows.*

Row 14: Ch 2, hdc in each hdc; join with sl st in 2nd ch of turning ch-2, turn.

Rows 15–39: Rep row 14.

Row 40: Ch 3, dc in each sc; join with sl st in 3rd ch of turning ch-3.

Fasten off and weave in ends.

SLEEVES
Row 1 (RS): Hold piece with RS facing you and beg ch at top; make slip knot on hook and join with sc in 3rd ch of 1 ch-5 sp on row 5; sc in next 2 chs, 2 sc in next sc; *sc in next 3 sts, 2 sc in next st; rep from * around; join with sl st in joining sc, turn.

Row 2: Ch 1, sc in each sc; join with sl st in first sc, turn.

Rows 3–17: Rep row 2.

Row 18: Ch 1, sc in each sc; join with sl st in first sc.

Fasten off and weave in ends.

Work 2nd Sleeve in same manner.

FINISHING
Step 1: With sewing needle and matching thread, sew buttons to last sts of rows 1 and 9.

Step 2: Thread ribbon through rnd 40. Gather and tie in bow.

HAT
Rnd 1 (RS): Ch 2, 6 sc in 2nd ch from hook; join with sl st in first sc. *(6 sc)*

Shown on doll

Rnd 2: Ch 1, 2 sc in each sc; join with sl st in first sc. *(12 sc)*

Rnd 3: Ch 1, sc in each sc; join with sl st in first sc.

Rnd 4: Ch 1, 2 sc in each sc; join with sl st in first sc. *(24 sc)*

Rnd 5: Ch 1, 2 sc in first sc; sc in next sc, [2 sc in next sc; sc in next sc] 11 times; join with sl st in first sc. *(36 sc)*

Rnds 6–18: Rep rnd 3.

Rnd 19: Ch 1, sc in each sc; join with sl st in **front lp** *(see Stitch Guide)* of first sc.

Rnd 20: Ch 2, hdc in same lp as joining; working in front lps only, hdc in each rem sc; join with sl st in 2nd ch of beg ch-2.

Rnd 21: Ch 2, hdc in same ch as joining and in each rem hdc; join with sl st in 2nd ch of beg ch-2.

Rnds 22 & 23: Rep rnd 21.

Fasten off and weave in ends.

Pillow Toys for Playtime

Designs by Svetlana Avrakh

School Bus Toy

SKILL LEVEL ◼◻◻ EASY

FINISHED SIZE
Approximately 10 long x 4½ inches wide x 6 inches tall

MATERIALS
- Patons Astra light (light worsted) weight yarn (1¾ oz/133 yds/50g per skein):
  3 skeins #02941 school bus yellow *(A)*
  1 skein #02753 sky *(B)*
  1 skein #02765 black *(C)*
  1 skein #02762 cardinal *(D)*
- Size E/4/3.5mm crochet hook or size needed to obtain gauge
- Tapestry needle
- Polyester fiberfill
- Stitch markers

GAUGE
18 sc = 4 inches

Instructions

LEFT SIDE
Row 1 (RS): With A, ch 44; sc in 2nd ch from hook and in each rem ch, turn. *(43 sc)*

Row 2: Ch 1, sc in each sc, turn.

Rep row 2 until piece measures 3¾ inches from beg, ending with a RS row.

Next row: Ch 1, sc in first 29 sc,

turn, leaving rem sc unworked. *(29 sc)*

Rep row 2 until piece measures 6 inches from beg, ending with a WS row.

ROOF, FRONT & BACK
Next row: Ch 42—*front made;* sc in 2nd ch from hook, in each rem ch and in each sc, turn. *(70 sc)*

Next row: Ch 28—*back made;* sc in 2nd ch from hook, in each ch and in each sc, turn. *(97 sc)*

Note: *Mark beg of last row.*

Rep row 2 until Roof, Front and Back section measures 4 inches, ending with a RS row.

Next row: Ch 1, sc first 56 sc, turn,

leaving rem sc unworked. *(56 sc)*

Note: *Mark beg of last row.*

Next row: Ch 1, sc in first 29 sc, turn, leaving rem sc unworked. *(29 sc)*

Rep row 2 on rem 29 sc for 2¼ inches, ending with a WS row.

RIGHT SIDE
Next row: Ch 15; sc in 2nd ch from hook, in each rem ch and in each sc, turn. *(43 sc)*

Rep row 2 until Right Side measures 3¾ inches, ending with a WS row.

BOTTOM
Rep row 2 until piece measures 7¾ inches from beg of Right Side,

ending with a WS row.

Fasten off and weave in ends.

WINDOW
MAKE 4.
Row 1 (RS): With B, ch 11; sc in 2nd ch from hook and each rem ch, turn.

Row 2: Ch 1, sc in each sc, turn.

Rep row 2 until piece measures 1¾ inches from beg, ending with a RS row.

Fasten off and weave in ends.

WINDSHIELD
Row 1 (RS): With B, ch 15; sc in 2nd ch from hook and each rem ch, turn.

Row 2: Ch 1, sc in each sc, turn.

Rep row 2 until piece measures 1¾ inches from beg, ending with a RS row.

Fasten off and weave in ends.

TIRE
MAKE 4.

OUTER SIDE
Rnd 1 (RS): With A, ch 3; join with sl st to form ring; ch 1, 8 sc in ring; join with sl st in first sc. *(8 sc)*

Rnd 2: Ch 1, 2 sc in each sc; join with sl st in first sc; change to C by drawing lp through; cut A. *(16 sc)*

Rnd 3: Ch 1, 2 sc in same sc; sc in next sc, [2 sc in next sc, sc in next sc] 7 times; join with sl st in first sc. *(24 sc)*

Rnd 4: Ch 1, 2 sc in same sc; sc in next 2 sc, [2 sc in next sc, sc in next 2 sc] 7 times; join with sl st in

back lp *(see Stitch Guide)* of first sc. *(32 sc)*

Rnd 5: Ch 1, sc in same lp; working in back lps only, sc in each rem sc; join with sl st in back lp of first sc.

Rnd 6: Rep rnd 5.

Fasten off and weave in all ends.

INNER SIDE
Rnd 1 (RS): With C, ch 3; join with sl st to form ring; ch 1, 8 sc in ring; join with sl st in first sc. *(8 sc)*

Rnd 2: Ch 1, 2 sc in each sc; join with sl st in first sc. *(16 sc)*

Rnd 3: Ch 1, 2 sc in same sc; sc in next sc, [2 sc in next sc, sc in next sc] 7 times; join with sl st in first sc. *(24 sc)*

Rnd 4: Ch 1, 2 sc in same sc; sc in next 2 sc, [2 sc in next sc, sc in next 2 sc] 7 times; join with sl st in back lp of first sc. *(32 sc)*

Fasten off and weave in ends.

FRONT LIGHT
MAKE 2.
Rnd 1 (RS): With C, ch 2; 8 sc in 2nd ch from hook; join with sl st in first sc. *(8 sc)*

Rnd 2: Ch 1, sc in each sc; join with sl st in first sc.

Fasten off and weave in ends.

RADIATOR GRILL
With C, ch 10; tr in 4th ch from hook, [ch 1, sk next ch, tr in next ch] 4 times.

Fasten off and weave in ends.

FINISHING
Step 1: Referring to photo for placement, sew Windshield and Windows to Sides and Front of bus.

Step 2: Referring to Assembly Diagram, sew School Bus sections tog, leaving opening for stuffing. Stuff firmly with fiberfill and sew opening closed.

Step 3: With WS tog, sew Outer and Inner Sides of each Tire tog, leaving opening for stuffing. Stuff firmly with fiberfill and sew openings closed. Sew Tires to Bus.

Step 4: Referring to photo for placement and with tapestry needle and C, tack Front Lights and Radiator Grill to Front of School Bus.

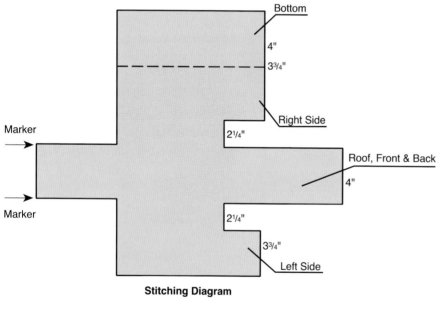

Stitching Diagram

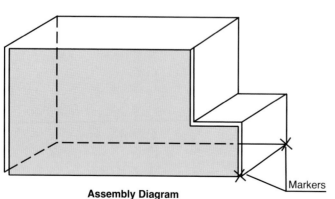

Assembly Diagram

Car Toy

SKILL LEVEL
EASY

FINISHED SIZE
Approximately 9 inches long x 4½ inches wide x 7 inches tall

MATERIALS
- Patons Astra light (light worsted) weight yarn (1¾ oz/133 yds/50g per skein):
    - 3 skeins #08742 hot blue *(A)*
    - 1 skein #02212 mint *(B)*
    - 1 skein #08628 hot orange *(C)*
    - 1 skein #08712 hot green *(D)*
    - 1 skein #02765 black *(E)*
- Size E/4/3.5mm crochet hook or size needed to obtain gauge
- Tapestry needle
- Polyester fiberfill
- Stitch markers

GAUGE
18 sc = 4 inches

Instructions

LEFT SIDE
Row 1 (RS): With A, ch 43; sc in 2nd ch from hook and in each rem ch, turn. *(42 sc)*

Row 2: Ch 1, sc in each sc, turn.

Rep row 2 until piece measures 4 inches from beg, ending with a RS row.

Next row: Sl st in first 12 sc, ch 1, sc in same sc as last sl st and in next 19 sc, turn, leaving rem sc unworked. *(20 sc)*

Rep row 2 until piece measures 7 inches from beg, ending with a WS row.

ROOF, FRONT & BACK
Next row: Ch 44—*front made;* sc in 2nd ch from hook, in each rem ch and in each sc, turn. *(63 sc)*

Next row: Ch 44—*back made;* sc in 2nd ch from hook, in each ch and in each sc, turn. *(106 sc)*

Note: Mark beg of last row.

Rep row 2 until Roof, Front and Back section measures 4½ inches, ending with a RS row.

Next row: Ch 1, sc first 63 sc, turn, leaving rem sc unworked. *(63 sc)*

Note: Mark beg of last row.

Next row: Ch 1, sc in first 20 sc, turn, leaving rem sc unworked. *(20 sc)*

Rep row 2 on rem 20 sc for 3 inches, ending with a WS row.

RIGHT SIDE
Next row: Ch 12; sc in 2nd ch from hook, in each rem ch and in each sc, turn. *(31 sc)*

Next row: Ch 12—*trunk made;* sc in 2nd ch from hook, in each rem ch and in each sc, turn. *(42 sc)*

Rep row 2 until Right Side measures 4 inches, ending with a WS row.

BOTTOM
Rep row 2 until piece measures

8½ inches from beg of Right Side, ending with a WS row.

Fasten off and weave in ends.

WINDOW
MAKE 3.
Row 1 (RS): With B, ch 14; sc in 2nd ch from hook; [ch 1, sk next ch, sc in next ch] 6 times, turn.

Row 2: Ch 1, sc in first sc, [ch 1, sc in next ch-1 sp] 6 times; sc in last sc, turn.

Rep row 2 until piece measures 2 inches from beg, ending with a RS row. At end of last row, change to C by drawing lp; cut B.

TRIM
Ch 1, sc in first sc, [ch 1, sc in next ch-1 sp] 6 times; sc in next sc; working across next side in ends of rows, ch 1, work (sc, ch 1) in each row; working across next side in unused lps of beg ch, sc in first lp, [ch 1, sk next lp, sc in next lp] 6 times; working across next side in ends of rows, ch 1, work (sc, ch 1) in each row; join with sl st in first sc.

Fasten off and weave in all ends.

TIRE
MAKE 4.
OUTER SIDE

Rnd 1 (RS): With D, ch 3; join with sl st to form ring; ch 1, 8 sc in ring; join with sl st in first sc. *(8 sc)*

Rnd 2: Ch 1, 2 sc in each sc; join with sl st in first sc; change to E by drawing lp through; cut D. *(16 sc)*

Rnd 3: Ch 1, 2 sc in same sc; sc in next sc, [2 sc in next sc, sc in next sc] 7 times; join with sl st in first sc. *(24 sc)*

Rnd 4: Ch 1, 2 sc in same sc; sc in next 2 sc, [2 sc in next sc, sc in next 2 sc] 7 times; join with sl st in **back lp** *(see Stitch Guide)* of first sc. *(32 sc)*

Rnd 5: Ch 1, sc in same lp; working in back lps only, sc in each rem sc; join with sl st in back lp of first sc.

Rnd 6: Rep rnd 5.

Fasten off and weave in all ends.

INNER SIDE
Rnd 1 (RS): With E, ch 3; join with sl st to form ring; ch 1, 8 sc in ring; join with sl st in first sc. *(8 sc)*

Rnd 2: Ch 1, 2 sc in each sc; join with sl st in first sc. *(16 sc)*

Rnd 3: Ch 1, 2 sc in same sc; sc in next sc, [2 sc in next sc, sc in next

sc] 7 times; join with sl st in first sc. *(24 sc)*

Rnd 4: Ch 1, 2 sc in same sc; sc in next 2 sc, [2 sc in next sc, sc in next 2 sc] 7 times; join with sl st in back lp of first sc. *(32 sc)*

Fasten off and weave in ends.

FRONT LIGHT
MAKE 2.
Rnd 1 (RS): With E, ch 2; 8 sc in 2nd ch from hook; join with sl st in first sc. *(8 sc)*

Rnd 2: Ch 1, sc in each sc; join with sl st in first sc.

Fasten off and weave in ends.

FINISHING
Step 1: Referring to photo for placement, sew windows to Sides and Front of car.

Step 2: Referring to Assembly Diagram, sew Car sections tog, leaving opening for stuffing. Stuff firmly with fiberfill and sew opening closed.

Step 3: With WS tog, sew Inner and Outer Sides of each Tire tog, leaving opening for stuffing. Stuff firmly with fiberfill and sew openings closed. Sew Tires to Car.

Step 4: Referring to photo for placement and details, use tapestry needle and E to tack on Front Lights and add eyelashes; with C, add highlight sts to Front Lights, and use chain st (see Fig. 1) to embroider smile on front of Car below Front Lights.

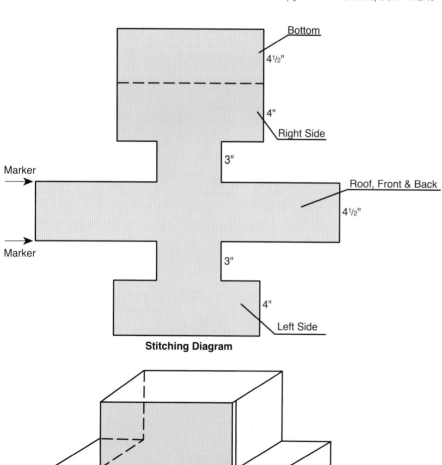

Stitching Diagram

Assembly Diagram

Fig. 1

Ladybug Toy

SKILL LEVEL ■■□□
EASY

FINISHED SIZE
Approximately 16 x 11½ inches

MATERIALS
- Patons Astra light (light worsted) weight yarn (1¾ oz/133 yds/50g per skein):
  - 2 skeins #02762 cardinal (A)
  - 1 skeins #02765 black (B)
- Size E/4/3.5mm crochet hook or size needed to obtain gauge
- Tapestry needle
- Polyester fiberfill

GAUGE
18 sc = 4 inches

Instructions

TOP/BOTTOM
Make 2.
Row 1 (RS): Starting at small end with A, ch 4; 2 sc in 2nd ch from hook; sc in next ch, 2 sc in last ch, turn. *(5 sc)*

Row 2: Ch 1, 2 sc in first sc; sc in each sc to last sc; 2 sc in last sc, turn. *(7 sc)*

Rows 3–14: Rep row 2. *(31 sc at end of row 14)*

Row 15: Ch 1, sc in each sc, turn.

Row 16: Ch 1, 2 sc in first sc; sc in each sc to last sc; 2 sc in last sc, turn. *(33 sc)*

Rows 17–24: [Work rows 15 and 16] 4 times. *(41 sc at end of row 14)*

Rep row 15 until piece measures 11 inches from beg, ending with a WS row.

FRONT SECTION
Row 1 (RS): Ch 1, sk first sc, sc in each sc to last 2 sc; sk next sc, sc in last sc, turn. *(39 sc)*

Row 2: Ch 1, sc in each sc, turn.

Rows 3–8: [Work rows 1 and 2] 3 times. *(33 sc at end of row 8)*

Row 9: Sl st in first 3 sc; ch 1, sc in same sc as last sl st made and in next 28 sc, turn, leaving rem sts unworked. *(29 sc)*

Row 10: Sl st in first 4 sc; ch 1, sc in same sc as last sl st made and in next 22 sc, turn, leaving rem sts unworked. *(23 sc)*

Row 11: Sl st in first 4 sc, ch 1, sc in same sc as last sl st made and in next 16 sc; change to B by drawing lp through; cut A, turn, leaving rem sts unworked. *(17 sc)*

HEAD
Row 1 (RS): Ch 1, sc in each sc, turn.

Rows 2–6: Rep row 1.

Row 7: Ch 1, sk first sc, sc in next 14 sc, sk next sc, sc in last sc, turn. *(15 sc)*

Row 8: Rep row 1.

Row 9: Ch 1, sk first sc, sc in next 12 sc, sk next sc, sc in last sc, turn. *(13 sc)*

Row 10: Sl st in first 3 sc, ch 1, sc in same sc and in next 8 sc, turn, leaving rem sts unworked. *(9 sc)*

Row 11: Sl st in first 3 sc, ch 1, sc in same sc as last sl st made and in next 4 sc, turn, leaving rem sts unworked. *(5 sc)*

Fasten off and weave in all ends.

BLACK SPOT
MAKE 6.
Rnd 1 (WS): With B, ch 3; join with sl st to form ring; ch 1, 8 sc in ring, join with sl st in first sc. *(8 sc)*

Rnd 2: Ch 1, 2 sc in each sc; join with sl st in first sc. *(16 sc)*

Rnd 3: Ch 1, sc in first sc, 2 sc in next sc; [sc in next sc, 2 sc in next sc] 7 times; join with sl st in first sc. *(24 sc)*

Fasten off and weave in ends.

ANTENNA
Make 2.
With A, ch 10; dc in 3rd ch from hook and in next ch, sc in next ch, sl st in next 6 chs.

Fasten off and weave in ends.

FINISHING
Step 1: With tapestry needle and B, sew Black Spots randomly to Top piece, adding small amount of fiberfill to each as you sew.

Step 2: Referring to photo for placement, sew antennae to top of Head section of Top piece.

Step 3: With WS tog, sew Top and Bottom pieces tog, leaving opening for stuffing. Stuff firmly with fiberfill and sew opening closed.

Daisy Toy

SKILL LEVEL ■■□□ EASY

FINISHED SIZE
Approximately 12 inches in diameter, excluding petals

MATERIALS

- Patons Astra light (light worsted) weight yarn (1¾ oz/133 yds/50g per skein):
  - 4 skeins #02751 white *(A)*
  - 3 skeins #02943 maize yellow *(B)*
  - small amount #02765 black *(C)*
- Size E/4/3.5mm crochet hook or size needed to obtain gauge
- Tapestry needle
- Polyester fiberfill

GAUGE
18 sc = 4 inches

Instructions

FRONT/BACK
Make 2.
Rnd 1 (RS): With B, ch 3; join with sl st to form ring; ch 2, 12 hdc in ring; join with sl st in first hdc. *(12 hdc)*

Rnd 2: Ch 2, 2 hdc in each hdc; join with sl st in first hdc. *(24 hdc)*

Rnd 3: Ch 2, 2 hdc in first hdc; hdc in next 2 hdc; *2 hdc in next hdc; hdc in next 2 hdc; rep from * around; join with sl st in first hdc. *(32 hdc)*

Rnd 4: Ch 2, 2 hdc in first hdc; hdc in next 3 hdc; *2 hdc in next hdc; hdc in next 3 hdc; rep from * around; join with sl st in first hdc. *(40 hdc)*

Rnd 5: Ch 2, 2 hdc in first hdc; hdc in next 4 hdc; *2 hdc in next hdc; hdc in next 4 hdc; rep from * around; join with sl st in first hdc. *(48 hdc)*

Rnd 6: Ch 2, 2 hdc in first hdc; hdc in next 5 hdc; *2 hdc in next hdc; hdc in next 5 hdc; rep from * around; join with sl st in first hdc. *(56 hdc)*

Rnd 7: Ch 2, 2 hdc in first hdc; hdc in next 6 hdc; *2 hdc in next hdc; hdc in next 6 hdc; rep from * around; join with sl st in first hdc. *(64 hdc)*

Rnd 8: Ch 2, 2 hdc in first hdc; hdc in next 7 hdc; *2 hdc in next hdc; hdc in next 7 hdc; rep from * around; join with sl st in first hdc. *(72 hdc)*

Rnd 9: Ch 2, 2 hdc in first hdc; hdc in next 8 hdc; *2 hdc in next hdc; hdc in next 8 hdc; rep from * around; join with sl st in first hdc. *(80 hdc)*

Rnd 10: Ch 2, 2 hdc in first hdc; hdc in next 9 hdc; *2 hdc in next hdc; hdc in next 9 hdc; rep from * around; join with sl st in first hdc. *(88 hdc)*

Rnd 11: Ch 2, 2 hdc in first hdc; hdc in next 10 hdc; *2 hdc in next hdc; hdc in next 10 hdc; rep from * around; join with sl st in first hdc. *(96 hdc)*

Rnd 12: Ch 2, 2 hdc in first hdc; hdc in next 11 hdc; *2 hdc in next hdc; hdc in next 11 hdc; rep from * around; join with sl st in first hdc. *(104 hdc)*

Rnd 13: Ch 2; hdc in each hdc; join with sl st in first hdc.

Rnd 14: Ch 2, 2 hdc in first hdc; hdc in next 12 hdc; *2 hdc in next hdc; hdc in next 12 hdc; rep from * around; join with sl st in first hdc. *(112 hdc)*

Rnd 15: Rep rnd 13.

Rnd 16: Ch 2, 2 hdc in first hdc; hdc in next 13 hdc; *2 hdc in next hdc; hdc in next 13 hdc; rep from * around; join with sl st in first hdc. *(120 hdc)*

Rnd 17: Rep rnd 13.

Rnd 18: Ch 2; *2 hdc in first hdc; hdc in next 14 hdc; rep from * around; join with sl st in first hdc. *(128 hdc)*

Rnd 19: Rep rnd 13.

Rnd 20: Ch 2, 2 hdc in first hdc; hdc in next 14 hdc; *2 hdc in next hdc; hdc in next 14 hdc; rep from * around; join with sl st in first hdc. (136 hdc)

Fasten off and weave in ends.

PETAL
FRONT/BACK
MAKE 12.
Row 1 (RS): Beg at base of petal with A, ch 38; sc in 2nd ch from hook; *ch 1, sk next ch, sc in next ch; rep from * across, turn. (37 sts)

Row 2: Ch 1, sc in first sc; *sc in next ch-1 sp, ch 1; rep from * to last ch-1 sp; sc in last ch-1 sp and in last sc, turn.

Row 3: Ch 1, sc in first sc; *ch 1, sc in next ch-1 sp; rep from * to last 2 sc; ch 1, sk next sc, sc in last sc, turn.

Rep rows 2 and 3 until piece measures approximately 3½ inches from beg, ending with a WS row.

OUTER SHAPING
Row 1 (RS): Ch 1, sc in first sc; *ch 1, sc in next ch-1 sp; rep from * to last 4 sts; sc in next sc, turn leaving rem sts unworked. (34 sts)

Row 2: Ch 1, sc in first sc; *ch 1, sc in next ch-1 sp; rep from * to last 3 sts, turn leaving rem sts unworked. (31 sts)

Row 3: Ch 1, sc in first sc; *sc in next ch-1 sp, ch 1; rep from * to last 4 sts; sc in next sc, turn leaving rem sts unworked. (28 sts)

Row 4: Ch 1, sc in first sc; *sc in next ch-1 sp, ch 1; rep from * to last 5 sts; sc in next ch-1 sp and in next sc, turn leaving rem sts unworked. (25 sts)

Row 5: Ch 1, sc in first sc; *ch 1, sc

in next ch-1 sp; rep from * to last 4 sts; sc in next sc, turn leaving rem sts unworked. (22 sts)

Row 6: Ch 1, sc in first sc; *ch 1, sc in next ch-1 sp; rep from * across, turn leaving rem sts unworked. (19 sts)

Row 7: Ch 1, sc in first sc; *sc in next ch-1 sp, ch 1; rep from * to last 4 sts; sc in next ch-1 sp, turn leaving rem sts unworked. (16 sts)

Row 8: Ch 1, sc in first sc; *sc in next ch-1 sp, ch 1; rep from * to last 5 sts; sc in next ch-1 sp and in next sc, turn leaving rem sts unworked. (13 sts)

Row 9: Ch 1, sc in first sc; *ch 1, sc in next ch-1 sp; rep from * to last 5 sts; sc in next ch-1 sp and in next sc, turn leaving rem sts unworked. (10 sts)

Row 10: Ch 1, sc in first sc; [ch 1, sc in next ch-1 sp] 3 times, turn leaving rem sts unworked. (7 sts)

Fasten off and weave in ends.

FINISHING
Step 1: With tapestry needle and B, sew Front and Back tog, leaving opening for stuffing. Stuff lightly and sew opening closed.

Step 2: Sew 1 Front and Back tog for each Petal, leaving opening at base for stuffing. Stuff lightly and sew openings closed.

Step 3: Sew Petals to center, easing to fit.

Step 4: With tapestry needle and C, stitch eyes and mouth.

Wrapped In Love

Every baby needs a choice of blankets
for comfort. This chapter features
delightfully new ideas for gift blankets.

Heirloom Aran Afghan

Design by Nazanin S. Fard

SKILL LEVEL
INTERMEDIATE

FINISHED SIZE
Approximately 35 x 36 inches

MATERIALS
- Red Heart Sport light (light worsted) weight yarn (2½ oz/240 yds/70g per skein):
  10 skeins #4 off-white
- Size H/8/5mm crochet hook or size needed to obtain gauge
- Tapestry needle

GAUGE
18 sc = 4 inches

SPECIAL STITCHES
Front post double crochet (fpdc): Yo, insert hook from front to back to front around **post** *(see Stitch Guide)* of st indicated, draw lp through, [yo, draw through 2 lps on hook] twice.

Back post double crochet (bpdc): Yo, insert hook from back to front to back around **post** *(see Stitch Guide)* of st indicated, draw lp through, [yo, draw through 2 lps on hook] twice.

Instructions

AFGHAN
Note: *Afghan is worked lengthwise.*

Row 1 (RS): Ch 139, dc in 3rd ch from hook *(beg 2 sk chs count as a dc)* and in each rem ch, turn. *(138 dc)*

Row 2: Ch 2 *(counts as a dc on this and following rows)*, ***fpdc** *(see Special Stitches)* around each of next 2 dc; **bpdc** *(see Special Stitches)* around each of next 2 dc; rep from * to beg 2 sk chs; dc in 2nd ch of beg 2 sk chs, turn.

Row 3: Ch 2; *bpdc around each of next 2 sts; fpdc around each of next 2 sts; rep from * to turning ch-2; dc in 2nd ch of turning ch-2, turn.

Row 4: Ch 2; *fpdc around each of next 2 sts; bpdc around each

of next 2 sts; rep from * to turning ch-2; dc in 2nd ch of turning ch-2, turn.

Rows 5 & 6: Rep rows 3 and 4.

Row 7: Ch 1, sc in each st. Do not turn.

Row 8: Ch 1, working from left to right, work reverse sc in **front lps** *(see Stitch Guide)* only of sc on row 7. Do not turn.

Row 9: Ch 1, working in unused **back lps** *(see Stitch Guide)* of sc on row 7, sc in each lp, turn.

Row 10: Ch 1, sc in each sc, turn.

Row 11: Ch 1, sc in front lp of first sc; *ch 3, sk next 2 sc, sc in front lp of next sc, turn; 4 sc in ch-3 sp just made, turn; sc in front lp of each of 2 previously sk sc; rep from * to last sc; sc in front lp of last sc, turn.

Row 12: Ch 1, working in unused lps of previous row, sc in each lp, turn.

Rows 13–15: Rep rows 7–9.

Row 16: Ch 1, sc in each sc, turn.

Row 17: Ch 3 *(count as a dc on this and following row)*, dc in next sc; *sk next 3 sc, tr in next sc, working behind tr just made, dc in each sk sc; rep from * to last 2 sc; dc in last 2 sc, turn.

Row 18: Ch 3, dc in next dc; *sk next 3 sts, tr in next st, working in front of tr just made, dc in each sk st; rep from * to last dc and turning ch-3; dc in last dc and in 3rd ch of turning ch-3, turn.

Row 19: Ch 1, sc in each st and in 3rd ch of turning ch-3, turn.

Row 20: Rep row 16.

Rows 21–26: Rep rows 7–12.

Rows 27–29: Rep rows 7–9.

Row 30: Ch 3, dc in each sc, turn.

Row 31: Rep row 4.

Rows 32 & 33: Rep rows 3 and 4.

Row 34: Rep row 4.

Rows 35–146: [Work rows 7–34] 4 times.

Row 147: Ch 2; *fpdc around each of next 2 sts; bpdc around each of next 2 sts; rep from * to turning ch-2; dc in 2nd ch of turning ch-2.

BORDER
Rnd 1 (RS): Working across next side, work 2 sc in end of each dc row and sc in end of each sc row; working across next side in unused lps of beg ch, sc in each lp; working across next side, work 2 sc in end of each dc row and sc in end of each sc row; working across row 147, sc in each st; join in first sc.

Rnd 2: Ch 1, working from left to right in front lps only, work **reverse sc** *(see Stitch Guide)* in each sc; join in first reverse sc.

Rnd 3: Ch 1, working in unused lps of sc on rnd 1, sc in each lp; join in first sc.

Rnd 4: Ch 1, working from left to right, work reverse sc in each sc; join in first reverse sc.

Fasten off and weave in all ends.

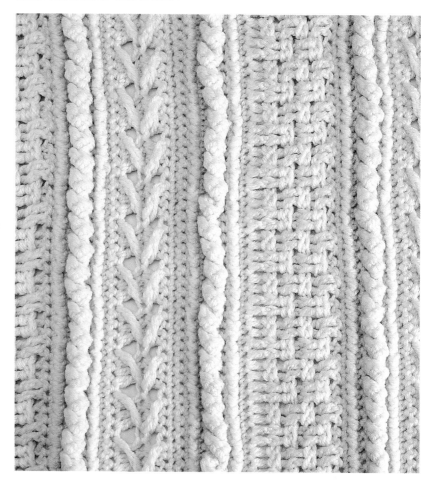

Lullaby Lamb

Design by Debbie Tabor

SKILL LEVEL
EASY

FINISHED SIZE
Approximately 11 x 12 inches

MATERIALS
- TLC Amore medium (worsted) weight yarn (6 oz/278 yds/170g per skein):
  1 skein #3103 vanilla *(A)*
  small amount #3002 black *(B)*
- Red Heart Baby Clouds bulky (chunky) weight yarn (6 oz/140 yds/170g per skein):
  1 skein #9311 cloud *(C)*
- Moda Dea Cutesie bulky (chunky) weight yarn (1¾ oz/46 yds/50g per skein):
  1 skein #3943 sherbert *(D)*
- Size H/8/5mm crochet hook or size needed to obtain gauge
- Tapestry needle
- Polyester fiberfill
- Wrights satin blanket binding: 3 yds #927 baby maize
- Sewing needle and matching thread

GAUGE
12 sts = 3 inches

Instructions

LAMB
HEAD
Note: *Head is worked in continuous rnds. Do not join; mark beg of rnds.*

Rnd 1 (RS): With A, ch 4; join with sl st to form ring; 2 sc in each ch. *(8 sc)*

Rnd 2: [2 sc in next sc, sc in next sc] 4 times. *(12 sc)*

Rnd 3: [2 sc in next sc, sc in next sc] 6 times. *(18 sc)*

Rnd 4: Sc in each sc.

Rnd 5: Rep rnd 4. Change to C by drawing lp through; cut A.

Rnd 6: [2 sc in next sc, sc in next sc] 9 times. *(27 sc)*

Rnd 7: Rep rnd 4.

Rnd 8: [Sc in next sc, 2 sc in next sc, sc in next sc] 9 times. *(36 sc)*

Rnd 9: Rep rnd 4.

Rnd 10: [Sc in next sc, sk next sc, sc in next sc] 12 times. *(24 sc)*

Rnd 11: [Sc in next sc, sk next sc, sc in next sc] 8 times. *(16 sc)*

Fill with fiberfill.

Rnd 12: [Sk next sc, sc in next sc] 8 times. *(8 sc)*

Rnd 13: [Sk next sc, sc in next sc] 4 times. *(4 sc)*

Rnd 14: [Sk next sc, sl st in next sc] twice.

Fasten off and weave in ends.

FOOT
MAKE 4.
Note: *Foot is worked in continuous rnds. Do not join; mark beg of rnds.*

Rnd 1 (RS): With A, ch 8; sc in 2nd ch from hook and in each rem ch; working on opposite side in unused lps of beg ch, sc in next 7 lps. *(14 sc)*

Rnd 2: Sc in each sc.

Rnd 3: Rep rnd 2. Change to C by drawing lp through; cut A.

Rnd 4: Rep rnd 2.

Rnd 5: Fold piece in half, carefully matching sc; working through both pieces at same time, sc in next 7 sc.

Fasten off, leaving a 10-inch end for sewing.

EAR
Make 2 with A and 2 with C.
Row 1 (RS): Ch 4; sc in 2nd ch from hook, 2 sc in next ch; sc in last ch, turn. *(4 sc)*

Row 2: Ch 1, sc in first sc, 2 sc in next sc; sc in next sc, 2 sc in next sc, turn. *(6 sc)*

Row 3: Ch 1, sc in each sc, turn.

Row 4: Ch 1, sc in first sc, sk next sc, sc in next 2 sc, sk next sc, sc in next sc, turn. *(4 sc)*

Row 5: Ch 1, sc in first sc, sk next sc, sc in next 2 sc.

Fasten off and weave in ends.

CENTER
Row 1 (RS): With D, ch 35; sc in

2nd ch from hook and in each rem ch, turn. *(34 sc)*

Row 2: Ch 1 sc in each sc, turn.

Rows 3–31: Rep row 2.

Fasten off and weave in ends.

FINISHING
Step 1: With sewing needle and matching thread, sew blanket binding to Center, folding as you turn corners.

Step 2: Referring to photo for placement and with tapestry needle and B, sew eyes, nose and mouth.

Step 3: Hold 1 A and 1 C Ear pieces with WS tog; with matching yarn, sew pieces tog. Rep with rem pieces. Sew Ears to top of Head, tacking sides of each Ear tog at base for shaping.

Step 4: Referring to photo for placement, sew Head to top of Center.

Step 5: With A, tack center of each Foot for toe shaping. With C, sew 2 Feet to bottom of Center, and 2 Feet near top of each side as shown.

Warm & Cuddly

Design by Mary Ann Sipes

SKILL LEVEL

■■□□ **EASY**

FINISHED SIZE

Approximately 27 x 39 inches

MATERIALS

- Red Heart Baby Clouds bulky (chunky) weight yarn (solids: 6 oz/140 yds/170g; swirls: 4½ oz/105 yds/127g per skein):
  3 skeins each #9832 blue swirl *(A)* and #9321 pale yellow *(B)*
- Size M/13/9mm crochet hook or size needed to obtain gauge
- Tapestry needle

GAUGE

4 sc = 2 inches

PATTERN NOTE

To change color, work last stitch until 2 loops remain on hook; with new color, yarn over and draw through 2 loops on hook. Cut old color.

Instructions

CENTER

Row 1 (RS): With A, ch 70; sc in 2nd ch from hook and in each rem ch, turn. *(69 sc)*

Row 2: Ch 1, working in **front lps** *(see Stitch Guide)* only, sc in each sc, turn.

Row 3: Ch 1, sc in first sc; *dc in unused lp of next sc on row 1, sk next sc on working row behind dc just made, sc in next sc; rep from * across. *(69 sts)*

Row 4: Ch 1, working in front lps only, sc in each st, turn.

Row 5: Ch 1, sc in first sc; *dc in unused lp of next sc on row 3, sk next sc on working row behind dc just made, sc in next sc; rep from * across, turn.

Row 6: Rep row 4, changing to B in last sc, turn.

Row 7: Ch 1, sc in first sc; *dc in unused lp of next dc 1 row below, sk next sc on working row behind dc just made, sc in next sc; rep from * across, turn.

Row 8: Rep row 4.

Row 9: Ch 1, sc in first sc; *dc in unused lp of next dc 1 row below, sk next sc on working row behind dc just made, sc in next sc; rep from * across, turn.

Row 10: Rep row 4, changing to A in last sc, turn.

Row 11: Ch 1, sc in first sc; *dc in unused lp of next dc 1 row below, sk next sc on working row behind dc just made, sc in next sc; rep from * across, turn.

Row 12: Rep row 4.

Row 13: Ch 1, sc in first sc; *dc in unused lp of next dc 1 row below, sk next sc on working row behind sc just made, sc in next sc; rep from * across, turn.

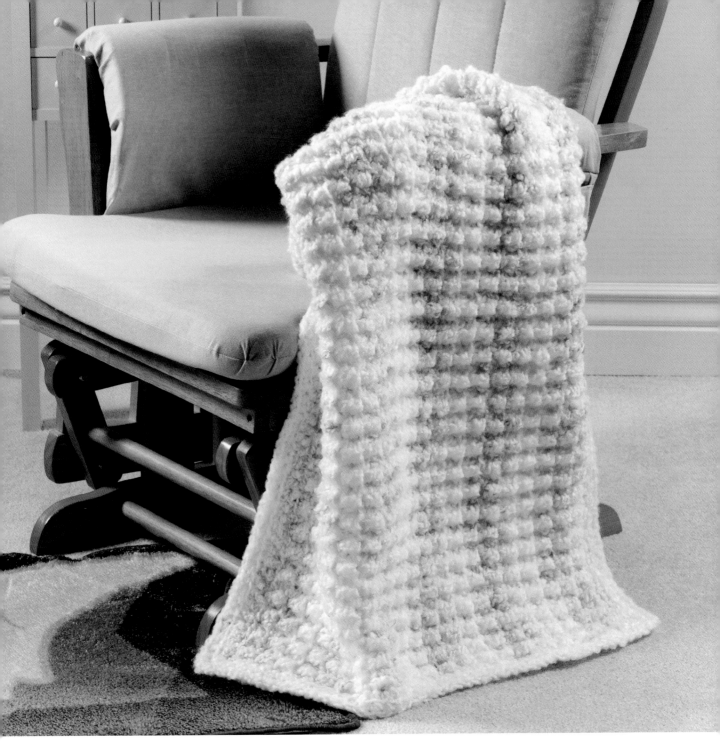

Row 14: Rep row 4.

Rows 15–46: [Work rows 7–14] 4 times.

Fasten off and weave in all ends.

BORDER
Rnd 1 (RS): Hold center with RS facing you and 1 short end at top; join B with sl st in first sc in upper right-hand corner; ch 1, 3 sc in same sc—*corner made*; sc in each sc to last sc; 3 sc in last sc—*corner made*; working across next side in ends of rows, sc in each row; working across next side in unused lps of beg ch, 3 sc in first lp—*corner made*; sc in each lp to last lp; 3 sc in last lp—*corner made*; working across next side in ends of rows, sc in each row; join with sl st in **back lp** *(see Stitch Guide)* only of first sc.

Rnd 2: Ch 1, sc in same lp as joining; working in back lps only, corner in next sc; *sc in each sc to 2nd sc of next corner; corner in 2nd sc; rep from * twice; sc in each sc to first sc; join with sl st in first sc.

Grandma's Double Delight

Design by Elaine Bartlett

SKILL LEVEL
■■□□ EASY

FINISHED SIZE
Approximately 30 x 36 inches

MATERIALS
- Red Heart Super Saver medium (worsted) weight yarn (7 oz/364 yds/198g per skein):
  - 2 skeins #311 white (A)
  - 1 skein each #381 light blue (B), #724 baby pink (C), #322 pale yellow (D), #363 pale green (E)
- Size I/9/5.5mm crochet hook or size needed to obtain gauge
- Tapestry needle

GAUGE
Motif = 4½ x 4½ inches

Instructions

MOTIF
Make 7 each of Motifs A–F.
Note: *See Motif Chart for color sequence.*

Rnd 1 (RS): With A, ch 4; join with sl st to form ring; ch 3 *(counts as a dc)*, 2 dc in ring; ch 2, in ring work [3 dc, ch 2] 3 times; join with sl st in first sc. Fasten off. *(12 dc)*

Rnd 2: With 2nd color, make slip knot on hook and join with sc in **back lp** *(see Stitch Guide)* only of first dc of any 3-dc group; sc in back lp of next 2 dc; *3 sc in next ch-2 sp—corner made; sc in back lp of next 3 dc; rep from * twice; 3 sc in next ch-2 sp—corner made; join with sl st in first sc. Fasten off. *(24 sc)*

Rnd 3: With 3rd color, make slip knot on hook and join with sc in back lp of 3rd sc of any corner; *[dc in unused **front lp** *(see Stitch Guide)* of next dc on rnd 1; sk next sc on working rnd behind dc just made, sc in back lp of next sc] twice; corner in next sc; sc in back lp of next sc; rep from * twice; [dc in unused front lp of next dc on rnd 1, sk next sc on working rnd behind dc just made, sc in back lp of next sc] twice; corner in next sc; join with sl st in first sc. Fasten off. *(32 sts)*

Rnd 4: With 4th color, make slip knot on hook and join with sc in back lp of 3rd sc of any corner; *[dc in unused front lp of next st 1 rnd below, sk next st on working rnd behind dc just made, sc in back lp of next st] 3 times; corner in next sc; sc in back lp of next st; rep from * twice; [dc in unused front lp of next st 1 rnd below, sk next st on working rnd behind dc just made, sc in back lp of next st] 3 times; corner in next sc; join with sl st in joining sc. Fasten off. *(40 sts)*

Rnd 5: With 5th color, make slip knot on hook and join with sc in back lp of 3rd sc of any corner; *[dc in unused front lp of next st 1 rnd below, sk next sc on working rnd behind dc just made, sc in back lp of next sc] 4 times; corner in next sc; sc in back lp of next sc; rep from * twice; [dc in unused front lp of next st 1 rnd below, sk next sc on working rnd behind dc just made, sc in back lp of next sc] 4 times; corner in next sc; join with sl st in joining sc. Fasten off. *(48 sts)*

Rnd 6: With A, make slip knot on hook and join with sc in back lp of 3rd sc of any corner; *[dc in unused front lp of next st 1 rnd

Motif	Rnd 1	Rnd 2	Rnd 3	Rnd 4	Rnd 5	Rnds 6 & 7
A	white	yellow	pink	blue	green	white
B	white	green	yellow	blue	pink	white
C	white	pink	blue	green	yellow	white
D	white	yellow	green	pink	blue	white
E	white	blue	pink	yellow	green	white
F	white	green	blue	pink	yellow	white

Motif Chart

A	B	C	D	E	F
B	C	D	E	F	A
C	D	E	F	A	B
D	E	F	A	B	C
E	F	A	B	C	D
F	A	B	C	D	E
A	B	C	D	E	F

Assembly Diagram

below, sk next sc on working rnd behind dc just made, sc in back lp of next sc] 5 times; corner in next sc; sc in back lp of next sc; rep from * twice; [dc in unused front lp of next st 1 rnd below, sk next sc on working rnd behind dc just made, sc in back lp of next sc] 5 times; corner in next sc; join in joining sc. *(56 sts)*

Rnd 7: Ch 1, hdc in same sc as joining; *sc in next 9 sts, hdc in next 2 sts, 3 dc in center sc of corner**, hdc in next 2 sts, rep from * twice; ending at ** on last rep, hdc in last st; join with sl st in first hdc. *(64 sts)*

Fasten off and weave in all ends.

ASSEMBLY
Following Assembly Diagram for color placement, join Motifs in 7 rows of 6 Motifs each. To join Motifs, hold 2 Motifs with WS tog; with tapestry needle and A and working in back lps only, sew Motifs tog, beg and ending in 2nd dc of corners. Secure corners by working in both lps of each corner st.

EDGING
Rnd 1 (RS): Hold piece with RS facing you and 1 short end at top; with A make slip knot on hook and join with sc in 3rd dc of upper right-hand corner; sc in next 14 sts; ***hdc dec** (see Stitch Guide) in next 2 joined dc; sc in next 15 sts; rep from * to 2nd dc on next outer corner; 3 sc in 2nd dc—*corner made*; sc in next 15 sts; **hdc dec in next 2 joined dc; sc in next 15 sts; rep from ** to 2nd dc on next outer corner; 3 sc in 2nd dc—*corner made*; sc in next 15 sts, ***hdc dec in next 2 joined dc; sc in next 15 sts; rep from *** to 2nd dc on next outer corner; 3 sc in 2nd dc—*corner made*; sc in next 15 sts, ****hdc dec in next 2 joined dc; sc in next 15 sts; rep from **** to 2nd dc on next outer

corner; 3 sc in 2nd dc—*corner made*; join with sl st in first hdc. Fasten off.

Rnd 2: With B, make slip knot on hook and join with sc in 2nd sc of any corner; 2 sc in same sc; *working in back lps only, sc in each sc to 2nd sc of next corner; working through both lps of sc, corner in 2nd sc; rep from * twice; working in back lps only, sc in each sc to first sc; join with sl st in joining sc. Fasten off.

Rnd 3: With C, make slip knot on hook and join with sc in back lp of 3rd sc of any corner; *dc in unused front lp of next sc 1 rnd below, sk next sc on working rnd behind dc just made, sc in back lp of next sc; rep from * to 2nd sc of next corner; working through both lps of sc, corner in 2nd sc; sc in back lp of next sc, **dc in unused front lp of next sc 1 rnd below, sk next sc on working rnd behind dc just made, sc in back lp of next sc; rep from ** to 2nd sc of next corner; working through both lps of sc, corner in 2nd sc; sc in back lp of next sc, ***dc in unused front lp of next sc 1 rnd

below, sk next sc on working rnd behind dc just made, sc in back lp of next sc; rep from *** to 2nd sc of next corner; working through both lps of sc, corner in 2nd sc; sc in back lp of next sc, ****dc in unused front lp of next sc 1 rnd below, sk next sc on working rnd behind dc just made, sc in back lp of next sc; rep from **** to 2nd sc of next corner; working through both lps of sc, corner in 2nd sc; join with sl st in joining sc. Fasten off.

Rnd 4: With D, rep rnd 3.

Rnd 5: With E, rep rnd 3.

Rnd 6: With A, rep rnd 3. At end of rnd, do not fasten off.

Rnd 7: Ch 1, hdc in same sc as joining; *sc in each st to last 2 sts before 2nd sc of next corner, hdc in next 2 sts, 3 dc in 2nd sc of corner; hdc in next 2 sts, rep from * twice; sc in each st to last 2 sts before 2nd sc of next corner; hdc in next 2 sts, 3 dc in 2nd sc of corner; hdc in next st; join in first hdc.

Fasten off and weave in all ends.

Sweet Posies

Design by Joyce Nordstrom

SKILL LEVEL

■■□□ EASY

FINISHED SIZE

Approximately 37½ x 38½ inches

MATERIALS

- Red Heart Soft Baby light (light worsted) weight yarn (solids: 7 oz/575 yds/198g; prints: 6 oz/430 yds/170g per skein):
  4 skeins #8889 laddie print *(A)*
  1 skein #7624 lime *(B)*
- Size G/6/4mm crochet hook or size needed to obtain gauge
- Tapestry needle

GAUGE

16 hdc = 4 inches

SPECIAL STITCHES

Front post double crochet (fpdc): Yo, insert hook from front to back to front around **post** *(see Stitch Guide)* of st indicated, draw lp through, [yo, draw through 2 lps on hook] twice. Always sk st on working row behind fpdc.

V-stitch (V-st): In sp indicated work (hdc, ch 1, hdc).

Instructions

BOTTOM BORDER

Row 1 (RS): With A, ch 163; hdc in 2nd ch from hook and in each rem ch, turn. *(162 hdc)*

Row 2: Ch 2, hdc in each hdc, turn.

Rep row 2 until piece measures 5 inches from beg.

CENTER

Foundation row: Ch 2, hdc in first 19 hdc; ***fpdc** (see Special Stitches) around next st 1 row below; hdc in next hdc; rep from * to last 20 hdc; fpdc around next st 1 row below, hdc in last 19 hdc, turn.

Row 1 (WS): Ch 2, hdc in first 20 sts, [sk next 2 sts, **V-st** *(see Special Stitches)* in next st] 40 times; sk next 2 sts, hdc in next 20 sts, turn.

Row 2 (RS): Ch 2, hdc in first 19 hdc, fpdc around next fpdc 2 rows below, [V-st between next 2 V-sts] 39 times; fpdc around next fpdc 2 rows below; hdc in last 19 hdc, turn.

Row 3: Ch 2, hdc first 20 sts, V-st in sp between last st worked and

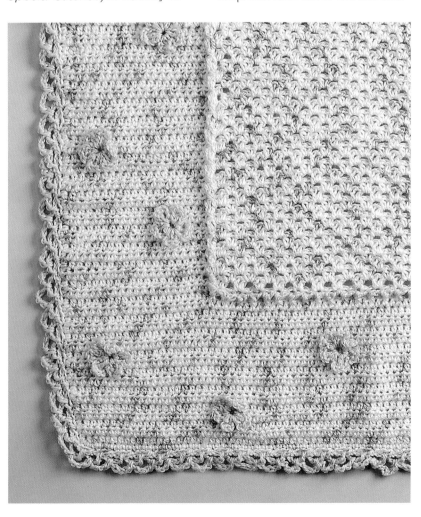

next V-st, [V-st between next 2 V-sts] 38 times; sk last V-st, V-st in sp between sk V-st and next st, hdc in next 20 sts, turn.

Rep rows 2 and 3 until piece measures approximately 32 inches from beg, ending with a RS row.

Last row: Ch 2, hdc in first 20 sts, sc in each hdc and in each ch-1 sp to last 20 sts; hdc in last 20 sts, turn.

TOP BORDER
Row 1 (RS): Ch 2, hdc in first 19 hdc; *fpdc around next st 1 row below; hdc in next sc; rep from * to last 20 hdc; fpdc around next st 1 row below, hdc in last 19 hdc, turn.

Row 2: Ch 2, hdc in each st, turn.

Row 3: Ch 2, hdc in each hdc, turn.

Rep row 3 until Top Border measures same as Bottom Border, ending with a WS row. At end of last row, ch 1, turn.

EDGING
Working around piece, sc evenly across each side to first sc; join in first sc.

Fasten off and weave in ends.

INSIDE TRIM
Hold afghan with RS facing you and 1 short end at top; join B around last fpdc in upper left-hand corner; ch 1, working left to right, work **reverse sc** *(see Stitch Guide)* around next fpdc, ch 2; rep from * around ; join in first reverse sc.

OUTSIDE EDGING
Row 1 (RS): Hold afghan with RS facing you and 1 short end at top; join B in last st in upper left-hand corner; ch 1, working left to right, work reverse sc in same st; *ch 2, sk next st, sc in next st; rep from

* around; join with sl st in first reverse sc.

Row 2: Ch 4; *sc in next ch-2 sp, ch 4; rep from * around; join with sl st in joining sl st.

Row 3: Ch 5, *sc in next ch-4 sp, ch 5; rep from * around; join with sl st in joining sl st.

Fasten off and weave in ends.

SMALL FLOWER
MAKE 19.
With B, ch 5; join to form ring; ch 3, dc in ring, ch 3, [sl st in next ch, ch 3, dc in ring, ch 3] 4 times; join with sl st in joining sl st.

Fasten off and weave in ends.

LARGE FLOWER
MAKE 11.
With B, ch 6; join to form ring; ch 3, dc in ring, ch 3, [sl st in next ch, ch 3, dc in ring, ch 3] 5 times; join with sl st in joining sl st.

Fasten off and weave in ends.

FINISHING
Referring to photo for placement and with tapestry needle and B, sew Flowers to afghan as desired.

Surround Him With Stripes

Design by Marty Miller

FINISHED SIZE
Approximately 31 x 39 inches

MATERIALS
• Lion Brand Homespun bulky (chunky) weight yarn (6 oz/185 yds/170g per skein):
  2 skeins each #369 Florida Keys green *(A)* and 2 skeins #379 cobalt *(B)*
• Size N/15/10mm crochet hook or size needed to obtain gauge
• Tapestry needle

GAUGE
12 sts = 3 inches

PATTERN NOTE
To change color, work last stitch until 2 loops remain on hook; with new color, yarn over and draw through 2 loops on hook. Cut old color.

Instructions

AFGHAN
Row 1 (RS): With A, ch 3; insert hook in 2nd sc from hook, yo, draw lp through, yo, draw through 1 lp on hook—*ch st made;* yo and draw through 2 lps on hook; *insert hook in ch st just made, yo, draw lp through, yo, draw through 1 lp on hook—*ch st made;* yo and draw through 2 lps on hook; rep from * 64 times, turn.

Row 2: Ch 1, sc in first st; *ch 1, sk next st, sc in next st; rep from * to last st; sc in last st, turn.

Row 3: Ch 1, sc in first sc; *ch 1, sc in next ch-1 sp; rep from * to last sc; sc in last sc, turn.

Rows 4–8: Rep row 3, changing to B in last sc of row 8.

Rows 9–81: Rep row 3 working in following color sequence: 1 row B, 5 rows A, 1 row B, 3 rows A, 2 rows B, 2 rows A, 3 rows B, 1 row A, 5 rows B, 1 row A, 8 rows B, 1 row A, 8 rows B, 1 row A, 5 rows B, 1 row A, 3 rows B, 2 rows A, 2 rows B, 3 rows A, 1 row B, 5 rows A, 1 row B, 8 rows A.

Fasten off and weave in all ends.

BORDER
Rnd 1 (RS): Hold piece with RS facing you and last row worked at top; join B in first sc in upper right-hand corner; ch 1, 3 sc in same sc—*corner made;* *sc in each sc and in each ch-1 sp to last sc; 3 sc in last sc—*corner made;* working across next side in ends of rows, sc evenly, keeping work flat; working across next side, 3 sc in first st—*corner made;* sc in each st to last st; 3 sc in last st—*corner made;* working across next side in ends of rows, sc evenly, keeping work flat; join with sl st in first sc. Change to A by drawing lp through; cut B. Turn.

Rnd 2: Ch 1, sc in first sc, *ch 1, sk next sc, sc in next sc; rep from * to 2nd sc of next corner; corner in 2nd sc; **ch 1, sk next sc, sc in next sc; rep from ** to 2nd sc of next corner; corner in 2nd sc; ***ch 1, sk next sc, sc in next sc; rep from *** to 2nd sc of next corner; corner in 2nd sc; ****ch 1, sk next sc, sc in next sc; rep from **** to 2nd sc of next corner; corner in 2nd sc; join with sl st in first sc. Change to B by drawing lp through; cut A. Turn.

Note: *On following rnds, to work in pattern as established, adjust beg of reps by working 2 sc in a row if necessary.*

Rnd 3: Ch 1, sc in first sc, ch 1, sk next sc; corner in next sc; ch 1; *sc in next ch-1 sp, ch 1; rep from * to 2nd sc of next corner; corner in 2nd sc; ch 1; **sc in next ch-1 sp, ch 1; rep from ** to 2nd sc of next corner; corner in 2nd sc; ch 1; ***sc in next ch-1 sp, ch 1; rep from *** to 2nd sc of next corner; corner in 2nd sc; ch 1; ****sc in next ch-1 sp, ch 1; rep from **** to first sc; join with sl st in first sc. Turn.

Rnd 4: Ch 1, sc in first sc and in next ch-1 sp, ch 1; *sc in next ch-1 sp, ch 1; rep from * to 2nd sc of next corner; corner in 2nd sc; ch 1; **sc in next ch-1 sp, ch 1; rep from ** to 2nd sc of next corner; corner in 2nd sc; ch 1; ***sc in next ch-1 sp, ch 1; rep from *** to 2nd sc of next corner; corner in 2nd sc; ch 1; ****sc in next ch-1 sp, ch 1; rep from **** to 2nd sc of next corner; corner in 2nd sc; ch 1, sc in next ch-1 sp; join with sl st in first sc.

Fasten off and weave in all ends.

Swirly-Fringed Blanket

Design by Karen Hay

SKILL LEVEL ■■□□
EASY

FINISHED SIZE
Approximately 48 x 48 inches including spiral edging

MATERIALS

- Bernat Baby Coordinates Sweet Stripes light (light worsted) weight yarn (5¼ oz/404 yds/150g per skein): 3 balls #09414 candy stripes
- Size H/8/5mm crochet hook or size needed to obtain gauge
- Tapestry needle

GAUGE
In pattern: 14 sts = 4 inches

Instructions

Row 1: Ch 149; sc in 2nd ch from hook, dc in next ch; *sc in next ch, dc in next ch, rep from * across, turn. *(148 sts)*

Row 2: Ch 17, 2 dc in 3rd ch from hook and in each of next 14 chs—*spiral made*; *sc in next dc, dc in next sc; rep from * across, turn.

Row 3: Rep row 2.

Row 4: Ch 1, sc in first dc, dc in next sc; * sc in next dc, dc in next sc; rep from * across, turn.

Rows 5 & 6: Rep row 4.

Rep Rows 2–6 until piece measures approximately 42 inches from beg.

Last row: Ch 1, sc in first dc, dc in next sc; *ch 17, 2 dc in 3rd ch from hook and in each of next 14 chs—*spiral made*; [sc in next dc, dc in next sc] twice; rep from * to last 2 sts; ch 17, 2 dc in 3rd ch from hook and in each of next 14 chs—*spiral made*; sc in next dc, dc in last sc.

Fasten off and weave in ends.

LOWER EDGING
Hold piece with RS facing you

and beg ch at top; join yarn in first unused lp of beg ch; ch 1, sc in same lp; working in rem unused lps of beg ch, dc in next lp; *ch 17, 2 dc in 3rd ch from hook and in each of next 14 chs—*spiral made*; [sc in next lp, dc in next lp] twice; rep from * to last 2 lps; ch 17, 2 dc in 3rd ch from hook and in each of next 14 chs—*spiral made*; sc in next lp, dc in last lp.

Fasten off and weave in ends.

Baby Burrito Blanket

Design by Cindy Adams

SKILL LEVEL

EASY

FINISHED SIZE
Approximately 36 inches in diameter

MATERIALS
- Red Heart Baby Econo medium (worsted) weight yarn (6 oz/460 yds/170g per skein): 2 skeins #1984 citrus multi
- Size G/6/4mm crochet hook or size needed to obtain gauge
- Tapestry needle

GAUGE
Rnds 1–3 = 4 inches

SPECIAL STITCHES
Beginning cluster (beg cl): Ch 2, [yo, draw up lp in sp indicated, yo, draw through 2 lps on hook] twice; yo and draw through all 3 lps on hook.

Cluster (cl): [Yo, draw up lp in sp indicated, yo, draw through 2 lps on hook] 3 times; yo and draw through all 4 lps on hook.

Instructions

BLANKET
Rnd 1 (RS): Ch 5, dc in 5th ch from hook (*beg 4 sk chs count as a dc and a ch-1 sp*), ch 1, in same ch work [dc, ch 1] 6 times; join with sl st in 4th ch of beg 4 sk chs. (*8 ch-1 sps*)

Rnd 2: Sl st in next ch-1 sp; **beg cl** (*see Special Stitches*) in same sp, ch 2, *cl (*see Special Stitches*) in next ch-1 sp, ch 2; rep from * around; join with sl st in top of beg cl.

Rnd 3: Sl st in next ch-2 sp, in same sp work (beg cl, ch 2, cl); ch 2, in each rem ch-2 sp work [cl, ch 2] twice; join with sl st in top of beg cl. (*16 ch-2 sps*)

Rnd 4: Sl st in next ch-2 sp, in same sp work (beg cl, ch 2, cl); ch 2, cl in next ch-2 sp, ch 2; *in next ch-2 sp work [cl, ch 2] twice; cl in next ch-2 sp, ch 2; rep from * around; join with sl st in top of beg cl. (*24 ch-2 sps*)

Rnd 5: Sl st in next ch-2 sp, beg cl in same sp; ch 2, cl in next ch-2 sp; ch 2, in next ch-2 sp work [cl, ch 2] twice; *[cl in next ch-2 sp, ch 2] twice; in next ch-2 sp work [cl, ch 2] twice; rep from * around; join with sl st in top of beg cl. (*32 ch-2 sps*)

Rnd 6: Sl st in next ch-2 sp, beg cl in same sp; ch 2, [cl in next ch-2 sp, ch 2] 6 times; in next ch-2 sp work [cl, ch 2] twice; *[cl in next ch-2 sp, ch 2] 7 times; in next ch-2 sp work [cl, ch 2] twice; rep from * around; join with sl st in top of beg cl. (*36 ch-2 sps*)

Rnd 7: Sl st in next ch-2 sp, beg cl in same sp; ch 2, [cl in next ch-2 sp, ch 2] 4 times; in next ch-2 sp work [cl, ch 2] twice; *[cl in next ch-2 sp, ch 2] 8 times; in next ch-2 sp work [cl, ch 2] twice; rep from * twice, [cl in next ch-2 sp, ch 2] 3

times; join with sl st in top of beg cl. *(40 ch-2 sps)*

Rnd 8: Sl st in next ch-2 sp, in same sp work (beg cl, ch 2, cl); ch 2, [cl in next ch-2 sp, ch 2] 9 times; *in next ch-2 sp work [cl, ch 2] twice; [cl in next ch-2 sp, ch 2] 9 times; rep from * around; join with sl st in top of beg cl. *(44 ch-2 sps)*

Rnd 9: Sl st in next ch-2 sp, beg cl in same sp; ch 2, [cl in next ch-2 sp, ch 2] 5 times; in next ch-2 sp work [cl, ch 2] twice; *[cl in next ch-2 sp, ch 2] 10 times; in next ch-2 sp work [cl, ch 2] twice; rep from * twice; [cl in next ch-2 sp, ch 2] 4 times; join with sl st in top of beg cl. *(48 ch-2 sps)*

Rnd 10: Sl st in next ch-2 sp, in same sp work (beg cl, ch 2, cl); ch 2, [cl in next ch-2 sp, ch 2] 11 times; *in next ch-2 sp work [cl, ch 2] twice; [cl in next ch-2 sp, ch 2] 11 times; rep from * around; join with sl st in top of beg cl. *(52 ch-2 sps)*

Rnd 11: Sl st in next ch-2 sp, beg cl in same sp, ch 2, [cl in next ch-2 sp, ch 2] 5 times; in next ch-2 sp work [cl, ch 2] twice; *[cl in next ch-2 sp, ch 2] 12 times; in next ch-2 sp work [cl, ch 2] twice; rep from * twice; [cl in next ch-2 sp, ch 2] 6 times; join with sl st in top of beg cl. *(56 ch-2 sps)*

Rnd 12: Sl st in next ch-2 sp, in same sp work (beg cl, ch 2, cl); ch 2, [cl in next ch-2 sp, ch 2] 13 times; *in next ch-2 sp work [cl, ch 2] twice; [cl in next ch-2 sp, ch 2] 13 times; rep from * around; join with sl st in top of beg cl. *(60 ch-2 sps)*

Rnd 13: Sl st in next ch-2 sp, beg cl in same sp; ch 2, [cl in next ch-2 sp, ch 2] 5 times; in next ch-2 sp work [cl, ch 2] twice; *[cl in next ch-2 sp, ch 2] 14 times; in next ch-2 sp work [cl, ch 2] twice; rep from

* twice; [cl in next ch-2 sp, ch 2] 8 times; join with sl st in top of beg cl. *(64 ch-2 sps)*

Rnd 14: Sl st in next ch-2 sp, in same sp work (beg cl, ch 2, cl); ch 2, [cl in next ch-2 sp, ch 2] 15 times; *in next ch-2 sp work [cl, ch 2] twice; [cl in next ch-2 sp, ch 2] 15 times; rep from * around; join with sl st in top of beg cl. *(68 ch-2 sps)*

Rnd 15: Sl st in next ch-2 sp, beg cl in same sp, ch 2, [cl in next ch-2 sp, ch 2] 5 times; in next ch-2 sp work [cl, ch 2] twice; *[cl in next ch-2 sp, ch 2] 16 times; in next ch-2 sp work [cl, ch 2] twice; rep from * twice; [cl in next ch-2 sp, ch 2] 10 times; join with sl st in top of beg cl. *(72 ch-2 sps)*

Rnd 16: Sl st in next ch-2 sp, in same sp work (beg cl, ch 2, cl); ch 2, [cl in next ch-2 sp, ch 2] 8 times; *in next ch-2 sp work [cl, ch 2] twice; [cl in next ch-2 sp, ch 2] 8 times; rep from * around; join with sl st in top of beg cl. *(80 ch-2 sps)*

Rnd 17: Sl st in next ch-2 sp, beg cl in same sp, ch 2, [cl in next ch-2 sp, ch 2] 3 times; in next ch-2 sp work [cl, ch 2] twice; *[cl in next ch-2 sp, ch 2] 9 times; in next ch-2 sp work [cl, ch 2] twice; rep from * 6 times; [cl in next ch-2 sp, ch 2] 5 times; join with sl st in top of beg cl. *(88 ch-2 sps)*

Rnd 18: Sl st in next ch-2 sp, in same sp work (beg cl, ch 2, cl); ch 2, [cl in next ch-2 sp, ch 2] 10 times; *in next ch-2 sp work [cl, ch 2] twice; [cl in next ch-2 sp, ch 2] 10 times; rep from * around; join with sl st in top of beg cl. *(96 ch-2 sps)*

Rnd 19: Sl st in next ch-2 sp, beg cl in same sp; ch 2, [cl in next ch-2 sp, ch 2] 3 times; in next ch-2 sp work [cl, ch 2] twice; *[cl in next ch-2 sp, ch 2] 11 times; in next ch-

2 sp work [cl, ch 2] twice; rep from

* 6 times; [cl in next ch-2 sp, ch 2] 7 times; join with sl st in top of beg cl. *(104 ch-2 sps)*

Rnd 20: Sl st in next ch-2 sp, in same sp work (beg cl, ch 2, cl); ch 2, [cl in next ch-2 sp, ch 2] 12 times; *in next ch-2 sp work [cl, ch 2] twice; [cl in next ch-2 sp, ch 2] 12 times; rep from * around; join with sl st in top of beg cl. *(112 ch-2 sps)*

Rnd 21: Sl st in next ch-2 sp, beg cl in same sp, ch 2, [cl in next ch-2 sp, ch 2] twice; in next ch-2 sp work [cl, ch 2] twice; *[cl in next ch-2 sp, ch 2] 6 times; in next ch-2 sp work [cl, ch 2] twice; rep from * 14 times; [cl in next ch-2 sp, ch 2] 3 times; join with sl st in top of beg cl. *(128 ch-2 sps)*

Rnd 22: Sl st in next ch-2 sp, in same sp work (beg cl, ch 2, cl); ch 2, [cl in next ch-2 sp, ch 2] 7 times; *in next ch-2 sp work [cl, ch 2] twice; [cl in next ch-2 sp, ch 2] 7 times; rep from * around; join with sl st in top of beg cl. *(144 ch-2 sps)*

Rnd 23: Sl st in next ch-2 sp, beg cl in same sp, ch 2, [cl in next ch-2 sp, ch 2] twice; in next ch-2 sp work [cl, ch 2] twice; *[cl in next ch-2 sp, ch 2] 8 times; in next ch-2 sp work [cl, ch 2] twice; rep from * 14 times; [cl in next ch-2 sp, ch 2) 5 times; join with sl st in top of beg cl. *(160 ch-2 sps)*

EDGING

Sl st in next ch-2 sp, ch 1, sc in same sp; ch 3, dc in 3rd ch from hook; *sc in next ch-2 sp, ch 3, dc in 3rd ch from hook; rep from * around; join with sl st in first sc.

Fasten off and weave in ends.

Sugar & Spice Baby Girls

Feminine clothes for baby girls in 3 month to 24 month sizes. These include special occasion dresses, romper, jumper, sundress and even a bikini with matching poncho.

Lil' Lamb Cardigan & Hat

Design by Darla Sims

FINISHED SIZES
Instructions given for Cardigan and Hat fit size 6 months; changes for 12 months and 24 months are in [ ].

FINISHED GARMENT MEASUREMENTS
Chest: 20 [22, 24] inches

Hat: 16 [18, 20]-inch circumference

MATERIALS
- Bernat Baby Bouclé bulky (chunky) weight yarn (3½ oz/180 yds/100g per ball):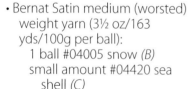
  2 [2, 3] balls #00101 soft white (A)
- Bernat Satin medium (worsted) weight yarn (3½ oz/163 yds/100g per ball):
  1 ball #04005 snow (B) small amount #04420 sea shell (C)
- Sizes G/6/4mm and H/8/5mm crochet hooks or size needed to obtain gauge
- Tapestry needle
- Polyester fiberfill
- Plastic stitch markers
- 5 pink satin roses
- Sewing needle and matching thread

GAUGE
Size H hook: 7 hdc = 2 inches

Take time to check gauge.

Instructions

CARDIGAN
Row 1 (RS): With H hook and A, ch 41 [45, 47]; hdc in 3rd ch (*beg 2 sk chs count as a hdc*) and each rem ch, turn. (*40 [44, 46] hdc*)

Row 2: Ch 2 (*counts as a hdc on this and following rows*), hdc in each hdc and in 2nd ch of beg 2 sk chs, turn.

Row 3: Ch 2, **hdc dec** (*see Stitch Guide*) in next 2 hdc; hdc to last hdc and turning ch-2; hdc dec in last hdc and in 2nd ch of turning ch-2, turn. (*38 [42, 44] hdc*)

Row 4: Ch 2, hdc in each hdc and in 2nd ch of turning ch-2, turn.

Row 5: Ch 2, hdc dec in next 2 hdc; hdc to last hdc and turning ch-2; hdc dec in last hdc and in 2nd ch of turning ch-2, turn. (*36 [40, 42] hdc*)

Rows 6–11: [Work rows 4 and 5] 3 times. (*30, [34, 36] hdc at end of row 11*)

Rep row 2 until piece measures 7½ [8, 9] inches from beg, ending with a WS row.

SLEEVES
Note: *Join separate strand of A in turning ch-2 of last row worked; ch 20 [22, 26] for sleeve. Fasten off.*

Row 1: Ch 21 [23, 27]; dc in 3rd ch from hook (*beg 2 sk chs count as a hdc*), in each rem ch, in each hdc,

in 2nd ch of turning ch-2, and in each ch, turn. *(70 [78, 88] hdc)*

Row 2: Ch 2, hdc in each hdc and in 2nd ch of beg 2 sk chs, turn.

Row 3: Ch 2, hdc in each hdc and in 2nd ch of turning ch-2, turn.

Rows 4–8 [4–10, 4–12]: Rep row 3.

NECK & FIRST FRONT SHAPING

Row 1: Ch 2, hdc in next 29 [32, 37] hdc, turn, leaving rem hdc unworked. *(30 [33, 38] hdc)*

Row 2: Ch 2, hdc in first hdc, in each rem hdc and in 2nd ch of turning ch-2, turn. *(31 [34, 39] hdc)*

Row 3: Ch 2, hdc in each hdc and in 2nd ch of turning ch-2, turn.

Row 4: Ch 2, hdc in first hdc, in each rem hdc and in 2nd ch of turning ch-2, turn. *(32 [35, 40] hdc)*

Note: *Join separate strand of A in turning ch-2 of last row; ch 3 [4, 4]. Fasten off.*

Row 5: Ch 2, hdc in each hdc, in 2nd ch of turning ch-2 and in each ch, turn. *(35 [39, 44] hdc)*

Rows 6–8 [6–10, 6–12]: Rep row 3. Fasten off.

FIRST LOWER FRONT SECTION
Row 1 (RS): Sk first 20 [22, 26] sts; with H hook, join A with sl st in next hdc; ch 2, hdc in each rem hdc and in 2nd ch of turning ch-2, turn. *(15 [17, 18] hdc)*

Row 2: Ch 2, hdc in each hdc and in 2nd ch of beg ch-2, turn.

Row 3: Ch 2, hdc in first hdc, in each rem hdc and in 2nd ch of turning ch-2, turn. *(16 [18, 19] hdc)*

Row 4: Ch 2, hdc in each hdc and in 2nd ch of turning ch-2, turn.

Row 5: Ch 2, hdc in first hdc, in each rem hdc and in 2nd ch of turning ch-2, turn. *(17 [19, 20] hdc)*

Rows 6–11: [Work rows 4 and 5] 3 times. *(20 [22, 23] hdc at end of row 11)*

Rows 12 & 13: Rep row 4.

Fasten off.

NECK & 2ND FRONT SHAPING
Row 1: Sk center back 10 [12, 12] hdc; with H hook, join A with sl st in next hdc; ch 2, hdc in each rem hdc and in 2nd ch of turning ch-2, turn. *(30 [33, 38] hdc)*

Row 2: Ch 2, hdc in each hdc to beg ch-2; 2 hdc in 2nd ch of beg ch-2, turn. *(31 [34, 39] hdc)*

Row 3: Ch 2, hdc in each hdc and in 2nd ch of turning ch-2, turn.

Row 4: Ch 2, hdc in each hdc to turning ch-2; 2 hdc in 2nd ch of turning ch-2, turn. *(32 [35, 40] hdc)*

Row 5: Ch 4 [5, 5], hdc in 3rd ch

from hook *(beg 2 sk chs count as a hdc)*, in next 1 [2, 2] chs, in each hdc and in 2nd ch of turning ch-2, turn. *(35 [39, 44] hdc)*

Row 6: Ch 2, hdc in each hdc and in 2nd ch of beg 2 sk chs, turn.

Rows 7 & 8 [7–10, 7–12]: Rep row 3.

2ND LOWER FRONT SECTION
Row 1: Ch 2, hdc in next 14 [16, 17] hdc, leaving rem sts unworked; turn. *(15 [17, 18] hdc)*

Row 2: Ch 2, hdc in each hdc and in 2nd ch of turning ch-2, turn.

Row 3: Ch 2, hdc in each hdc to turning ch-2; 2 hdc in 2nd ch of turning ch-2, turn. *(16 [18, 19] hdc)*

Row 4: Ch 2, hdc in each hdc and in 2nd ch of turning ch-2, turn.

Row 5: Ch 2, hdc in first hdc, in each rem hdc and in 2nd ch of turning ch-2, turn. *(17 [19, 20] hdc)*

Rows 6–11: [Work rows 4 and 5] 3 times. *(20 [22, 23] hdc at end of row 11)*

Rows 12 & 13: Rep row 4.

Fasten off and weave in all ends.

ASSEMBLY
With tapestry needle and A, sew side and Sleeve seams in 1 continuous seam.

EDGINGS
SLEEVE EDGING
Rnd 1 (RS): Hold Cardigan with RS facing you; with G hook, join B with sl st in seam of 1 Sleeve; ch 1, sc in same sp; working in ends of rows, sc in each row; join with sl st in first sc.

Rnd 2: Ch 1, sc in same sc and in each rem sc; join with sl st in first sc.

Fasten off and weave in ends.

Rep on 2nd Sleeve.

OUTER EDGING
Rnd 1 (RS): Hold Cardigan with RS facing you; with G hook, join B in 1 side seam; ch 1, sc in same sp; sc evenly spaced around outer edge of Cardigan, working 3 sc in each corner; join in first sc.

Note: *Place markers for 3 evenly spaced roses on right front, having first marker at neck edge and last marker 4 inches from neck edge.*

Rnd 2: Ch 1, 1 sc in same sc; sc in each sc to first marker; ch 4—*button lp made*; sl st in last sc made; [sc to next marker, ch 4—*button lp made*; sl st in last sc made] twice; sc in each rem sc and work 3 sc in 2nd sc of each corner; join in first sc.

Fasten off and weave in ends.

LOWER CARDIGAN EDGING
Hold Cardigan with RS facing you and lower edge at top; with G hook, join C in 2nd sc of right-hand corner of Cardigan; *ch 5, [sl st in 4th ch from hook, ch 4] 3 times; ch 1, sk next 2 sc, sl st in next sc; rep from * to 2nd sc of next corner, adjusting last rep as necessary to end evenly.

Fasten off and weave in ends.

FINISHING
With sewing needle and matching thread, sew 3 ribbon roses to left front opposite button lps.

HAT
Note: *Hat is worked in continuous rnds. Do not join unless specified; mark end of rnds.*

Rnd 1 (RS): Beg at top, with H hook and A, ch 2; 8 sc in 2nd ch from hook.

Rnd 2: 2 sc in each sc. *(16 sc)*

Rnd 3: *Sc in next sc, 2 sc in next sc; rep from * around. *(24 sc)*

Rnd 4: *Sc in next 2 sc, 2 sc in next sc; rep from * around. *(32 sc)*

Rnd 5: *Sc in next 3 sc, 2 sc in next sc; rep from * around. *(40 sc)*

Rnd 6: *Sc in next 4 sc, 2 sc in next sc; rep from * around. *(48 sc)*

Rnd 7: *Sc in next 5 sts, 2 sc in next st; rep from * around. *(56 sc)*

For Size 6 Months Only
Continue with Lower Section.

For Size 12 Months Only
Rnd 8: *Sc in next 6 sc, 2 sc in next sc; rep from * around. *(64 sc)*

Continue with Lower Section.

For Size 24 Months Only
Rnd 8: *Sc in next 6 sc, 2 sc in next sc; rep from * around. *(64 sc)*

Rnd 9: *Sc in next 7 sc, 2 sc in next sc; rep from * around. *(72 sc)*

Continue with Lower Section.

LOWER SECTION
Rnd 8 [9, 10]: Sc in each sc.

Rep last rnd until piece measures 5 [5½, 6] inches from center of top. At end of last rnd, join with sl st in first sc. Change to B by drawing lp through; cut A. Change to G hook.

LOWER BAND
Rnd 1: Ch 1, sc in same sc as joining and in each rem sc; join in first sc.

Rnds 2–4: Rep rnd 1.

Fasten off and weave in all ends.

EAR
Make 2.

OUTER EAR
Row 1 (RS): With H hook and A, ch 5; hdc in 3rd ch from hook *(beg 2 sk chs count as a hdc)* and in each rem ch, turn. *(4 hdc)*

Row 2: Ch 2 *(counts as a hdc on this and following rows)*, hdc in first hdc and in next 2 hdc, 2 hdc in 2nd ch of beg 2 sk chs, turn. *(6 hdc)*

Row 3: Ch 2, hdc in each hdc and in 2nd ch of turning ch-2, turn.

Row 4: Ch 2, hdc in first hdc and in next 4 hdc, 2 hdc in 2nd ch of turning ch-2, turn. *(8 hdc)*

Row 5: Ch 2, **hdc dec** *(see Stitch Guide)* in next 2 hdc; hdc in next 2 hdc, [yo, draw up lp in next hdc] 3 times; yo and draw through all 7 lps on hook, turn. *(5 hdc)*

Row 6: Ch 2, [hdc dec] twice.

Fasten off and weave in ends.

INNER EAR
With H hook and C, work same as Outer Ear.

ASSEMBLY
Place 1 Inner Ear and 1 Outer Ear with WS tog. With G hook, join A with sl st through bottom of both pieces; ch 1, sc evenly around outer edge, working 2 sc in center top; join in first sc. Fasten off. Pinch lower ends of 1 Ear tog and sew for approximately 1 inch. Rep for rem Ear.

FINISHING
Step 1: Referring to photo for placement, sew Ears to sides of Hat.

Step 2: With sewing needle and matching thread, sew 1 ribbon rose to base of each Ear.

Beach Baby Ensemble

Design by Mary Ann Sipes

SKILL LEVEL ■■■□ INTERMEDIATE

FINISHED SIZES

Bikini Set: Instructions given fit child's size 3 months; changes for 6, 12 and 18 months are in [ ].

Poncho: Instructions given fit child's size 3–6 months; changes for 6–12 months and 12–18 months are in [ ].

MATERIALS

- Bernat Cottontots medium (worsted) weight yarn (solids: 3½ oz/171 yds/100g per ball; ombrés: 3 oz/150 yds/85g per ball):
    - 3 [3, 3, 3] balls #90129 blue berry *(A)*
    - 1 [1, 1, 2] balls #91713 koolade *(B)*
- DMC embroidery floss:
    - small amount white *(C)*
    - small amount #727 yellow *(D)*
- Sizes E/4/3.5mm and G/6/4mm crochet hooks or sizes needed to obtain gauge
- Size 5/1.90mm steel crochet hook (for flower)
- Tapestry needle
- Stitch markers
- 1 yd ⅛-inch-wide elastic (for bikini top)
- ½ yd ½-inch-wide elastic (for panty)
- Sewing needle and matching thread

GAUGE
Size E hook: 9 sc = 2 inches
Size G hook: 7 sc = 2 inches

Instructions

BIKINI
HALTER FRONT
Row 1 (RS): With E hook and B, ch 10 [10, 12, 12]; working in back bumps only, sc in 2nd ch from hook and in each rem ch, turn. *(9 [9, 11, 11] sc)*

Row 2: Ch 1, working in **back lps** (see Stitch Guide) only, sc in each sc, turn. *(9 [9, 11, 11] sc)*

Rows 3–30 [3–32, 3–34, 3–36]: Rep row 2.

***Note:** Place marker in first sc of last row to mark end of Halter Front.*

HALTER BACK
Row 1: Ch 1, **sc dec** (see Stitch Guide) in first 2 sc; working in back

lps only, sc in each rem sc, turn. *(8 [8, 10, 10] sc)*

Row 2: Ch 1, working in back lps only, sc in first 6 [6, 8, 8] sc, sc dec in last 2 sc, turn. *(7 [7, 9, 9] sc)*

Row 3: Ch 1, sc dec in first 2 sc; working in back lps only, sc in each rem sc, turn. *(6 [6, 8, 8] sc)*

Row 4: Ch 1, working in back lps only, sc in first 4 [4, 6, 6] sc, sc dec in last 2 sc, turn. *(5 [5, 7, 7] sc)*

Row 5: Rep row 2. *(4 [4, 6, 6] sc at end of row)*

Row 6: Ch 1, working in back lps only, sc in first 2 [2, 4, 4] sc, sc dec over last 2 sc, turn. *(3 [3, 5, 5] sc)*

Row 7: Ch 1, working in back lps only, sc in each sc, turn.

Rows 8–24: [8–26, 8–28, 8–30]: Rep row 7.

Row 25 [27, 29, 31]: Ch 1, working in back lps only, 2 sc in first sc; sc in each rem sc, turn. *(4 [4, 6, 6] sc)*

Row 26 [28, 30, 32]: Ch 1, working in back lps only, sc in first 3 [3, 5, 5] sc, 2 sc in last sc, turn. *(5 [5, 7, 7] sc)*

Row 27 [29, 31, 33]: Rep row 25 [27, 29, 31]. *(6 [6, 8, 8] sc at end of row)*

Row 28 [30, 32, 34]: Ch 1, working in back lps only, sc in first 5 [5, 7, 7] sc, 2 sc in last 2 sc, turn. *(7 [7, 9, 9] sc)*

Row 29 [31, 33, 35]: Rep row 25 [27, 29, 31]. *(8 [8, 10, 10] sc at end of row)*

Row 30 [32, 34, 36]: Ch 1, working in back lps only, sc in first 7 [7, 9, 9] sc, 2 sc in last sc. *(9 [9, 11, 11] sc)*

Fasten off, leaving an 8-inch end for sewing. Weave in other end.

ASSEMBLY
Hold beg and end of Halter with WS tog; with tapestry needle and long end left for sewing and working in back lps of sc only, sew ends tog through back lps only of corresponding sc.

LOWER CASING
Rnd 1: Hold piece with RS facing you and 1 long edge at top; with E hook, join A with sl st in end of center row of Halter Back; ch 1, sc in same sp as joining; working in ends of rem rows, sc in each row; join with sl st in first sc.

Rnd 2: Ch 1, sc in same sc and in each rem sc; join with sl st in first sc. Fasten off.

TOP CASING
Rnd 1: Hold piece with RS facing you and unworked long edge at top; with E hook, join A with sl st in end of center row of Halter Back; ch 1, sc in same sp as joining, ch 1; working in ends of rows, *sk next row, sc in next row, ch 1; rep from * around, join with sl st in **front lp** *(see Stitch Guide)* of first sc.

Rnd 2: Ch 1, sc in same sc; working in front lps only, sc in

each ch and in each rem sc; join with sl st in back lp of first sc.

Rnd 3: Ch 1, sc in lp as joining and in back lp of each rem sc; join with sl st in back lp of first sc.

Fasten off, leaving a 24-inch end for sewing.

Fold last rnd toward WS of piece. With tapestry needle and A, sew through back lp of sc of last rnd and unused lp of corresponding sc 2 rows below to form casing. Leave small opening for threading elastic through casing.

TOP CASING EDGING
Hold piece with RS facing you; with E hook, join A with sl st in front lp of first st of row 2 of Top Casing; *ch 2, sl st in back bump of 2nd ch from hook—*picot made*; sk next 2 sc, sl st in next sc; rep from * around; join with sl st in joining sl st.

Fasten off and weave in ends.

STRAP
Make 2.
With E hook and A, ch 29 [31, 33, 35]; working in back bumps only, sl st in 2nd ch from hook and in each rem ch.

Fasten off and weave in ends.

FINISHING
Step 1: On top edge, place marker in center st of both Halter Back and Front. Place markers 1½, [1¾, 2, 2¼] inches from center st on Halter Front and ¾ inch from center st on Halter Back. Sew RS of Strap ends at base of casings, left Strap on front marker and back marker, and right Strap on front marker and back marker.

Step 2: Cut 2 pieces of ⅛-inch-wide elastic approximately 2–3 inches less than finished Halter circumference, or desired length for comfort. Place safety pin at end of each piece of elastic, pull through each Casing to desired tightness. Overlap ends of elastic about 1 inch; with sewing needle and matching thread, st ends securely. Sew opening closed.

PANTY FRONT

Row 1: Starting at front crotch, with G hook and B, ch 11 [12, 13, 14]; working in back bumps only, sc in 2nd ch from hook and in each rem ch, turn. *(10 [11, 12, 13] sc)*

Row 2: Ch 1, sc in each sc, turn.

Rows 3–8: Rep row 2.

Row 9: Ch 1, 2 sc in first sc, sc in each sc to last sc; 2 sc in last sc, turn. *(12 [13, 14, 15] sc)*

Row 10: Rep row 2.

Rows 11 & 12 [11–14, 11–14, 11–16]: [Work rows 9 and 10] 1 [2, 2, 3 times. *(14 [17, 18, 21] sc at end of last row)*

Row 13 [15, 15, 17]: Ch 5 [6, 7, 7], sc in 2nd ch from hook, in next 3 [4, 5, 5] chs, and in each sc, turn. *(18 [22, 24, 27] sc)*

Row 14 [16, 16, 18]: Ch 5 [6, 7, 7], sc in 2nd ch from hook, in next 3 [4, 5, 5] chs, and in each sc, turn. *(22 [27, 30, 33] sc)*

Rows 15–24 [17–26, 17–28, 19–30]: Rep row 2.

Row 25 [27, 29, 31]: Ch 1, sc dec, in first 2 sc; sc in each sc to last 2 sc; sc dec in last 2 sc. *(20 [25, 28, 31] sc)*

Fasten off and weave in ends.

PANTY BACK

Row 1: Starting at back crotch, with G hook and B, ch 11 [12, 13, 14], working in back bumps only, sc in 2nd ch from hook and in each rem ch, turn. *(10 [11, 12, 13] sc)*

Row 2: Ch 1, sc in each sc, turn.

Row 3: Ch 1, 2 sc in first sc; sc in next 8 [9, 10, 11] sc, 2 sc in last sc, turn. *(12 [13, 14, 15] sc)*

Row 4: Rep row 2.

Row 5: Ch 1, 2 sc in first sc; sc in each sc to last sc; 2 sc in last sc, turn. *(14 [15, 16, 17] sc)*

Rows 6–11 [6–13, 6–13, 6–15]: [Work rows 4 and 5] 3 [4, 4, 5 times. *(20 [23, 24, 27] sc at end of last row)*

Row 12 [14, 14, 16]: Rep row 2.

Row 13 [15, 15, 17]: Ch 4, sc in 2nd ch from hook, in next 2 chs, and in each sc, turn. *(23 [26, 28, 30] sc)*

Row 14 [16, 16, 18]: Ch 4, sc in 2nd ch from hook, in next 2 chs, and in each sc, turn. *(26 [29, 31, 33] sc)*

Rows 15–24 [17–26, 17–28, 19–30]: Rep row 2.

Row 25 [27, 29, 31]: Ch 1, sc dec in first 2 sc; sc in each sc to last sc; sc dec.

Fasten off and weave in ends.

ASSEMBLY

Hold pieces with RS tog; with tapestry needle and B, sew side and crotch seams.

WAISTBAND

Rnd 1 (RS): With G hook, join A with sl st in front lp of center sc of Panty Back; ch 1, sc in same lp; working in front lps only, sc in each sc; join with sl st in first sc.

Rnd 2: Ch 1, sc in same sc and in each rem sc; join with sl st in first sc.

Rnd 3: Ch 1, sc in same sc and in each rem sc; join with sl st in back lp of first sc.

Rnd 4: Ch 1, sc in same lp and in back lp of each rem sc; join with sl st in first sc.

Rnds 5 & 6: Rep rnd 2.

Fasten off, leaving a 24-inch end for sewing. Weave in rem end.

FINISHING
Step 1: Fold Waistband in half. On WS, with tapestry needle and long end, sew edge to unused lps of rnd 1, forming casing.

Step 2: Cut piece of ½-inch-wide elastic approximately 4 inches less than waist size. Place safety pin at end of elastic, pull through casing to desired tightness. With sewing needle and matching thread, overlap elastic ends 1 inch and sew to secure. Sew opening of Waistband closed.

LEG EDGING
Hold piece with RS facing you; with G hook, join A with sl st in first st to left of crotch seam; *ch 2, sl st in back bump of 2nd ch from hook—*picot made*; sk next 2 sc rows, sl st in end of next sc row; rep from * around, join with sl st in joining sl st.

Fasten off and weave in all ends.

Rep on rem Leg.

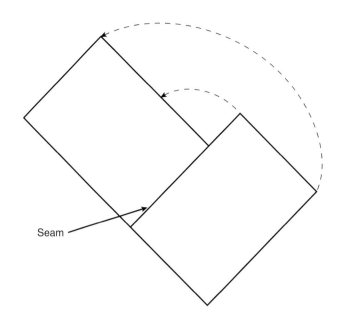

Seam

PONCHO PANEL
Make 2.

Row 1: With G hook and A, ch 57 [60, 63], sc in 2nd ch from hook and in each rem sc, turn. *(56 [59, 62] sc)*

Row 2 (RS): Ch 3 *(counts as a dc on this and following rows)*; *sk next sc, dc in next 2 sc, working around last 2 dc made, dc in sk sc; rep from * to last sc; dc in last sc, turn.

Row 3: Ch 1, sc in each st, turn. *(56 [59, 62] sc)*

Rep rows 2 and 3 until piece measures 5¾ [6½, 7¼] inches from beg.

EDGING
Ch 1, 3 sc in first sc; sc in each sc to last sc; 3 sc in last sc; working across next side in sps formed by edge dc and turning chs, *ch 1, 2 sc in end of next dc row; sk next sc row; rep from * to next corner; working across next side in unused lps of beg ch, 3 sc in first lp; sc in each lp to last lp; 3 sc in last lp; working across next side in sps formed by edge dc and turning chs, **ch 1, 2 sc in end of next dc row, sk next sc row; rep from ** to first sc; ch 1; join with sl st in first sc.

Fasten off and weave in all ends.

ASSEMBLY
Referring to Assembly Diagram and with tapestry needle and A, sew Panels tog.

DAISY
Rnd 1 (RS): With size 5 hook and D, ch 5; join with sl st to form a ring; ch 1, 8 sc in ring. Fasten off.

Rnd 2: With size 5 hook, join C with sl st in any sc; *ch 3, in same sc work (tr, ch 3, sl st)—*petal made*; in each rem sc work (sl st, ch 3, tr, sl st)—*petal made*; join with sl st in joining sl st.

Fasten off and weave in all ends.

FINISHING
Referring to photo for placement, sew Daisy to center front of Poncho.

Little Princess

Design by Laura Gebhardt

FINISHED SIZES
Instructions given fit child's size 6 months; changes for 12, 18 and 24 months are in [ ].

FINISHED GARMENT MEASUREMENTS
Chest: 19 [20, 21, 22] inches

MATERIALS
- Bernat Baby Coordinates light (DK) weight yarn (6 oz/471 yds/170g per skein):
  - 1 [1, 2, 2] skeins #01100 aqua/pink *(A)*
  - 1 [1, 2, 2] skeins #01008 baby pink *(B)*
- Size G/6/4mm crochet hook or size needed to obtain gauge
- Tapestry needle
- 2 coordinating ⅜-inch diameter buttons

GAUGE
18 sc = 5 inches

Take time to check gauge.

SPECIAL STITCHES
V-stitch (V-st): In st indicated work (dc, ch 1, dc).

Beginning shell (beg shell): Ch 3, in sp indicated work (dc, ch 2, 2 dc).

Shell: In sp indicated work (2 dc, ch 2, 2 dc).

Instructions

DRESS
BACK BODICE
Row 1 (RS): With A, ch 35 [37, 39, 41]; sc in 2nd ch from hook, dc in next ch; *sc in next ch, dc in next ch; rep from * across, turn. *(34 [36, 38, 40] sts)*

Row 2: Ch 1, sc in first dc, dc in next sc; *sc in next dc, dc in next sc, rep from * across, turn.

Rows 3 & 4: Rep row 2.

ARMHOLE SHAPING
Row 5: Sl st in first 4 sts, ch 1; *sc in next dc, dc in next sc; rep from * to last 4 sts, turn, leave rem sts unworked. *(26 [28, 30, 32] sts)*

Row 6: Ch 1, sc in first dc, dc in next sc; *sc in next dc, dc in next sc; rep from * across, turn.

RIGHT SHOULDER

For Size 6 Months Only
Row 1: Ch 1, sc in first dc, dc in next sc; [sc in next dc, dc in next sc] 5 times; sc in next dc, turn, leaving rem sts unworked. *(13 sts)*

Row 2: Ch 3 *(counts as a dc on this and following rows)*, [sc in next dc, dc in next sc] 6 times, turn.

Row 3: Ch 1, sc in first dc, dc in next sc, [sc in next dc, dc in next sc] 5 times; sc in 3rd ch of turning ch-3, turn.

Rows 4–7: [Work rows 2 and 3] twice.

Row 8: Rep row 2.

Row 9: Ch 1, sc in first dc, dc in next sc, [sc in next dc, dc in next sc] twice; **sc dec** *(see Stitch Guide)* in next 2 sts, turn, leaving rem sts unworked. *(7 sts)*

Row 10: Ch 3, [sc in next dc, dc in next sc] 3 times. Fasten off.

Continue with Left Shoulder.

For Size 12 Months Only
Row 1: Ch 1, sc in first dc, dc in next sc; [sc in next dc, dc in next sc] 6 times, turn, leaving rem sts unworked. *(14 sts)*

Row 2: Ch 1, sc in first dc, dc in next sc, [sc in next dc, dc in next sc] 6 times, turn.

Row 3: Ch 1, sc in first dc, dc in next sc, [sc in next dc, dc in next sc] 6 times, turn.

Rows 4–9: [Work rows 2 and 3] 3 times.

Row 10: Rep row 2.

Row 11: Ch 1, sc in first dc, dc in next sc, [sc in next dc, dc in next sc] twice; sc in next dc, **dc dec** *(see Stitch Guide)* in next 2 sts, turn, leaving rem sts unworked. *(8 sts)*

Row 12: Ch 1, sc in first dc, dc in next sc, [sc in next dc, dc in next sc] 3 times. Fasten off.

Continue with Left Shoulder.

For Size 18 Months Only
Row 1: Ch 1, sc in first dc, dc in next sc; [sc in next dc, dc in next sc] 6 times; sc in next dc, turn, leaving rem sts unworked. *(15 sts)*

Row 2: Ch 3 *(counts as a dc on this and following rows)*, [sc in next dc, dc in next sc] 7 times, turn.

Row 3: Ch 1, sc in first dc, dc in next sc, [sc in next dc, dc in next sc] 6 times; sc in 3rd ch of turning ch-3, turn.

Rows 4–11: [Work rows 2 and 3] 4 times.

Row 12: Rep row 2.

Row 13: Ch 1, sc in first dc, dc in next sc, [sc in next dc, dc in next sc] 3 times; **sc dec** *(see Stitch Guide)* in next 2 sts, turn, leaving rem sts unworked. *(9 sts)*

Row 14: Ch 3, [sc in next dc, dc in next sc] 4 times. Fasten off.

Continue with Left Shoulder.

For Size 24 Months Only
Row 1: Ch 1, sc in first dc, dc in next sc; [sc in next dc, dc in next sc] 7 times, turn, leaving rem sts unworked. *(16 sts)*

Row 2: Ch 1, sc in first dc, dc in next sc, [sc in next dc, dc in next sc] 7 times, turn.

Row 3: Ch 1, sc in first dc, dc in next sc, [sc in next dc, dc in next sc] 7 times, turn.

Rows 4–11: [Work rows 2 and 3] 4 times.

Row 12: Rep row 2.

Row 13: Ch 1, sc in first dc, dc in next sc, [sc in next dc, dc in next sc] 3 times; sc in next dc, **dc dec** *(see Stitch Guide)* in next 2 sts, turn, leaving rem sts unworked. *(10 sts)*

Row 14: Ch 1, sc in first dc, dc in next sc, [sc in next dc, dc in next sc] 4 times. Fasten off.

Continue with Left Shoulder.

LEFT SHOULDER

For Size 6 Months Only
Row 1 (RS): Join A with sl st in first unworked sc on row 6 from Right Shoulder; ch 3, [sc in next dc, dc in next sc] 6 times, turn. *(13 sts)*

Row 2: Ch 1, sc in first dc, dc in next sc, [sc in next dc, dc in next sc] 5 times; sc in 3rd ch of beg ch-3, turn.

Row 3: Ch 3, [sc in next dc, dc in next sc] 6 times, turn.

Row 4: Ch 1, sc in first dc, dc in next sc, [sc in next dc, dc in next sc] 5 times; sc in 3rd ch of turning ch-3, turn.

Rows 5–8: [Work rows 3 and 4] twice.

Row 9: Sl st in first 5 sts, ch 1, **dc dec** (see Stitch Guide) in next 2 sts; [sc in next dc, dc in next sc] 3 times, turn, leaving rem sts unworked. (7 sts)

Row 10: Ch 1, sc in first dc, dc in next sc, [sc in next dc, dc in next sc] twice; sc in next dc. Fasten off.

Continue with Front.

For Size 12 Months Only
Row 1 (RS): Join A with sl st in first unworked dc on row 6 from Right Shoulder; ch 1, sc in same dc, dc in next sc; [sc in next dc, dc in next sc] 6 times, turn. (14 sts)

Row 2: Ch 1, sc in first dc, dc in next sc, [sc in next dc, dc in next sc] 6 times, turn.

Row 3: Ch 1, sc in first dc, dc in next sc, [sc in next dc, dc in next sc] 6 times, turn.

Rows 4–9: [Work rows 2 and 3] 3 times.

Row 10: Rep row 2.

Row 11: Sl st in first 5 sts, ch 1, **sc dec** (see Stitch Guide) in next 2 sts; dc in next sc, [sc in next dc, dc in next sc] 3 times, turn, leaving rem sts unworked. (8 sts)

Row 12: Ch 1, sc in first dc, dc in next sc, [sc in next dc, dc in next sc] 3 times. Fasten off.

Continue with Sleeve.

For Size 18 Months Only
Row 1 (RS): Join A with sl st in first unworked sc on row 6 from Right Shoulder; ch 3, [sc in next dc, dc in next sc] 7 times, turn. (15 sts)

Row 2: Ch 1, sc in first dc, dc in next sc, [sc in next dc, dc in next sc] 6 times; sc in 3rd ch of beg ch-3, turn.

Row 3: Ch 3, [sc in next dc, dc in next sc] 7 times, turn.

Row 4: Ch 1, sc in first dc, dc in next sc, [sc in next dc, dc in next sc] 6 times; sc in 3rd ch of turning ch-3, turn.

Rows 5–12: [Work rows 3 and 4] 4 times.

Row 13: Sl st in first 5 sts, ch 1, **dc dec** (see Stitch Guide) in next 2 sts; [sc in next dc, dc in next sc] 4 times, turn, leaving rem sts unworked. (9 sts)

Row 14: Ch 1, sc in first dc, dc in next sc, [sc in next dc, dc in next sc] 4 times; sc in next dc. Fasten off.

Continue with Front.

For Size 24 Months Only
Row 1 (RS): Join A with sl st in first unworked dc on row 6 from Right Shoulder; ch 1, sc in same dc, dc in next sc; [sc in next dc, dc in next sc] 7 times, turn. (16 sts)

Row 2: Ch 1, sc in first dc, dc in next sc, [sc in next dc, dc in next sc] 7 times, turn.

Row 3: Ch 1, sc in first dc, dc in next sc, [sc in next dc, dc in next sc] 7 times, turn.

Rows 4–11: [Work rows 2 and 3] 4 times.

Row 12: Rep row 2.

Row 13: Sl st in first 5 sts, ch 1, **sc dec** (see Stitch Guide) in next 2 sts;

dc in next sc, [sc in next dc, dc in next sc] 4 times, turn, leaving rem sts unworked. *(10 sts)*

Row 14: Ch 1, sc in first dc, dc in next sc, [sc in next dc, dc in next sc] 4 times. Fasten off.

Continue with Front.

FRONT BODICE
Work same as Back through row 6 of Armhole Shaping.

Rows 7–12 [7–14, 7–16, 7–16]: Rep row 6.

LEFT SHOULDER

For Size 6 Months Only
Row 13: Ch 1, sc in first dc, [dc in next sc, sc in next dc] 3 times; dc in next sc, turn, leaving rem sts unworked. *(8 sts)*

Row 14: Ch 1, sc in first dc, [dc in next sc, sc in next dc] 3 times; dc in last sc, turn.

Row 15: Ch 1, sc in first dc, [dc in next sc, sc in next dc] twice; dc in next sc, sc dec in next 2 sts, turn. *(7 sts)*

Row 16: Ch 1, sc in first 2 sts, [dc in next sc, sc in next dc] twice; dc in last sc. Fasten off.

Continue with Right Shoulder.

For Size 12 Months Only
Row 15: Ch 1, sc in first dc; [dc in next sc, sc in next dc] 4 times, turn, leaving rem sts unworked. *(9 sts)*

Row 16: Ch 3, [sc in next dc, dc in next sc] 4 times, turn.

Row 17: Ch 1, sc in first dc, [dc in next sc, sc in next dc] 3 times; sc dec in next sc and in 3rd ch of beg ch-3, turn. *(8 sts)*

Row 18: Ch 1, sc in first st, [dc in

next sc, sc in next dc] 3 times; dc in last sc. Fasten off.

Continue with Right Shoulder.

For Size 18 Months Only
Row 17: Ch 1, sc in first dc; [dc in next sc, sc in next dc] 4 times; dc in next sc, turn, leaving rem sts unworked. *(10 sts)*

Row 18: Ch 1, sc in first dc, [dc in next sc, sc in next dc] 4 times; dc in last sc, turn.

Row 19: Ch 1, sc in first dc, [dc in next sc, sc in next dc] 3 times; dc in next sc, sc dec in next 2 sts, turn. *(9 sts)*

Row 20: Ch 1, sc in first 2 sts, [dc in next sc, sc in next dc] 3 times; dc in last sc. Fasten off.

Continue with Right Shoulder.

For Size 24 Months Only
Row 17: Ch 1, sc in first dc; [dc in next sc, sc in next dc] 5 times, turn, leaving rem sts unworked. *(11 sts)*

Row 18: Ch 3, [sc in next dc, dc in

next sc] 5 times, turn.

Row 19: Ch 1, sc in first dc, [dc in next sc, sc in next dc] 4 times; sc dec in next sc and in 3rd ch of beg ch-3, turn. *(10 sts)*

Row 20: Ch 1, sc in first st, [dc in next sc, sc in next dc] 4 times; dc in last sc. Fasten off.

Continue with Right Shoulder.

RIGHT SHOULDER

For Size 6 Months Only
Row 1 (RS): Hold piece with RS facing you; sk next 10 sts from Left Shoulder, join yarn with sl st in next dc; ch 1, sc in same dc; [dc in next sc, sc in next dc] 3 times; dc in last sc, turn. *(8 sts)*

Row 2: Ch 1, sc in first dc, [dc in next sc, sc in next dc] 3 times; dc in last sc, turn.

Row 3: Ch 1, [dc in next sc, sc in next dc] 3 times; dc in last sc, turn. *(7 sts)*

Row 4: Ch 1, sc in first dc, [dc in

next sc, sc in next dc] 3 times. Fasten off.

Continue with Sleeve.

For Size 12 Months Only
Row 1 (RS): Hold piece with RS facing you; sk next 10 sts from Left Shoulder, join yarn with sl st in next dc; ch 3, [sc in next dc, dc in next sc] 4 times, turn. *(9 sts)*

Row 2: Ch 1, sc in first dc, [dc in next sc, sc in next dc] 3 times; dc in next sc, sc in 3rd ch of beg ch-3, turn.

Row 3: Ch 1, [sc in next dc, dc in next sc] 4 times, turn. *(8 sts)*

Row 4: Ch 1, sc in first dc, [dc in next sc, sc in next dc] 3 times, dc in last sc. Fasten off.

Continue with Sleeve.

For Size 18 Months Only
Row 1 (RS): Hold piece with RS facing you; sk next 10 sts from Left Shoulder, join yarn with sl st in next dc; ch 1, sc in same dc; [dc in next sc, sc in next dc] 4 times; dc in last sc, turn. *(10 sts)*

Row 2: Ch 1, sc in first dc, [dc in next sc, sc in next dc] 4 times; dc in last sc, turn.

Row 3: Ch 1, [dc in next sc, sc in next dc] 4 times; dc in last sc, turn. *(9 sts)*

Row 4: Ch 1, sc in first dc, [dc in next sc, sc in next dc] 4 times. Fasten off.

Continue with Sleeve.

For Size 24 Months Only
Row 1 (RS): Hold piece with RS facing you; sk next 10 sts from Left Shoulder, join yarn with sl st in next dc; ch 3, [sc in next dc, dc in next sc] 5 times, turn. *(11 sts)*

Row 2: Ch 1, sc in first dc, [dc in next sc, sc in next dc] 4 times; dc in next sc, sc in 3rd ch of beg ch-3, turn.

Row 3: Ch 1, [sc in next dc, dc in next sc] 5 times, turn. *(10 sts)*

Row 4: Ch 1, sc in first dc, [dc in next sc, sc in next dc] 4 times, dc in last sc. Fasten off.

Continue with Sleeve.

SLEEVE
Make 2.
Row 1 (RS): With A, ch 23 [23, 27, 27]; sc in 2nd ch from hook, dc in next ch; *sc in next ch, dc in next ch; rep from * across, turn. *(22 [22, 26, 26] sts)*

Row 2: Ch 1, sc in first dc, dc in next sc; *sc in next dc, dc in next sc, rep from * across, turn.

Row 3: Ch 3 *(counts as a dc on this and following rows)*, sc in first dc, dc in next sc; *sc in next dc, dc in next sc, rep from * to last 2 sts; sc in next dc, in last sc work (dc, sc), turn. *(24 [24, 28, 28] sts)*

Row 4: Ch 3; *sc in next dc, dc in next sc; rep from * to turning ch-3; sc in 3rd ch of turning ch-3.

Rows 5 & 6: Rep row 4.

Row 7: Ch 1, in first sc work (sc, dc); *sc in next dc, dc in next sc; rep from * to turning ch-3; in 3rd ch of turning ch-3 work (sc, dc), turn. *(26 [26, 30, 30] sts)*

Rows 8–10: Rep row 2.

Row 11: Ch 3, sc in first dc, dc in next sc; *sc in next dc, dc in next sc, rep from * to last 2 sts; sc in next dc, in last sc work (dc, sc), turn. *(28 [28, 32, 32] sts)*

Rows 12–14: Rep row 4.

Row 15: Ch 1, in first sc work (sc, dc); *sc in next dc, dc in next sc; rep from * to turning ch-3; in 3rd ch of turning ch-3 work (sc, dc), turn. *(30 [30, 34, 34] sts)*

For Size 6 Months Only
Rep row 2 until piece measures 6½ inches from beg. Fasten off and weave in ends.

Continue with Assembly.

For Size 12 Months Only
Rows 16–18: Rep row 2.

Row 19: Ch 3, sc in first dc, dc in next sc; *sc in next dc, dc in next sc, rep from * to last 2 sts; sc in next dc, in last sc work (dc, sc), turn. *(32 sts)*

Rep row 4 until piece measures 7½ inches from beg. Fasten off and weave in ends.

Continue with Assembly.

For Size 18 Months Only
Rows 16–18: Rep row 2.

Row 19: Ch 3, sc in first dc, dc in next sc; *sc in next dc, dc in next sc, rep from * to last 2 sts; sc in next dc, in last sc work (dc, sc), turn. *(28 [28, 32, 32] sts)*

Rows 20–22: Rep row 4.

Row 23: Ch 1, in first sc work (sc, dc); *sc in next dc, dc in next sc; rep from * to turning ch-3; in 3rd ch of turning ch-3 work (sc, dc), turn. *(36 sts)*

Rep row 2 until piece measures 8 inches from beg. Fasten off and weave in ends.

Continue with Assembly.

For Size 24 Months Only
Rows 16–18: Rep row 2.

Row 19: Ch 3, sc in first dc, dc in

next sc; *sc in next dc, dc in next sc, rep from * to last 2 sts; sc in next dc, in last sc work (dc, sc), turn. (32 sts)

Rows 20–22: Rep row 4.

Row 23: Ch 1, in first sc work (sc, dc); *sc in next dc, dc in next sc; rep from * to turning ch-3; in 3rd ch of turning ch-3 work (sc, dc), turn. (36 sts)

Rep row 2 until piece measures 8½ inches from beg. Fasten off and weave in ends.

Continue with Assembly.

ASSEMBLY
With tapestry needle and A, sew shoulder seams. Sew Sleeves in armhole openings, then sew Sleeve and side seams.

SKIRT
Rnd 1 (RS): Hold Bodice with RS facing you and beg ch at top; join A in first unused lp of beg ch from 1 side seam; ch 1, sc in same lp and in each rem unused lp; join with sl st in first sc. (68 [72, 76, 80] sc)

Rnd 2: Ch 4 (counts as a dc and a ch-1 sp), dc in same sc; *sk next sc, in next sc work **V-st** (see Special Stitches); rep from * around; join with sl st in 3rd ch of beg ch-4. (34 [36, 38, 40] V-sts)

Rnd 3: Sl st in next ch-1 sp, **beg shell** (see Special Stitches) in same sp; in ch-1 sp of each rem V-st work **shell** (see Special Stitches); join with sl st in 3rd ch of beg ch-3.

Rnd 4: Sl st in next dc and in next ch-2 sp, beg shell in same sp; shell in ch-2 of each rem shell; join with sl st in 3rd ch of beg ch-3.

Rep rnd 4 until piece measures approximately 8 [9, 10, 11] inches from beg. Fasten off.

EDGING
Join B in any ch-2 sp of last rnd of Skirt; beg shell in same sp; shell in ch-2 sp of each rem shell; join with sl st in 3rd ch of beg ch-3.

Fasten off and weave in all ends.

NECK EDGING
Rnd 1 (RS): Join B in first st at top of left-back neck opening; ch 1, work 35 [39, 43, 43] sc evenly around neck edge to top of right-back neck opening; working in ends of rows of right-back opening sc in each row; working in ends of rows of left-back opening, sc in next 4 [5, 6, 5] rows, ch 3—button lp made; sc in next 4 [5, 5, 5] rows, ch 3—button lp made; sc in next 2 [2, 3, 3] rows; join with sl st in first sc.

Rnd 2: Ch 1, sc in same sc; *ch 3, hdc in top of sc just made, sk next sc, sc in next sc; rep from * to top corner of right back neck opening Fasten off and weave in ends.

SLEEVE EDGING
Rnd 1 (RS): Join B in first unused lp of beg ch to left of 1 Sleeve seam; ch 1, sc in same unused lp and in each rem unused lp; join with sl st in first sc. (22 [22, 26, 26] sc)

Rnd 2: Ch 1, sc in same sc; ch 3, hdc in sc just made, sk next sc; *sc in next sc, ch 3, hdc in sc just made; rep from * around; join with sl st in first sc.

Fasten off and weave in ends.

Rep on rem Sleeve.

FINISHING
With sewing needle and matching thread, sew buttons opposite button lps.

JACKET
BACK
Row 1: With B, ch 43 [45, 47, 49]; sc in 2nd ch from hook, dc in next ch; *sc in next ch, dc in next ch; rep from * across, turn. (42 [44, 46, 48] sts)

Row 2: Ch 1, sc in first dc, dc in next sc; *sc in next dc, dc in next sc; rep from * across, turn.

Rows 3–14 [3–14, 3–16, 3–16]: Rep row 2.

ARMHOLE SHAPING
Row 15 [15, 17, 17]: Sl st in first 4 sts, ch 1; *sc in next dc, dc in next sc; rep from * to last 4 sts, turn, leave rem sts unworked. (34 [36, 38, 40] sts)

Rows 16–24 [16–26, 18–30, 18–30]: Rep row 2.

Fasten off and weave in ends.

LEFT FRONT
Row 1: Ch 21 [23, 25, 27]; sc in 2nd ch from hook, dc in next ch; *sc in next ch, dc in next ch; rep from * across, turn. (20 [22, 24, 26] sts)

Row 2: Ch 1, sc in first dc, dc in next sc; *sc in next dc, dc in next sc; rep from * across, turn.

Rows 3–14 [3–14, 3–16, 3–16]: Rep row 2.

ARMHOLE SHAPING

For Size 6 Months Only
Row 15: Sl st in first 4 sts, ch 1; *sc in next dc, dc in next sc; rep from * to last 2 sts; **sc dec** (see Stitch Guide) in last 2 sts, turn. (15 sts)

Row 16: Ch 3 (counts as a dc on this and following rows); *sc in next dc, dc in next sc; rep from * across, turn.

Row 17: Ch 1, sc in first dc, [dc in next sc, sc in next dc] 6 times; **dc dec** (see Stitch Guide) in next st and in 3rd ch of turning ch-3, turn. (14 sts)

Row 18: Ch 1, sc in first dc, dc in next dc, [sc in next dc, dc in next sc] 6 times, turn.

Row 19: Ch 1, sc in first dc, dc in next sc, [sc in next dc, dc in next sc] 5 times; sc dec in last 2 sts, turn. *(13 sts)*

Row 20: Ch 3, *sc in next dc, dc in next sc; rep from * across, turn.

Row 21: Ch 1, sc in first dc, [dc in next sc, sc in next dc] 5 times; dc dec in next st and in 3rd ch of turning ch-3, turn. *(12 sts)*

Row 22: Ch 1, sc in first dc, dc in next dc, [sc in next dc, dc in next sc] 5 times, turn.

Row 23: Ch 1, sc in first dc, dc in next sc, [sc in next dc, dc in next sc] 4 times; sc dec in last 2 sts, turn. *(11 sts)*

Row 24: Ch 3, [sc in next dc, dc in next sc] 5 times.

Fasten off and weave in ends.

Continue with Right Front.

For Size 12 Months Only
Row 15: Sl st in first 4 sts, ch 1; *sc in next dc, dc in next sc; rep from * to last 2 sts; **sc dec** *(see Stitch Guide)* in last 2 sts, turn. *(17 sts)*

Row 16: Ch 3 *(counts as a dc on this and following rows)*; *sc in next dc, dc in next sc; rep from * across, turn.

Row 17: Ch 1, sc in first dc, [dc in next sc, sc in next dc] 7 times; **dc dec** *(see Stitch Guide)* in next st and in 3rd ch of turning ch-3, turn. *(16 sts)*

Row 18: Ch 1, sc in first dc, dc in next dc, [sc in next dc, dc in next sc] 7 times, turn.

Row 19: Ch 1, sc in first dc, dc in

next sc, [sc in next dc, dc in next sc] 6 times; sc dec in last 2 sts, turn. *(15 sts)*

Row 20: Ch 3, *sc in next dc, dc in next sc; rep from * across, turn.

Row 21: Ch 1, sc in first dc, [dc in next sc, sc in next dc] 6 times; dc dec in next st and in 3rd ch of turning ch-3, turn. *(14 sts)*

Row 22: Ch 1, sc in first dc, dc in next dc, [sc in next dc, dc in next sc] 6 times, turn.

Row 23: Ch 1, sc in first dc, dc in next sc, [sc in next dc, dc in next sc] 5 times; sc dec in last 2 sts, turn. *(13 sts)*

Row 24: Ch 3, *sc in next dc, dc in next sc; rep from * across, turn.

Row 25: Ch 1, sc in first dc, [dc in next sc, sc in next dc] 5 times; dc dec in next st and in 3rd ch of turning ch-3, turn. *(12 sts)*

Row 26: Ch 1, sc in first dc, dc in next sc, [sc in next dc, dc in next sc] 5 times.

Fasten off and weave in ends.

Continue with Right Front.

For Size 18 Months Only
Row 17: Sl st in first 4 sts, ch 1; *sc

in next dc, dc in next sc; rep from * to last 2 sts; **sc dec** *(see Stitch Guide)* in last 2 sts, turn. *(19 sts)*

Row 18: Ch 3 *(counts as a dc on this and following rows)*; *sc in next dc, dc in next sc; rep from * across, turn.

Row 19: Ch 1, sc in first dc, [dc in next sc, sc in next dc] 8 times; dc dec in next st and in 3rd ch of turning ch-3, turn. *(18 sts)*

Row 20: Ch 1, sc in first dc, dc in next dc, [sc in next dc, dc in next sc] 8 times, turn.

Row 21: Ch 1, sc in first dc, dc in next sc, [sc in next dc, dc in next sc] 7 times; sc dec in last 2 sts, turn. *(17 sts)*

Row 22: Ch 3, *sc in next dc, dc in next sc; rep from * across, turn.

Row 23: Ch 1, sc in first dc, [dc in next sc, sc in next dc] 7 times; **dc dec** *(see Stitch Guide)* in next st and in 3rd ch of turning ch-3, turn. *(16 sts)*

Row 24: Ch 1, sc in first dc, dc in next dc, [sc in next dc, dc in next sc] 7 times, turn.

Row 25: Ch 1, sc in first dc, dc in next sc, [sc in next dc, dc in next sc] 6 times; sc dec in last 2 sts, turn. *(15 sts)*

Row 26: Ch 3, [sc in next dc, dc in next sc] 7 times.

Row 27: Ch 1, sc in first dc, [dc in next sc, sc in next dc] 6 times; dc dec in next st and in 3rd ch of turning ch-3, turn. *(14 sts)*

Row 28: Ch 1, sc in first dc, dc in next dc, [sc in next dc, dc in next sc] 6 times, turn.

Rows 29 & 30: Rep row 28.

Fasten off and weave in ends.

Continue with Right Front.

For Size 24 Months Only
Row 17: Sl st in first 4 sts, ch 1; *sc in next dc, dc in next sc; rep from * to last 2 sts; sc dec in last 2 sts, turn. *(21 sts)*

Row 18: Ch 3 *(counts as a dc on this and following rows);* *sc in next dc, dc in next sc; rep from * across, turn.

Row 19: Ch 1, sc in first dc, [dc in next sc, sc in next dc] 8 times; dc dec in next st and in 3rd ch of turning ch-3, turn. *(20 sts)*

Row 20: Ch 1, sc in first dc, dc in next dc, [sc in next dc, dc in next sc] 9 times, turn.

Row 21: Ch 1, sc in first dc, dc in next sc, [sc in next dc, dc in next sc] 8 times; **sc dec** *(see Stitch Guide)* in last 2 sts, turn. *(19 sts)*

Row 22: Ch 3, *sc in next dc, dc in next sc; rep from * across, turn.

Row 23: Ch 1, sc in first dc, [dc in next sc, sc in next dc] 8 times; **dc dec** *(see Stitch Guide)* in next st and in 3rd ch of turning ch-3, turn. *(18 sts)*

Row 24: Ch 1, sc in first dc, dc in next dc, [sc in next dc, dc in next sc] 8 times, turn.

Row 25: Ch 1, sc in first dc, dc in next sc, [sc in next dc, dc in next sc] 7 times; sc dec in last 2 sts, turn. *(17 sts)*

Row 26: Ch 3, [sc in next dc, dc in next sc] 8 times.

Row 27: Ch 1, sc in first dc, [dc in next sc, sc in next dc] 7 times; dc dec in next st and in 3rd ch of turning ch-3, turn. *(16 sts)*

Row 28: Ch 1, sc in first dc, dc in next dc, [sc in next dc, dc in next sc] 7 times, turn.

Row 29: Ch 1, sc in first dc, dc in next sc, [sc in next dc, dc in next sc] 6 times; sc dec in last 2 sts, turn. *(15 sts)*

Row 30: Ch 3, [sc in next dc, dc in next sc] 7 times, turn.

Fasten off and weave in ends.

Continue with Right Front.

RIGHT FRONT
Work same as Left Front to Armhole Shaping.

ARMHOLE SHAPING

For Size 6 Months Only
Row 15: Ch 1, [dc in next sc, sc in next dc] 7 times; dc in next sc, turn. *(15 sts)*

Row 16: Ch 1, sc in first dc, dc in next sc, [sc in next dc, dc in next sc] 6 times; sc in next dc, turn.

Row 17: Ch 1, [sc in next dc, dc in next sc] 7 times, turn. *(14 sts)*

Row 18: Ch 1, sc in first dc, dc in next sc, [sc in next dc, dc in next sc] 6 times, turn.

Row 19: Ch 1, dc in next sc, [sc in next dc, dc in next sc] 6 times, turn. *(13 sts)*

Row 20: Ch 1, sc in first dc, dc in next sc, [sc in next dc, dc in next sc] 5 times; sc in next dc, turn.

Row 21: Ch 1, [sc in next dc, dc in next sc] 6 times, turn. *(12 sts)*

Row 22: Ch 1, sc in first dc, dc in next sc, [sc in next dc, dc in next sc] 5 times, turn.

Row 23: Ch 1, [dc in next sc, sc in next dc] 5 times; dc in next sc, turn. *(11 sts)*

Row 24: Ch 1, sc in first dc, [dc in next sc, sc in next dc] 5 times.

Fasten off and weave in ends.

Continue with Sleeve.

For Size 12 Months Only
Row 15: Ch 1, [dc in next sc, sc in next dc] 8 times; dc in next sc, turn. *(17 sts)*

Row 16: Ch 1, sc in first dc, dc in next sc, [sc in next dc, dc in next sc] 7 times; sc in next dc, turn.

Row 17: Ch 1, [sc in next dc, dc in next sc] 8 times, turn. *(16 sts)*

Row 18: Ch 1, sc in first dc, dc in next sc, [sc in next dc, dc in next sc] 7 times, turn.

Row 19: Ch 1, dc in next sc, [sc in next dc, dc in next sc] 7 times, turn. *(15 sts)*

Row 20: Ch 1, sc in first dc, dc in next sc, [sc in next dc, dc in next sc] 6 times; sc in next dc, turn.

Row 21: Ch 1, [sc in next dc, dc in next sc] 6 times, turn. *(14 sts)*

Row 22: Ch 1, sc in first dc, dc in next sc, [sc in next dc, dc in next sc] 6 times, turn.

Row 23: Ch 1, [dc in next sc, sc in next dc] 6 times; dc in next sc, turn. *(13 sts)*

Row 24: Ch 1, sc in first dc, [dc in next sc, sc in next dc] 6 times.

Row 25: Ch 1, [sc in next dc, dc in next sc] 6 times, turn. (12 sts)

Row 26: Ch 1, sc in first dc, dc in next sc, [sc in next dc, dc in next sc] 5 times.

Fasten off and weave in ends.

Continue with Sleeve.

For Size 18 Months Only
Row 17: Ch 1, [dc in next sc, sc in next dc] 9 times; dc in next sc, turn. (19 sts)

Row 18: Ch 1, sc in first dc, dc in next sc, [sc in next dc, dc in next sc] 8 times; sc in next dc, turn.

Row 19: Ch 1, [sc in next dc, dc in next sc] 7 times, turn. (18 sts)

Row 20: Ch 1, sc in first dc, dc in next sc, [sc in next dc, dc in next sc] 8 times, turn.

Row 21: Ch 1, dc in next sc, [sc in next dc, dc in next sc] 8 times, turn. (17 sts)

Row 22: Ch 1, sc in first dc, dc in next sc, [sc in next dc, dc in next sc] 7 times; sc in next dc, turn.

Row 23: Ch 1, [sc in next dc, dc in next sc] 8 times, turn. (16 sts)

Row 24: Ch 1, sc in first dc, dc in next sc, [sc in next dc, dc in next sc] 7 times, turn.

Row 25: Ch 1, [dc in next sc, sc in next dc] 7 times; dc in next sc, turn. (15 sts)

Row 26: Ch 1, sc in first dc, [dc in next sc, sc in next dc] 7 times.

Row 27: Ch 1, [sc in next dc, dc in next sc] 7 times, turn. (14 sts)

Row 28: Ch 1, sc in first dc, dc in next sc, [sc in next dc, dc in next sc] 6 times, turn.

Rows 29 & 30: Rep row 28.

Fasten off and weave in ends.

Continue with Sleeve.

For Size 24 Months Only
Row 17: Ch 1, [dc in next sc, sc in next dc] 10 times; dc in next sc, turn. (21 sts)

Row 18: Ch 1, sc in first dc, dc in next sc, [sc in next dc, dc in next sc] 9 times; sc in next dc, turn.

Row 19: Ch 1, [sc in next dc, dc in next sc] 10 times, turn. (20 sts)

Row 20: Ch 1, sc in first dc, dc in next sc, [sc in next dc, dc in next sc] 9 times, turn.

Row 21: Ch 1, dc in next sc, [sc in next dc, dc in next sc] 9 times, turn. (19 sts)

Row 22: Ch 1, sc in first dc, dc in next sc, [sc in next dc, dc in next sc] 8 times; sc in next dc, turn.

Row 23: Ch 1, [sc in next dc, dc in next sc] 9 times, turn. (18 sts)

Row 24: Ch 1, sc in first dc, dc in next sc, [sc in next dc, dc in next sc] 8 times, turn.

Row 25: Ch 1, [dc in next sc, sc in next dc] 8 times; dc in next sc, turn. (17 sts)

Row 26: Ch 1, sc in first dc, [dc in next sc, sc in next dc] 8 times.

Row 27: Ch 1, [sc in next dc, dc in next sc] 8 times, turn. (16 sts)

Row 28: Ch 1, sc in first dc, dc in next sc, [sc in next dc, dc in next sc] 7 times, turn.

Row 29: Ch 1, [dc in next sc, sc in next dc] 7 times; dc in next sc, turn. (15 sts)

Row 30: Ch 1, sc in first dc, [dc in next sc, sc in next dc] 7 times.

Fasten off and weave in ends.

Continue with Sleeve.

SLEEVE
Make 2.
Row 1: With B, ch 33 [35, 39, 39]; sc in 2nd ch from hook, dc in next ch; *sc in next ch, dc in next ch; rep from * across, turn. (32 [34, 38, 38] sts)

Row 2: Ch 1, sc in first dc, dc in next sc; *sc in next dc, dc in next sc; rep from * across, turn.

Rep row 2 until piece measures 7 [8, 8½, 9] inches from beg.

Fasten off and weave in ends.

ASSEMBLY
With tapestry needle and B, sew shoulder seams. Sew Sleeves in armhole openings; sew Sleeve and side seams.

EDGING
Rnd 1: Hold Jacket with RS facing you; join B in first st of back neck to left of right shoulder seam; ch 1, sc evenly spaced around outer edge of Jacket; join with sl st in first sc.

Rnd 2: Ch 1, sc in same sc, ch 3, hdc in top of sc just made, sk next sc; *sc in next sc, ch 3, hdc in top of sc just made; rep from * around; join with sl st in first sc.

Fasten off and weave in ends.

Mint Smoothie Jumper

Design by Cindy Adams

SKILL LEVEL

EASY

FINISHED SIZES
Instructions given fit child's size 6 months; changes for 12 months and 18 months are in [ ].

FINISHED GARMENT MEASUREMENTS
Chest: 17 [18, 19] inches

MATERIALS
- Red Heart Soft Baby light (light worsted) weight yarn (7 oz/575 yds/198g per skein):
   1 skein #7680 new mint *(A)*
   small amount #7001 white *(B)*
- Size G/6/4mm crochet hook or size needed to obtain gauge
- Tapestry needle
- 2 yds½-inch-wide white satin ribbon
- Sewing needle and matching thread
- Purchased hair clip

GAUGE
6 (sc, dc, sc) groups = 4 inches

Take time to check gauge.

Instructions

FRONT/BACK
Make 2.

Row 1 (RS): With A, ch 46 [49, 52]; in 3rd ch from hook (*beg 2 sk chs count as a dc*) work (sc, dc, sc); *sk next 2 chs; in next ch work (sc, dc, sc); rep from * to last ch; dc in last ch, turn.

Row 2: Ch 2 (*counts as a dc on this and following rows*), in each dc work (sc, dc, sc); dc in 2nd ch of beg 2 sk chs, turn.

Row 3: Ch 2, in each dc work (sc, dc, sc); dc in 2nd ch of turning ch-2, turn.

Rep row 3 until piece measures 9 [10, 11] inches from beg.

ARMHOLE SHAPING
Row 1: Sl st in first dc and in next 3 sts; ch 2; *in next dc work (sc, dc, sc); rep from * to last 3 sts and turning ch-2; dc in next sc, turn, leaving rem sts and turning ch-2 unworked.

Row 2: Sl st in first dc and in next 3 sts; ch 2; *in next dc work (sc, dc, sc); rep from * to last 3 sts and beg ch-2; dc in next sc, turn, leaving rem sts and beg ch-2 unworked.

Rows 3–5: Rep row 2.

Fasten off and weave in ends.

ASSEMBLY
Hold Front and Back with RS tog. Working through both pieces at same time, join A with sl st in edge of row 1; working across side, sl st in each row. Rep on opposite side.

LOWER EDGING
Hold piece with beg ch at top; join A with sl st in 1 side seam; ch 2, working in unused lp of beg ch at base of each (sc, dc, sc) group, in each lp work (sc, dc, sc); join in 2nd ch of beg ch-2.

Fasten off and weave in ends.

JUMPER FLOWER
Make 2.

Rnd 1 (RS): With A, ch 4; join to form ring; 10 sc in ring; join with sl st in first sc. Fasten off.

Rnd 2: Join B in any sc; ch 1, sc in same sc; [ch 3, sk next sc, sc in next sc] 4 times; ch 3, sk last sc; join with sl st in first sc.

Rnd 3: Sl st in next ch-3 sp; in same sp and in each rem ch-3 sp work (sc, ch 3, 4 dc, ch 3, sc); join with sl st in first sc.

Fasten off and weave in all ends.

HAIR-CLIP FLOWER
Rnd 1 (RS): With B, ch 4; join to form ring; 10 sc in ring; join with sl st in first sc. Fasten off.

Rnd 2: Join A in any sc; ch 1, sc in same sc; [ch 3, sk next sc, sc in next sc] 4 times; ch 3, sk last sc; join with sl st in first sc.

Rnd 3: Sl st in next ch-3 sp; in same sp and in each rem ch-3 sp work (sc, ch 3, 4 dc, ch 3, sc); join with sl st in first sc.

Fasten off and weave in all ends.

FINISHING
Step 1: Cut ribbon in 4 lengths, each 18 inches. Referring to photo for placement and with sewing needle and matching thread, sew 2 pieces to WS of Front and 2

pieces to WS of Back. Tie in bows at top of shoulders.

Step 2: Referring to photo for placement, sew Jumper Flowers to Front. Sew Hair Clip Flower to hair clip.

Play-Date Dress & Hat

Design by Cassie Hennen

FINISHED SIZES
Dress: Instructions given fit child's size 6 months; changes for 12, 18 and 24 months are in [ ].

Hat: Instructions given fit child's size 6–12 months; changes for size 12–24 months are in [ ].

MATERIALS
- Red Heart Soft Baby light (light worsted) weight yarn (solids: 7 oz/575 yds/198g; multis: 6 oz/430 yds/170g per skein):
    2 skeins #7959 giggle multi (A)
    1 skein #7001 white (B)
- Size G/6/4mm crochet hook or size needed to obtain gauge
- Tapestry needle
- 2 white ½-inch buttons
- Sewing needle and matching thread
- 1 yd ⅞-inch-wide white ribbon

Note: Yarn amounts sufficient for all sizes.

GAUGE
4 hdc = 1 inch

Take time to check gauge.

Instructions

DRESS
Row 1 (RS): Starting at neck with A, ch 53 [57, 59, 63]; hdc in 3rd ch from hook *(beg 2 sk chs count as a hdc)* and in each rem ch, turn. *(52 [56, 58, 62] hdc)*

Row 2: Ch 1, sk first hdc; * in next hdc work (sc, ch 2, hdc); sk next hdc; rep from * to beg 2 sk chs; sc in 2nd ch of beg 2 sk chs, turn.

Row 3: Ch 1, 2 sc in first sc; keeping ch-2 sps to front of work, 3 sc in each sc to last sc; 2 sc in last sc, turn.

Row 4: Ch 1, sk first sc; *in next sc work (sc, ch 2, hdc); sk next sc; rep from * to last sc; sc in last sc, turn.

Row 5: Ch 1, 2 sc in first sc; keeping ch-2 sps to front of work, 2 sc in each rem sc, turn.

Row 6: Rep row 4.

Rows 7–10: Rep rows 3–6.

Note: Remainder of Dress is worked in joined rows.

Row 11: Ch 1, 2 sc in first sc; *sk next ch-2 sp, sc in next sc; rep from * 7 [8, 9, 10] times; sk next 11 [12, 13, 14] ch-2 sps, 2 sc in each of next 18 [19, 20, 21] sts; sk next 11 [12, 13, 14] ch-2 sps, 2 sc in each of last 9 [10, 11, 12] sts; join with sl st in first sc, turn.

Row 12: Ch 1, sk first sc; *in next sc work (sc, ch 2, hdc); sk next sc; rep from * around; join with sl st in first sc, turn.

Row 13: Ch 3 *(counts as a dc on this and following rows)*, dc in same sc; 2 dc in each rem sc; join with sl st in 3rd ch of beg ch-3, turn.

Row 14: Ch 1, in same ch as joining, in each dc and in 3rd ch of turning ch-3 work (sc, ch 2, hdc); join with sl st in first sc, turn.

Row 15: Ch 1, 3 sc in each sc; join with sl st in first sc, turn.

Row 16: Ch 1, sk first sc; *in next sc work (sc, ch 2, hdc); sk next sc; rep from * around; join with sl st in first sc, turn.

Row 17: Ch 1, 2 sc in each sc; join with sl st in first sc, turn.

Rep rows 16 and 17 until piece measures 7 [8, 9, 10] inches from row 15, ending with a row 16. At end of last row, change to B by drawing lp through; cut A.

EDGING
Row 1: Ch 1, 2 sc in each sc; join with sl st in first sc, turn.

Row 2: Ch 1, sk first sc; *in next sc work (sc, ch 2, hdc); sk next sc; rep from * around; join with sl st in first sc, turn.

Row 3: Ch 1, keeping ch-2 sps to front of work, in each sc work (sc, ch 2, hdc); join with sl st in first sc.

Fasten off and weave in all ends.

ARMHOLE EDGING
Row 1 (RS): Hold piece with RS

facing you; with B make slip knot on hook and join with sc in center st of 1 underarm; sc in same st; working around armhole opening, 2 sc in each sc; join with sl st in joining sc, turn.

Row 2: Ch 1, sk first sc; *in next st work (sc, ch 2, hdc); sk next sc; rep from * around; join with sl st in first sc, turn.

Row 3: Ch 1, keeping ch-2 sps to front of work, in each sc work (sc, ch 2, hdc); join with sl st in first sc.

Fasten off and weave in ends.

Rep on rem armhole opening.

BACK OPENING EDGING
Row 1: Hold piece with RS facing you and neck edge to right; with A make slip knot on hook and join with sc in edge of row 1; working across side in ends of rows, work 10 sc across side, sl st in bottom center st, working across next side, work 11 sc across side, turn.

Row 2: Ch 1, sc in first sc, ch 1, sk next st—*buttonhole made*; sc in next 5 sc, ch 1, sk next sc—*button-hole made*; sc in next 3 sc, sl st in bottom center sc; working up next side, sc in each sc, turn.

Row 3: Ch 1, sl st in each sc and in each ch.

Fasten off and weave in ends.

NECK EDGING
Row 1: Hold back of Dress with RS facing you; with B make slip knot on hook and join with sc in left corner of neck edge; sc in end of each row of left edging, in each unused lp of beg ch of Dress and in end of each row of right edging, turn.

Row 2: Ch 1, sk first sc; *in next sc work (sc, ch 2, hdc); sk next sc, rep from * across, turn.

Row 3: Ch 1, keeping ch-2 sps to front of work, in each sc work (sc, ch 2, hdc).

Fasten off and weave in ends.

FINISHING
Step 1: With sewing needle and matching thread, sew buttons opposite buttonholes.

Step 2: Cut 30-inch length of ribbon. Beg and ending at center back of Dress, weave ribbon

through dc of row 13. Tie in bow at back of Dress.

HAT
Note: Hat is worked in joined rows.

Row 1: With A, ch 3; 15 sc in 3rd ch from hook; join with sl st in 2nd ch of beg 2 sk chs, turn.

Row 2: Ch 1, sk first sc; *in next sc work (sc, ch 2, hdc); sk next sc; rep from * around; join with sl st in first sc, turn.

Row 3: Ch 1, 3 sc in each sc; join with sl st in first sc, turn.

Row 4: Ch 1, sk first sc; *in next sc work (sc, ch 2, hdc); sk next sc; rep from * around; join with sl st in first sc, turn.

Rows 5 & 6: Rep rows 3 and 4.

For Size 6-12 Months Only
Row 7: Ch 1, 2 sc in first sc; *3 sc in next sc; 2 sc in next sc; rep from * around; join with sl st in first sc, turn.

Row 8: Ch 1, sk first sc; *in next sc work (sc, ch 2, hdc); sk next sc; rep from * around; join with sl st in first sc, turn.

Row 9: Ch 1, 2 sc in each sc; join with sl st in first sc, turn.

Rows 10–23: [Work rows 8 and 9] 7 times.

Row 24: Rep row 8.

Row 25: Ch 1, 3 sc in each sc; join in first sc, turn.

Row 26: Ch 1, sk first sc; *in next sc work (sc, ch 2, hdc); sk next sc; rep from * around; join with sl st in first sc, turn.

Row 27: Ch 1, 2 sc in each sc; join with sl st in first sc, turn.

Row 28: Ch 1, sk first sc; *in next sc work (sc, ch 2, hdc); sk next sc; rep from * around; join with sl st in first sc, turn.

Row 29: Ch 1, 3 sc in each sc; join with sl st in first sc, turn.

Row 30: Ch 1, sk first sc; *in next sc work (sc, ch 2, hdc); sk next sc; rep from * around; change to B by drawing lp through; cut A; join with sl st in first sc, turn.

Row 31: Ch 1, 2 sc in each sc; join with sl st in first sc, turn.

Row 32: Ch 1, sk first sc; *in next sc work (sc, ch 2, hdc); sk next sc; rep from * around; join with sl st in first sc, turn.

Row 33: Ch 1, keeping ch-2 sps to front of work, in each sc work (sc, ch 2, hdc); join with sl st in first sc.

Fasten off and weave in all ends.

Continue with Finishing.

For Size 18–24 Months Only
Row 7: Ch 1, 3 sc in each sc; join in first sc, turn.

Row 8: Ch 1, sk first sc; *in next sc work (sc, ch 2, hdc); sk next sc; rep from * around; join with sl st in first sc, turn.

Row 9: Ch 1, 2 sc in first sc; *3 sc in next sc; 2 sc in next sc; rep from * around; join with sl st in first sc, turn.

Row 10: Ch 1, sk first sc; *in next sc work (sc, ch 2, hdc); sk next sc; rep from * around; join with sl st in first sc, turn.

Row 11: Ch 1, 2 sc in each sc; join with sl st in first sc, turn.

Rows 12–25: [Work rows 10 and 11] 7 times.

Row 26: Rep row 10.

Row 27: Ch 1, 3 sc in each sc; join with sl st in first sc, turn.

Row 28: Ch 1, sk first sc; *in next sc work (sc, ch 2, hdc); sk next sc; rep from * around; join with sl st in first sc, turn.

Row 29: Ch 1, 2 sc in each sc; join with sl st in first sc, turn.

Row 30: Ch 1, sk first sc; *in next sc work (sc, ch 2, hdc); sk next sc; rep from * around; join with sl st in first sc, turn.

Row 31: Ch 1, 3 sc in each sc; join with sl st in first sc, turn.

Row 32: Ch 1, sk first sc; *in next sc work (sc, ch 2, hdc); sk next sc; rep from * around; change to B by drawing lp through; cut A; join with sl st in first sc, turn.

Row 33: Ch 1, 2 sc in each sc; join with sl st in first sc, turn.

Row 34: Ch 1, sk first sc; *in next sc work (sc, ch 2, hdc); sk next sc; rep from * around; join with sl st in first sc, turn.

Row 35: Ch 1, keeping ch-2 sps to front of work, in each sc work (sc, ch 2, hdc); join with sl st in first sc.

Fasten off and weave in all ends.

Continue with Finishing.

FINISHING
Tie rem ribbon into bow. Fold front of hat brim up at row 24 [26] and tack bow to brim.

Bright Times Romper

Design by Karen Hay

SKILL LEVEL ■■■□ INTERMEDIATE

FINISHED SIZES
Instructions given fit child's size 6 months; changes for 12, 18 and 24 months are in [ ].

FINISHED GARMENT MEASUREMENTS
Chest/Waist: 21 [22, 23, 24] inches

Inseam: 8 [9, 10, 11] inches

MATERIALS
• Lion Brand Babysoft light (light worsted) weight yarn (5 oz/459 yds/141g per skein):
   2 [2, 2, 2] skeins #143 lavender *(A)*
   1 [1, 1, 1] skein #103 bubblegum *(B)*
• Size G/6/4mm crochet hook or size needed to obtain gauge
• Tapestry needle
• 4 pink ¾-inch buttons
• Sewing needle and matching thread

GAUGE
16 sc = 4 inches

Take time to check gauge.

Instructions

LEG
Make 2.

Note: *Leg is worked lengthwise.*

Row 1 (RS): Starting at cuff edge with A, ch 53 [59, 65, 71]; sc in 2nd

ch from hook and in next 7 chs, hdc in rem ch, turn. *(52 [58, 64, 70] sts)*

Row 2: Ch 2, hdc in first 44 [50, 56, 62] hdc, sc in last 8 sc, turn.

Row 3: Ch 1, sc in first 8 sc, hdc in each hdc, turn.

Rep rows 2 and 3 until piece measures approximately 3 [3, 3½,

3½] inches from beg, measured along widest side (waist edge).

WAIST SHAPING
Row 1: Ch 1, sc in first 4 hdc, hdc in next 40 [46, 52, 58] hdc, sc in last 8 sc, turn.

Row 2: Ch 1, sc in first 8 sc, hdc in next 40 [46, 52, 58] hdc, sc in last 4 sc, turn.

Row 3: Ch 1, sc in first 4 sc, hdc in next 40 [46, 52, 58] hdc, sc in last 8 sc, turn.

Rep rows 2 and 3 until piece measures approximately 7½ [8, 8, 8½] inches from beg, measured along widest side (waist edge), ending with a row 2.

Next row: Ch 2, hdc in first 44 [50, 56, 62] sts, sc in last 8 sts, turn.

Next row: Ch 1, sc in first 8 sc, hdc in next each hdc, turn.

Next row: Ch 2, hdc in first 44 [50, 56, 62] hdc, sc in last 8 sts, turn.

Rep last 2 rows until piece measures approximately 10½ [11, 11½, 12] inches from beg, measured along widest side (waist edge). Fasten off.

ASSEMBLY
Fold 1 Leg lengthwise. Sew inside leg seam from cuff to Waist, leaving last 18 [20, 22, 24] hdc unsewn. Whipstitch through each unused lp of beg ch and through **back lp** *(see Stitch Guide)* of each st on last row. Rep with 2nd Leg. Sew Legs tog from top of inside leg to Waist edge of both front and back.

FRONT BODICE
Row 1 (RS): Hold piece with RS facing you and Waist edge at top; join A in end of first row at right edge of Waist; ch 1, working in ends of rows, work 42 [44, 46, 48] sc evenly spaced across edge to left side of Waist, turn. *(42 [44, 46, 48] sc)*

Row 2: Ch 1, sc in each sc, turn.

Rows 3 & 4: Rep row 2.

Row 5: Ch 1, **sc dec** *(see Stitch Guide)* in first 2 sc; sc in each sc to last 2 sc; sc dec in last 2 sc, turn. *(40 [42, 44, 46] sc)*

Rows 6–11: Rep row 5. *(28 [30, 32, 34] sc at end of row 11)*

Rep row 2 until Front Bodice measures 5½ [6, 6½, 7] inches, ending with a WS row.

LEFT SHOULDER STRAP
Row 1: Ch 1, sc in first 9 [9, 10, 10] sc, sc dec, turn, leaving rem sc unworked. *(10 [10, 11, 11] sc)*

Row 2: Ch 1, sc dec; sc in each rem sc, turn. *(9 [9, 10, 10] sc)*

Row 3: Ch 1, sc in each sc to last 2 sc; sc dec, turn. *(8 [8, 9, 9] sc)*

For Sizes 6 Months & 12 Months Only
Row 4: Ch 1, sc in each sc, turn.

Rep row 4 until Strap measures 4 inches.

Last row: Ch 1, sl st in each sc.

Fasten off and weave in ends.

Continue with Right Shoulder Strap.

For Sizes 18 Months & 24 Months Only
Row 4: Rep row 2. *(8 sc)*

Row 5: Ch 1, sc in each sc, turn.

Rep row 5 until Strap measures 4 inches.

Last row: Ch 1, sl st in each sc.

Fasten off and weave in ends.

Continue with Right Shoulder Strap.

RIGHT SHOULDER STRAP
Row 1: Sk next 6 [8, 8, 10] unused sc on last row of Front Bodice from Left Shoulder Strap; join A in next sc; ch 1, sc dec in same sc and in next sc; sc in each rem sc, turn. *(10 [10, 11, 11] sc)*

Row 2: Ch 1, sc in each sc to last 2 sc; sc dec, turn. *(9 [9, 10, 10] sc)*

Row 3: Ch 1, sc dec; sc in each rem sc, turn. *(8 [8, 9, 9] sc)*

For Sizes 6 Months & 12 Months Only
Row 4: Ch 1, sc in each sc, turn.

Rep row 4 until strap measures 4 inches.

Last row: Ch 1, sl st in each sc.

Fasten off and weave in ends.

Continue with Back Bodice.

For Sizes 18 Months & 24 Months Only
Row 4: Rep row 2. *(8 sc)*

Row 5: Ch 1, sc in each sc, turn.

Rep row 5 until strap measures 4 inches.

Last row: Ch 1, sl st in each sc.

Fasten off and weave in ends.

Continue with Back Bodice.

BACK BODICE
Work as same as Front Bodice through row 3 of Left Shoulder Strap.

For Sizes 6 Months & 12 Months Only
Row 4: Ch 1, sc in each sc, turn.

Rep row 4 until Strap measures 2 inches.

BUTTONHOLE SECTION
Row 1: Ch 1, sc in first 3 sc, ch 2—*buttonhole made*; sk next 2 sc, sc in next 3 sc, turn.

Row 2: Ch 1, sc in each sc and in each ch, turn. *(8 sc)*

Row 3: Ch 1, sc in each sc, turn.

Rows 4–6: Rep row 3.

Rows 7–9: Rep rows 1–3.

Row 10: Rep row 3.

Row 11: Ch 1, sl st in each sc. Fasten off.

Continue with Right Shoulder Strap.

For Sizes 18 Months & 24 Months Only
Row 4: Rep row 2. *(8 sc)*

Row 5: Ch 1, sc in each sc, turn.

Rep row 5 until Strap measures 2 inches.

BUTTONHOLE SECTION
Row 1: Ch 1, sc in first 3 sc, ch 2—*buttonhole made*; sk next 2 sc, sc in next 3 sc.

Row 2: Ch 1, sc in each sc and in each ch, turn. *(8 sc)*

Row 3: Ch 1, sc in each sc, turn.

Rows 4–6: Rep row 3.

Rows 7–9: Rep rows 1–3.

Row 10: Rep row 3.

Row 11: Ch 1, sl st in each sc. Fasten off.

Continue with Right Shoulder Strap.

RIGHT SHOULDER STRAP
Rows 1–3: Rep rows 1–3 of Right Shoulder Strap of Front Bodice.

For Sizes 6 Months & 12 Months Only
Row 4: Ch 1, sc in each sc, turn.

Rep row 4 until strap measures 2 inches.

BUTTONHOLE SECTION
Work same as Buttonhole Section of Left Shoulder Strap of Back Bodice.

Continue with Edging.

For Sizes 18 Months & 24 Months Only
Row 4: Rep row 2. *(8 sc)*

Row 5: Ch 1, sc in each sc, turn.

Rep row 5 until Strap measures 2 inches.

BUTTONHOLE SECTION
Work same as Buttonhole Section of Left Shoulder Strap of Back Bodice.

Continue with Edging.

EDGING
Hold piece with RS facing you; join A with sl st in end of first row of Back Bodice; ch 1, sc in same sp; working in ends of rows of Back Bodice, sc evenly spaced up side of Back Bodice and Strap; working across end of Strap, sl st in each sc; sc evenly spaced around neck opening and up side of next Strap; sl st in each sc of Strap; sc evenly spaced down next side of Strap and Back Bodice; work in same manner around Front Bodice; join with sl st in first sc.

Fasten off and weave in all ends.

POCKET
Make 2.

Row 1 (RS): With B, ch 25 [27, 29, 31]; sc in 2nd ch from hook and in each rem ch, turn. *(24 [26, 28, 30] sc)*

Row 2: Ch 1, sc in each sc, turn.

Rows 3–24 [3–26, 3–28, 3–30]: Rep row 2.

Row 25 [27, 29, 31]: Ch 1, sl st in each sc.

Fasten off and weave in ends.

FINISHING
Step 1: Place 1 Pocket with last row approximately ⅓ down from waist and centered over side of 1 Leg. With tapestry needle and A, sew Pocket in place. Rep with rem Pocket.

Step 2: With sewing needle and matching thread, sew 1 button centered over 3rd or 4th row from end of each Strap on Front Bodice and 2nd button centered over 9th or 10th row from end of same Straps.

Let's Go Play Romper & Jacket

Design by Ann E. Smith

SKILL LEVEL

INTERMEDIATE

FINISHED SIZES

Instructions given fit child's size 6 months; changes for 12, 18 and 24 months are in [ ].

FINISHED GARMENT MEASUREMENTS

Romper chest: 19 [21, 22½, 24] inches

Jacket chest: 20½ [22½, 24½, 26½] inches

MATERIALS

• Plymouth Wildflower D.K. light (light worsted) weight yarn (1¾ oz/136 yds/50g per ball):
   4 [5, 6, 7] balls #156 green *(A)*
   1 ball #48 yellow *(B)*
• Size D/3/3.25mm crochet hook or size needed to obtain gauge
• Tapestry needle
• 7 [7, 8, 8] ½-inch buttons
• Sewing needle and matching thread

GAUGE

21 sts = 4 inches

Take time to check gauge.

SPECIAL STITCHES

Puff stitch (puff st): In st indicated [yo, draw up lp] 3 times; yo, draw through 6 lps on hook, yo and draw through 2 lps on hook.

Front post double crochet (fpdc): Yo, insert hook from front to back to front around **post** *(see*

Stitch Guide) of st indicated, draw lp through, [yo, draw through 2 lps on hook] twice.

Instructions

ROMPER
FRONT

Row 1 (RS): Beg at lower edge with A, ch 14 [15, 19, 19]; sc in 2nd ch from hook and in each rem ch, turn. *(13 [14, 18, 18] sc)*

Row 2: Ch 1, working in **front lps** *(see Stitch Guide)* only, 3 sc in first sc; sc in each sc to last sc; 3 sc in last sc, turn. *(17 [18, 22, 22] sc)*

Rows 3–10 [3–11, 3–11, 3–12]: Rep row 2. At end of last row, change to B by drawing lp

through; cut A. *(49 [54, 58, 62] sc at end of last row)*

BODY
Note: *Rem of Romper is worked in front lps only.*

Row 1 (WS): Ch 1, sc in first 3 [2, 4, 6] sc; ***puff st** (see Special Stitches) in next sc; sc in next 6 sc; rep from * to last 4 [3, 5, 7] sc; puff st in next sc; sc in last 3 [2, 4, 6] sc, turn. Change to A by drawing lp through; cut B.

Row 2: Ch 1, sc in each st, turn.

Row 3: Ch 1, sc in each sc, turn.

Rows 4–10 [4–12, 4–12, 4–14]: Rep row 3.

Row 11 [13, 13, 15]: Ch 1, sc in first 3 [2, 4, 6] sc; *puff st in next sc; sc in next 6 sc; rep from * to last 4 [3, 5, 7] sc; puff st in next sc; sc in last 3 [2, 4, 6] sc, turn. Change to A by drawing lp through; cut B.

Rows 12–20 [14–24, 14–24, 16–28]: Rep row 3.

Rep rows 11–20 [13–24, 13–24, 15–28] until piece measures 9¼ [10½, 11, 11¾] inches from beg, ending with a WS row. Fasten off.

ARMHOLE SHAPING
Row 1: Hold piece with RS facing you; sk first 4 [5, 5, 5] sc on last row; join A with sl st in front lp of next sc; ch 1, sc in same lp; sc in next 40 [43, 47, 51] sc, turn, leaving rem sc unworked. *(41 [44, 48, 52] sc)*

Row 2: Ch 1, sc in first sc, **sc dec** *(see Stitch Guide)* in next 2 sc, sc in each sc to last 3 sc; sc dec in next 2 sc; sc in last sc, turn. *(39 [42, 46, 50] sc)*

For Size 6 Months Only
Row 3: Ch 1, sc in each sc, turn.

Rep row 3 until piece measures 11¼ inches from beg, ending with a WS row.

Continue with Left Strap Shaping.

For Size 12 Months Only
Row 3: Ch 1, sc in first sc, sc dec; sc in each sc to last 3 sc; sc dec; sc in last sc, turn. *(40 sc)*

Row 4: Ch 1, sc in each sc, turn.

Rep row 4 until piece measures 12½ inches from beg, ending with a WS row.

Continue with Left Strap Shaping.

For Size 18 Months Only
Row 3: Ch 1, sc in first sc, sc dec; sc in each sc to last 3 sc; sc dec; sc in last sc, turn. *(44 sc)*

Row 4: Rep row 3. *(42 sc at end of row)*

Row 5: Ch 1, sc in each sc, turn.

Rep row 5 until piece measures 13½ inches from beg, ending with a WS row.

Continue with Left Strap Shaping.

For Size 24 Months Only
Row 3: Ch 1, sc in first sc, sc dec; sc in each sc to last 3 sc; sc dec; sc in last sc, turn. *(48 sc)*

Rows 4 & 5: Rep row 3. *(44 sc at end of last row)*

Row 6: Ch 1, sc in each sc, turn.

Rep row 6 until piece measures 14¼ inches from beg, ending with a WS row.

Continue with Left Strap Shaping.

LEFT STRAP SHAPING
Row 1 (RS): Ch 1, sc in first 14 [14, 15, 16] sc, turn, leaving rem sts unworked.

Row 2: Ch 1, sc in first sc, sc dec; sc in each rem sc, turn. *(13 [13, 14, 15] sc)*

Row 3: Ch 1, sc in each sc to last 2 sc; sc dec, turn. *(12 [12, 13, 14] sc)*

Rows 4 & 5: Rep rows 2 and 3. *(10 [10, 11, 12] sc at end of last row)*

For Size 6 Months Only
Row 6: Ch 1, sc in each sc, turn.

Rep row 3 until piece measures 3½ inches from armhole, ending with a WS row.

BUTTONHOLE SECTION
Row 1: Ch 1, sc in first 2 sc, ch 2—*buttonhole made*; sk next 2 sc, sc in next 2 sc, ch 2—*buttonhole made*; sk next 2 sc, sc in last 2 sc, turn.

Row 2: Ch 1, sc in each sc and in each ch. Fasten off.

Continue with Right Strap Shaping.

For Size 12 Months Only
Row 6: Ch 1, sc in each sc, turn.

Rep row 6 until piece measures 4 inches from beg, ending with a WS row.

BUTTONHOLE SECTION
Row 1: Ch 1, sc in first 2 sc, ch 2—*buttonhole made*; sk next 2 sc, sc in next 2 sc, ch 2—*Buttonhole made*; sk next 2 sc, sc in last 2 sc, turn.

Row 2: Ch 1, sc in each sc and in each ch. Fasten off.

Continue with Right Strap Shaping.

For Size 18 Months Only
Row 6: Rep row 2. *(10 sc)*

Row 7: Ch 1, sc in each sc, turn.

Rep row 7 until piece measures 4½ inches from beg, ending with a WS row.

BUTTONHOLE SECTION
Row 1: Ch 1, sc in first 2 sc, ch 2—*buttonhole made*; sk next 2 sc, sc in next 2 sc, ch 2—*buttonhole made*; sk next 2 sc, sc in last 2 sc, turn.

Row 2: Ch 1, sc in each sc and in each ch. Fasten off.

Continue with Right Strap Shaping.

For Size 24 Months Only
Rows 6 & 7: Rep rows 2 and 3. *(10 sc at end of last row)*

Row 8: Ch 1, sc in each sc, turn.

Rep row 8 until piece measures 5 inches from beg, ending with a WS row.

BUTTONHOLE SECTION
Row 1: Ch 1, sc in first 2 sc, ch 2—*buttonhole made*; sk next 2 sc, sc in next 2 sc, ch 2—*buttonhole made*; sk next 2 sc, sc in last 2 sc, turn.

Row 2: Ch 1, sc in each sc and in each ch. Fasten off.

Continue with Right Strap Shaping.

RIGHT STRAP SHAPING
Row 1: Hold piece with RS facing you; sk next 11 [12, 12, 12] sc from Left Strap; join A with sl st in front lp of next sc; ch 1, sc in same lp; sc in each sc, turn. *(14 [14, 15, 16] sc)*

Row 2: Ch 1, sc in each sc to last 3 sc; sc dec; sc in last sc, turn.

Row 3: Ch 1, sc in first sc, sc dec; sc in each rem sc, turn.

For Size 6 Months Only
Row 6: Ch 1, sc in each sc, turn.

Rep row 3 until piece measures 3½ inches from armhole, ending with a WS row.

BUTTONHOLE SECTION
Row 1: Ch 1, sc in first 2 sc, ch 2—*buttonhole made*; sk next 2 sc, sc in next 2 sc, ch 2—*buttonhole made*; sk next 2 sc, sc in last 2 sc, turn.

Row 2: Ch 1, sc in each sc and in each ch. Fasten off.

Continue with Back.

For Size 12 Months Only
Row 6: Ch 1, sc in each sc, turn.

Rep row 6 until piece measures 4 inches from beg, ending with a WS row.

BUTTONHOLE SECTION
Row 1: Ch 1, sc in first 2 sc, ch 2—*buttonhole made*; sk next 2 sc, sc in next 2 sc, ch 2—*buttonhole made*; sk next 2 sc, sc in last 2 sc, turn.

Row 2: Ch 1, sc in each sc and in each ch. Fasten off.

Continue with Back.

For Size 18 Months Only
Row 6: Rep row 2. *(10 sc)*

Row 7: Ch 1, sc in each sc, turn.

Rep row 7 until piece measures 4½ inches from beg, ending with a WS row.

BUTTONHOLE SECTION
Row 1: Ch 1, sc in first 2 sc, ch 2—*buttonhole made*; sk next 2 sc, sc in next 2 sc, ch 2—*buttonhole made*; sk next 2 sc, sc in last 2 sc, turn.

Row 2: Ch 1, sc in each sc and in each ch. Fasten off.

Continue with Back.

For Size 24 Months Only
Rows 6 & 7: Rep rows 2 and 3. *(10 sc at end of last row)*

Row 8: Ch 1, sc in each sc, turn.

Rep row 8 until piece measures 5 inches from beg, ending with a WS row.

BUTTONHOLE SECTION
Row 1: Ch 1, sc in first 2 sc, ch 2—*Buttonhole made*; sk next 2 sc, sc in next 2 sc, ch 2—*Buttonhole made*; sk next 2 sc, sc in last 2 sc, turn.

Row 2: Ch 1, sc in each sc and in each ch. Fasten off.

Continue with Back.

BACK
Work same as Front to Armhole Shaping.

ARMHOLE SHAPING
Row 1: Hold piece with RS facing you; sk first 4 [5, 5, 5] sc on last row; join A with sl st in front lp of next sc; ch 1, sc in same lp; sc in next 40 [43, 47, 51] sc, turn, leaving rem sc unworked. *(41 [44, 48, 52] sc)*

Row 2: Ch 1, sc in first sc, sc dec in next 2 sc, sc in each sc to last 3 sc; sc dec in next 2 sc; sc in last sc, turn. *(39 [42, 46, 50] sc)*

For Size 6 Months Only
Row 3: Ch 1, sc in each sc, turn.

Rep row 3 until piece measures 12¼ inches from beg, ending with a WS row.

Continue with Right Strap Shaping.

For Size 12 Months Only
Row 3: Ch 1, sc in first sc, sc dec; sc in each sc to last 3 sc; sc dec; sc in last sc, turn. *(40 sc)*

Row 4: Ch 1, sc in each sc, turn.

Rep row 4 until piece measures 13½ inches from beg, ending with a WS row.

Continue with Right Strap Shaping.

For Size 18 Months Only
Row 3: Ch 1, sc in first sc, sc dec; sc in each sc to last 3 sc; sc dec; sc in last sc, turn. *(44 sc)*

Row 4: Rep row 3. *(42 sc at end of row)*

Row 5: Ch 1, sc in each sc, turn.

Rep row 5 until piece measures 14½ inches from beg, ending with a WS row.

Continue with Right Strap Shaping.

For Size 24 Months Only
Row 3: Ch 1, sc in first sc, sc dec; sc in each sc to last 3 sc; sc dec; sc in last sc, turn. *(48 sc)*

Rows 4 & 5: Rep row 3. *(44 sc at end of last row)*

Row 6: Ch 1, sc in each sc, turn.

Rep row 6 until piece measures 15¼ inches from beg, ending with a WS row.

Continue with Right Strap Shaping.

RIGHT STRAP SHAPING

For All Sizes
Row 1: Ch 1, sc in first 12 sc, turn, leaving rem sc unworked. *(12 sc)*

Row 2: Ch 1, sc in first sc, sc dec; sc in each rem sc, turn. *(11 sc)*

Row 3: Ch 1, sc in each sc to last 3 sc; sc dec; sc in last sc, turn. *(10 sc)*

Row 4: Ch 1, sc in each sc, turn.

Rep row 4 until Strap measures same as Right Strap on Front. Fasten off.

LEFT STRAP SHAPING

For All Sizes
Row 1: Hold piece with RS facing you; sk next 15 [16, 18, 20] sc from First Strap; join A with sl st in front lp of next sc; sc in same lp; sc in each rem sc, turn. *(12 sc)*

Row 2: Ch 1, sc in each sc to last 3 sc; sc dec; sc in last sc, turn. *(11 sc)*

Row 3: Ch 1, sc in first sc, sc dec; sc in each rem sc. *(10 sc)*

Row 4: Ch 1, sc in each sc, turn.

Rep row 4 until Strap measures same as Right Strap.

Fasten off and weave in all ends.

ASSEMBLY
With tapestry needle and A, sew side seams.

LOWER BAND
Hold piece with RS of Back facing you and beg ch at top; join A with sl st in end left edge of row 1 of Back; working around left leg opening in ends of rows, work 36 [40, 40, 44] sc evenly spaced; working in unused lps of beg ch of Front, work 12 [12, 16, 16] sc evenly spaced; working around right leg opening in ends of rows, work 36 [40, 40, 44] sc; working in unused lps of beg ch of Back, work 12 [12, 16, 16] sc evenly spaced; join with sl st in first sc.

Rnd 2: Ch 1, sc in same sc and in next 38 [40, 40, 44] sc, [ch 2—*buttonhole made*, sk next 2 sc, sc in next 2 sc] 2 [2, 3, 3] times; ch 2—*buttonhole made*; sk next 2 sc, sc in each rem sc; join with sl st in first sc.

Rnd 3: Ch 1, sc in same sc and in each rem sc and 2 sc in each ch-2 sp; join in first sc.

Fasten off and weave in ends.

EDGING
Hold Romper with RS of Front facing you; join A with sl st in end of first row of Left Strap at neck edge; working around neck edge, sl st evenly to first row of Right Strap.

Fasten off and weave in ends.

FINISHING
With sewing needle and matching thread, sew buttons opposite buttonholes at bottom of Romper and on Back Straps opposite buttonholes on Front Straps.

JACKET
BACK
Row 1 (WS): With A, ch 55 [60, 65, 71]; sc in 2nd ch from hook and in each rem ch, turn. *(54 [59, 64, 70] sc)*

Note: *Rem of Back is worked in front lps only.*

Row 2 (RS): Ch 1, sc in each sc, turn.

Rep Row 2 until piece measures 5 [6, 7, 7¾] inches from beg, ending with a WS row.

ARMHOLE SHAPING
Row 1: Working in front lps only, sl st in first 5 [5, 6, 7] sc, sc in each sc to last 5 [5, 6, 7] sc, turn, leaving rem sts unworked. *(44 [49, 52, 56] sc)*

Row 2: Ch 1, sc in each sc, turn.

Rep row 2 until piece measures 9½ [11, 12 ½, 13¼] inches from beg. Fasten off.

RIGHT FRONT
Row 1 (WS): With A, ch 24 [26, 30, 32]; sc in 2nd ch from hook and in next 4 [5, 7, 8] chs, [dc in next ch, sc in next 5 chs] twice; dc in next ch, sc in last 5 [6, 8, 9] chs, turn. *(23 [25, 29, 31] sts)*

Row 2 (RS): Ch 1, working in front lps only, sc in first 5 [6, 8, 9] sc, **fpdc** *(see Special Stitches)* around next dc, on working row, sk sc behind fpdc, [sc in next 5 sc, fpdc around next dc, sk sc behind fpdc] twice; sc in last 5 [6, 8, 9] sc, turn.

Row 3: Ch 1, working in front lps only, sc in each st, turn.

Rows 4–9: [Work rows 2 and 3] 3 times.

Row 10: Ch 1, working in front lps only, sc in first 3 [4, 6, 7] sc; *fpdc around next fpdc, sk sc behind fpdc, sc in next 3 sc, fpdc around same fpdc as previous fpdc worked, sk sc behind, sc in next sc; from * twice; fpdc around next fpdc, sk sc behind fpdc, sc in next 3 sc, fpdc around same fpdc as previous fpdc worked, sk sc behind, sc in last 3 [4, 6, 7] sc, turn.

Row 11: Ch 1, working in front

lps only, sc in first 5 [6, 8, 9] sts; *drop A; join B with sl st through both lps of next sc, [yo, draw up lp in same sc] 5 times; yo, draw through 10 lps on hook, yo and draw through 2 lps on hook; change to A by drawing lp through; cut B; ch 1—*bud made*; sc in next 5 sts; rep from * twice; sc in each rem st, turn.

Note: *Rem of Right Front is worked in front lps only.*

Row 12: Ch 1, sc in each st, turn.

Row 13: Ch 1, sc in each sc, turn.

Rep row 13 until piece measures 5 [6, 7, 7¾] inches from beg, ending with a WS row.

ARMHOLE SHAPING
Row 1: Ch 1, sc in each sc to last 5 [5, 6, 7] sc, turn, leaving rem sc unworked. *(18 [20, 23, 24] sc)*

Row 2: *Ch 1, sc in each sc, turn.*

Rep row 2 until piece measures 5½ [6½, 7½, 7¾] inches from beg, ending with a WS row.

NECK SHAPING
Row 1: Ch 1, sc in first sc, sc dec; sc in each rem sc, turn. *(17 [19, 22, 23] sc)*

Row 2: Ch 1, sc in each sc to last 3 sc; sc dec; sc in last sc, turn. *(16 [18, 21, 22] sc)*

For Size 6 Months Only
Rows 3 & 4: Rep rows 1 and 2. *(14 sc)*

Row 5: Ch 1, sc in each sc, turn.

Row 6: Ch 1, sc in each sc to last 3 sc; sc dec; sc in last sc, turn. *(13 sc)*

Rows 7–10: [Work rows 5 and 6] twice. *(11 sc at end of last row)*

Rep row 5 until piece measures same as Back.

Fasten off and weave in all ends.

Continue with Left Front.

For Size 12 Months Only
Rows 3 & 4: Rep rows 1 and 2. *(16 sc)*

Row 5: Ch 1, sc in each sc, turn.

Row 6: Ch 1, sc in each sc to last 3 sc; sc dec; sc in last sc, turn. *(15 sc)*

Rows 7–12: [Work rows 5 and 6] 3 times. *(12 sc at end of last row)*

Rep row 5 until piece measures same as Back.

Fasten off and weave in all ends.

Continue with Left Front.

For Size 18 Months Only
Rows 3 & 4: Rep rows 1 and 2. *(19 sc)*

Row 5: Ch 1, sc in each sc, turn.

Row 6: Ch 1, sc in first sc, sc dec; sc in each rem sc, turn. *(18 sc)*

Rows 7–16: [Work rows 5 and 6] 5 times. *(13 sc at end of last row)*

Rep row 5 until piece measures same as Back.

Fasten off and weave in all ends.

Continue with Left Front.

For Size 24 Months Only
Rows 3 & 4: Rep rows 1 and 2. *(20 sc)*

Row 5: Ch 1, sc in each sc, turn.

Row 6: Ch 1, sc in each sc to last 3 sc; sc dec; sc in last sc, turn. *(19 sc)*

Rows 7–16: [Work rows 5 and 6] 5 times. *(14 sc at end of last row)*

Rep row 5 until piece measures same as Back.

Fasten off and weave in all ends.

Continue with Left Front.

LEFT FRONT
Work same as Right Front to Armhole Shaping.

ARMHOLE SHAPING
Row 1: Sl st in first 5 [5, 6, 7] sc; ch 1, sc in each rem sc, turn. *(18 [20, 23, 24] sc)*

Row 2: Ch 1, sc in each sc, turn.

Rep row 2 until piece measures 5½ [6½, 7½, 7¾] inches from beg, ending with a WS row.

NECK SHAPING
Row 1: Ch 1, sc in each sc to last 3 sc; sc dec; sc in last sc, turn. *(17 [19, 22, 23] sc)*

Row 2: Ch 1, sc in first sc, sc dec; sc in each rem sc, turn. *(16 [18, 21, 22] sc)*

For Size 6 Months Only
Rows 3 & 4: Rep rows 1 and 2. *(14 sc)*

Row 5: Ch 1, sc in each sc, turn.

Row 6: Ch 1, sc in first sc, sc dec; sc in each rem sc, turn. *(13 sc)*

Rows 7–10: [Work rows 5 and 6] twice. *(11 sc at end of last row)*

Rep row 5 until piece measures same as Back.

Fasten off and weave in all ends.

Continue with Assembly.

For Size 12 Months Only
Rows 3 & 4: Rep rows 1 and 2. *(16 sc)*

Row 5: Ch 1, sc in each sc, turn.

Row 6: Ch 1, sc in first sc, sc dec; sc in each rem sc, turn. *(15 sc)*

Rows 7–12: [Work rows 5 and 6] 3 times. *(12 sc at end of last row)*

Rep row 5 until piece measures same as Back.

Fasten off and weave in all ends.

Continue with Assembly.

For Size 18 Months Only
Rows 3 & 4: Rep rows 1 and 2. *(19 sc)*

Row 5: Ch 1, sc in each sc, turn.

Row 6: Ch 1, sc in first sc, sc dec; sc in each rem sc, turn. *(18 sc)*

Rows 7–16: [Work rows 5 and 6] 5 times. *(13 sc at end of last row)*

Rep row 5 until piece measures same as Back.

Fasten off and weave in all ends.

Continue with Assembly.

For Size 24 Months Only
Rows 3 & 4: Rep rows 1 and 2. *(20 sc)*

Row 5: Ch 1, sc in each sc, turn.

Row 6: Ch 1, sc in first sc, sc dec; sc in each rem sc, turn. *(19 sc)*

Rows 7–16: [Work rows 5 and 6] 5 times. *(14 sc at end of last row)*

Rep row 5 until piece measures same as Back.

Fasten off and weave in all ends.

Continue with Assembly.

ASSEMBLY
With tapestry needle and A, sew shoulder seams.

SLEEVES
Row 1: Hold piece with RS facing you; join A with sl st in end of row 1 of Armhole Shaping on Left Front; ch 1, working in ends of rows of sleeve opening, work 42 [46, 50, 54] sc evenly spaced to row 1 of Armhole Shaping of Back, turn.

Note: Rem of Sleeve is worked in front lps only.

Row 2: Ch 1, sc in each sc, turn.

Row(s) 3 [3, 3 & 4, 3–5]: Rep row 2.

Row 4 [4, 5, 6]: Ch 1, sc in first sc, sc dec in next 2 sc; sc in each sc to last 3 sc; sc dec in next 2 sc; sc in last sc, turn. *(40 [44, 48, 52] sc)*

For Size 6 Months Only
Rows 5–7: Rep row 2.

Row 8: Rep row 4. *(38 sc at end of row)*

Rows 9–20: [Work rows 5–8] 3 times. *(32 sc at end of last row)*

Rep row 2 until piece measures 7¾ inches from beg.

Fasten off and weave in ends.

Continue with Assembly.

For Size 12 Months Only
Rows 5–7: Rep row 2.

Row 8: Rep row 4. *(42 sc at end of row)*

Rows 9–28: [Work rows 5–8] 5 times. *(32 sc at end of last row)*

Rep row 2 until piece measures 8½ inches from beg.

Fasten off and weave in ends.

Continue with Assembly.

For Size 18 Months Only
Rows 6–8: Rep row 5. *(42 sc at end of last row)*

Rows 9–11: Rep row 2.

Row 12: Rep row 5. *(40 sc at end of row)*

Rows 13–28: [Work rows 9–12] 4 times. *(32 sc at end of last row)*

Rep row 2 until piece measures 8¾ inches from beg.

Fasten off and weave in ends.

Continue with Assembly.

For Size 23 Months Only
Rows 7–13: Rep row 6. *(38 sc at end of last row)*

Rows 14–16: Rep row 2.

Row 17: Rep row 6. *(36 sc at end of row)*

Rows 18–25: [Work rows 9–12] twice. *(32 sc at end of last row)*

Rep row 2 until piece measures 9¼ inches from beg.

Fasten off and weave in ends.

Continue with Assembly.

ASSEMBLY
Sew sleeves sides to sk sts for square armholes. Sew Sleeve and side seams.

TRIM
Rnd 1 (RS): Hold Jacket with RS facing you; join B with sl st in 1 side seam; sl st loosely around body, being careful that sts do not pull; join with sl st in joining sl st. Fasten off.

Rnd 2: Hold Jacket with RS facing you; join A with sl st in **back lp** *(see Stitch Guide)* of first sl st; sc in same lp; working in back lps only, sc in each sl st, work 3 sc in each lower corner and in each corner of neck edge and sc dec at each shoulder seam; join in first sc.

Rnd 3: Ch 1, sc in each sc, 3 sc in 2nd sc of each corner and sc dec at each shoulder seam; join in first sc.

Rnd 4: Sl st in each sc; join in joining sl st.

Fasten off and weave in all ends.

FISH
Make 2.

Row 1: With B, ch 4; sc in 2nd ch from hook and in each rem ch, turn. *(3 sc)*

Row 2: Ch 1, 2 sc in first sc; sc in next sc, 2 sc in last sc, turn. *(5 sc)*

Row 3: Ch 1, sc in each sc, turn.

Row 4: Ch 1, sc dec in first 2 sc; sc in next sc, sc dec in last 2 sc; turn.

Row 5: Ch 1, draw up lp in each sc, yo and draw through all 4 lps on hook; ch 3, in st just made work (3 dc, ch 3, sl st)—*fin made*; ch 3, in same st work (3 dc, ch 3,

sl st)—*fin made*; ch 1, sl st in first row, (ch 1, sl st in each row and st around), ending before tail.

Fasten off and weave in ends.

TIE
Make 2.

With B, ch 30; join with sl st in center sl st between fins of 1 Fish, sl st in each ch of beg ch-30. Fasten off and weave in ends.

FINISHING
Thread 1 Tie from back to front through center of 3 sc worked on rnd 2 of Edging at 1 corner of neck edge. Tie knot in end. Rep with 2nd Tie on opposite side.

Bouncing Baby Boys

Clever sweater and hat designs especially for baby boys ages 3 months to 24 months. We've even included a crown for your young prince!

Prince Charming

Design by Darla Sims

SKILL LEVEL

INTERMEDIATE

FINISHED SIZES

Instructions given fit child's size 6 months; changes for 12 months and 24 months are in [ ].

FINISHED GARMENT MEASUREMENTS

Chest: 20 [22, 24] inches

Hat: 16 [18, 20]-inch circumference

MATERIALS

• Bernat Satin medium (worsted) weight yarn (3½ oz/163 yds/100g per skein):
    3 [3, 4] skeins #04307 sultana *(A)*
    2 [3, 3] skeins #04143 lapis *(B)*
• Patons Cha Cha super bulky (super chunky) weight yarn (1¾ oz/77 yds/50g per skein):
    2 [2, 3] skeins #02011 waltz *(C)*
• Sizes G/6/4mm and H/8/5mm crochet hooks or size needed to obtain gauge
• Tapestry needle
• Stitch markers
• 8mm beads:
    14 [16, 18] purple
    14 [16, 18] silver

GAUGE

Size H hook: 7 sts = 2 inches

Take time to check gauge.

Instructions

JACKET
BACK

Row 1 (RS): With H hook and A, ch 39 [41, 45]; 2 dc in 5th ch from hook; *sk next ch, 2 dc in next ch; rep from * to last 2 chs; sk next ch, dc in last ch. *(36 [38, 42] dc)* Fasten off.

Row 2: Hold piece with RS facing you; with B make slip knot on hook and join with sc in sp formed by beg 4 sk chs; *ch 1, sk next 2 dc, sc in sp between last

dc and next dc; rep from * across. Fasten off.

Row 3: Hold piece with RS facing you; join A with sl st in 4th ch of beg 4 sk chs at beg of row 1; ch 3 *(counts as a dc on this and following rows)*; *sk next sc, 2 dc in next ch-1 sp; rep from * to last dc of row 1; dc in last dc. Fasten off.

Row 4: Hold piece with RS facing you; with B make slip knot on hook and join with sc in sp between first 2 dc; *ch 1, sk next 2 dc, sc in sp between last dc and next dc; rep from * across. Fasten off.

Row 5: Hold piece with RS facing you; join A with sl st in 3rd ch of beg ch-3 of 2nd row below; ch 3; *sk next sc, 2 dc in next ch-1 sp; rep from * to last dc of 2nd row below; dc in last dc. Fasten off.

Rows 6–21 [6–25, 6–29]: [Work rows 4 and 5] 8 [10, 12] times.

Weave in all ends.

LEFT FRONT
Row 1: With H hook and A, ch 21 [23, 35]; 2 dc in 5th ch from hook, *sk next ch, 2 dc in next ch; rep from * to last 2 chs; sk next ch, dc in last ch. *(36 [38, 42] dc)* Fasten off.

Row 2: Hold piece with RS facing you; with B make slip knot on hook and join with sc in sp formed by beg 4 sk chs; *ch 1, sk next 2 dc, sc in sp between last dc and next dc; rep from * across. Fasten off.

Row 3: Hold piece with RS facing you; join A with sl st in 4th ch of beg 4 sk chs at beg of row 1; ch 3 *(counts as a dc on this and following rows)*; *sk next sc, 2 dc in next ch-1 sp; rep from * to last dc of row 1; dc in last dc. Fasten off.

Row 4: Hold piece with RS facing

you; with B make slip knot on hook and join with sc in sp between first 2 dc; *ch 1, sk next 2 dc, sc in sp between last dc and next dc; rep from * across. Fasten off.

Row 5: Hold piece with RS facing you; join A with sl st in 3rd ch of beg ch-3 of 2nd row below; ch 3; *sk next sc, 2 dc in next ch-1 sp; rep from * to last dc of 2nd row below; dc in last dc. Fasten off.

Rows 6–11 [6–13, 6–13]: [Work rows 4 and 5] 3 [4, 4] times.

Row 12 [14, 14]: Rep row 4.

V-NECK SHAPING
Row 1: Hold piece with RS facing you; join A with sl st in 3rd ch of beg ch-3 of 2nd row below; ch 3; *sk next sc, 2 dc in next ch-1 sp; rep from * to last ch-1 sp; **dc dec** *(see Stitch Guide)* in last ch-1 sp and in last dc on 2nd row below. Fasten off.

Row 2: Hold piece with RS facing you; with B make slip knot on hook and join with sc in sp between first 2 dc; *ch 1, sk next 2 dc, sc in sp between last dc and next dc; rep from * across. Fasten off.

Row 3: Hold piece with RS facing you; join A with sl st in 3rd ch of beg ch-3 of 2nd row below; ch 3; *sk next sc, 2 dc in next ch-1 sp; rep from * to last ch-1 sp; dc dec in last ch-1 sp and in last dc on 2nd row below. Fasten off.

Row 4: Hold piece with RS facing you; with B make slip knot on hook and join with sc in sp between first 2 dc; *ch 1, sk next 2 dc, sc in sp between last dc and next dc; rep from * across. Fasten off.

Row 5: Hold piece with RS facing you; join A with sl st in 3rd ch of beg ch-3 of 2nd row below; ch 3; *sk next sc, 2 dc in next ch-1 sp; rep from * to last ch-1 sp; dc in

last ch-1 sp, dc dec in last ch-1 sp and in last dc on 2nd row below. Fasten off.

Row 6: Hold piece with RS facing you; with B make slip knot on hook and join with sc in sp between first 2 dc; *ch 1, sk next 2 dc, sc in sp between last dc and next dc; rep from * across. Fasten off.

Row 7: Hold piece with RS facing you; join A with sl st in 3rd ch of beg ch-3 of 2nd row below; ch 3; *sk next sc, 2 dc in next ch-1 sp; rep from * to last ch-1 sp; dc in last ch-1 sp, dc dec in last ch-1 sp and in last dc on 2nd row below. Fasten off.

Rows 8–11: [Work rows 6 and 7] twice.

Weave in all ends.

RIGHT FRONT
Work same as Left Front to V-Neck Shaping.

Row 1: Hold piece with RS facing you; with H hook, join A with sl st in 3rd ch of turning ch-3 at beg of 2nd row below; ch 2, yo, insert hook in next ch-1 sp, [yo, draw through 2 lps on hook; dc in same ch-1 sp; *sk next sc, 2 dc in next ch-1 sp; rep from * to last dc; dc in last dc. Fasten off.

Row 2: Hold piece with RS facing you; sk first 2 dc, with H hook make slip knot on hook with B and join with sc in sp between last dc and next dc; *ch 1, sk next 2 dc, sc in sp between last dc and next dc; rep from * across. Fasten off.

Row 3: Hold piece with RS facing you; with H hook, join A with sl st in first st at beg of 2nd row below; ch 2, dc in next dc; *sk next sc, 2 dc in next ch-1 sp; rep from * to last dc; dc in last dc. Fasten off.

Row 4: Hold piece with RS facing

you; sk first 3 dc, with H hook make slip knot on hook with B and join with sc in sp between last sk dc and next dc; *ch 1, sk next 2 dc, sc in sp between last dc and next dc; rep from * across. Fasten off.

Row 5: Hold piece with RS facing you; with H hook, join A with sl st in first st at beg of 2nd row below; ch 2, sk next dc, dc in next dc; *sk next sc, 2 dc in next ch-1 sp; rep from * to last dc; dc in last dc. Fasten off.

Row 6: Rep row 4.

Row 7: Rep row 5.

Row 8: Hold piece with RS facing you; sk beg ch-2 and next dc on 2nd row below; with H hook make slip knot on hook with B and join with sc in sp between last sk dc and next dc; *ch 1, sk next 2 dc, sc in sp between last dc and next dc; rep from * across. Fasten off.

Row 9: Hold piece with RS facing you; with H hook, join A with sl st in first dc of 2nd row below; ch 3; *sk next sc, 2 dc in next ch-1 sp; rep from * to last dc; dc in last dc. Fasten off.

Row 10: Hold piece with RS facing you; sk beg ch-3 and next dc on 2nd row below; with H hook make slip knot on hook with B and join with sc in sp between last sk dc and next dc; *ch 1, sk next 2 dc, sc in sp between last dc and next dc; rep from * across. Fasten off.

Row 11: Hold piece with RS facing you; with H hook, join A with sl st in first dc of 2nd row below; ch 3; *sk next sc, 2 dc in next ch-1 sp; rep from * to last dc; dc in last dc. Fasten off.

Weave in all ends.

SLEEVE
Make 2.

Row 1: With H hook and A, ch 27 [31, 33]; 2 dc in 5th ch from hook, *sk next ch, 2 dc in next ch; rep from * to last 2 chs; sk next ch, dc in last ch. *(24 [28, 30] dc)*

Fasten off.

Row 2: Hold piece with RS facing you; with B make slip knot on hook and join with sc in sp formed by beg 4 sk chs; *ch 1, sk next 2 dc, sc in sp between last dc and next dc; rep from * across. Fasten off.

Row 3: Hold piece with RS facing you; join A with sl st in 4th ch of beg 4 sk chs at beg of row 1; ch 3 *(counts as a dc on this and following rows)*; *sk next sc, 2 dc in next ch-1 sp; rep from * to last dc of row 1; dc in last dc. Fasten off.

Rep rows 2 and 3 until piece measures 6½ [7½, 8½] inches from beg. Weave in all ends.

ASSEMBLY
On Back and both Fronts, place markers 3½ [4, 4½] inches down from top of each piece. Sew shoulder seams. Matching center of Sleeves to shoulder seams and edges to markers, sew in Sleeves. Sew side and Sleeve seams in 1 continuous seam.

EDGINGS
SLEEVE EDGING
Rnd 1: Hold 1 Sleeve with RS facing you; with G hook, join B in seam; ch 1, sc in same sp; working in unused lps of beg ch, work 18 [20, 24] sc evenly spaced; join with

sl st in first sc.

Rnd 2: Ch 1, sc in same sc and in each rem sc; join in first sc.

Fasten off and weave in ends.

Rep on rem Sleeve.

OUTER EDGING
Rnd 1: Hold Jacket with RS facing you; with G hook, join B in 1 side seam; ch 1, sc in same sp; sc evenly spaced around outer edge, working 3 sc in each corner; join in first sc; change to C by drawing lp through; cut B.

Rnd 2: Ch 1, sc in each sc; join with sl st in first sc.

Rnd 3: Rep rnd 2.

Fasten off and weave in all ends.

TIE
With G hook, join B in beg of V-Neck Shaping on 1 side of Jacket; ch 30; sc in 2nd ch from hook and in each rem ch; sl st in joining sl st. Fasten off. Work Tie in same manner on opposite side of Jacket.

HAT
Note: *Hat is worked in continuous rnds. Do not join unless specified; mark end of rnds.*

Rnd 1: Beg at top of Hat, with G hook and A, ch 2; 8 sc in 2nd ch from hook.

Rnd 2: 2 sc in each sc. *(16 sc)*

Rnd 3: *Sc in next sc, 2 sc in next sc; rep from * around. *(24 sc)*

Rnd 4: *Sc in next 2 sc, 2 sc in next sc; rep from * around. *(32 sc)*

Rnd 5: *Sc in next 3 sc 2 sc in next sc rep from * around. *(40 sc)*

Rnd 6: *Sc in next 4 sc, 2 sc in next sc; rep from * around. *(48 sc)*

Rnd 7: *Sc in next 5 sc, 2 sc in next sc; rep from * around. *(56 sc)*

For Size 6 Months Only
Continue with For All Sizes.

For Size 12 Months Only
Rnd 8: *Sc in next 6 sc, 2 sc in next sc; rep from * around. *(64 sc)*

Continue with For All Sizes.

For Size 24 Months Only
Rnd 8: *Sc in next 6 sc, 2 sc in next sc; rep from * around. *(64 sc)*

Rnd 9: *Sc in next 7 sc, 2 sc in next sc; rep from * around. *(72 sc)*

Continue with For All Sizes.

For All Sizes
Rnd 8 [9, 10]: Sc in each sc.

Rep last rnd until piece measures 5 [5½, 6] inches from center of top. At end of last rnd, join with sl st in first sc. Change to C by drawing lp through; cut A. Turn.

BRIM
Rnd 1 (WS): Ch 1, sc in each sc; join with sl st in first sc.

Note: *String beads on B, alternating colors.*

Rnds 2–4: Rep rnd 1. At end of rnd 4, change to B by drawing lp through; cut C. Turn.

Rnd 5: Rep rnd 1.

Rnd 6: Ch 1; *sc in first sc, slide bead up close to back of work, sc in next sc; rep from * around; join with sl st in first sc. Turn.

Rnd 7: Ch 1, sc in each sc; join with sl st in first sc.

Rnds 8 & 9: Rep rnd 7.

Rnd 10: Ch 1; *sc in next sc, hdc in next sc, dc in next sc, tr in next sc, dtr in next sc, tr in next sc, dc in next sc, hdc in next sc; rep from * around; join with sl st in first sc.

Fasten off and weave in all ends.

Sailor Baby

Design by Svetlana Avrakh

FINISHED SIZES
Instructions given fit 3 months; changes for 6, 12, 18 and 24 months are in [ ].

FINISHED GARMENT MEASUREMENTS
Chest: 18 [20, 22, 25, 26] inches

MATERIALS
- Patons Grace light (light worsted) weight yarn (1¾ oz/136 yds/50g per skein):
  1 [2, 2, 3, 3] skeins #60130 sky (A)
  1 [2, 2, 3, 3] skeins #60005 snow (B)
  1 skein #60104 azure (C)
- Size F/5/3.75mm crochet hook or size needed to obtain gauge
- Tapestry needle
- Stitch markers
- 5 white ⅜-inch shank buttons
- Sewing needle and matching thread

GAUGE
24 sts = 4 inches

Take time to check gauge.

Instructions

JACKET

BACK
Foundation row (RS): With A, ch 56 (62, 68, 76, 80]; sc in 2nd ch from hook; *ch 1, sk next ch, sc in next ch; rep from * across, turn. *(55 [61, 67, 75, 79] sts)*

Row 1: Ch 1, sc in first sc; *sc in next ch-1 sp, ch 1, sk next sc; rep from * to last ch-1 sp; sc in last ch 1 sp and in last sc, turn.

Row 2: Ch 1, sc in first sc, *ch 1, sc in next ch-1 sp; rep from * to last 2 sc; ch 1, sk next sc, sc in last sc, turn.

Rows 3 & 4: Rep rows 1 and 2. At end of row 4, change to C by drawing lp through; cut A.

Rows 5 & 6: Rep rows 1 and 2. At end of row 6, change to A by drawing lp through; cut C.

Rows 7 & 8: Rep rows 1 and 2. At end of row 8, change to C; cut A.

Rows 9 & 10: Rep rows 1 and 2. At end of row 10, change to A; cut C.

Rows 11–14: [Work rows 1 and 2] twice. At end of row 14, change to B; cut A.

Rows 15–18: [Work rows 1 and 2] twice. At end of row 18, change to A; cut B.

Rep rows 11–18 until piece measures 5 [6½, 7¾, 8½, 9½] inches from beg, ending with a WS row. Continue with color rep of 4 rows A and 4 rows B.

ARMHOLE SHAPING
Row 1: Sl st in first 5 sts; ch 1; sc in next sc and in next ch-1 sp; *ch 1, sc in next ch-1 sp; rep from * last 6 sts; sc in next sc,

turn, leaving rem sts unworked. *(45 [51, 57, 65, 69] sts)*

Row 2: Ch 1, sc in first sc, *ch 1, sc in next ch-1 sp; rep from * to last sc; sc in last sc, turn.

Row 3: Ch 1, sc in first sc; *sc in next ch-1 sp, ch 1; rep from * to last ch-1 sp; sc in last ch 1 sp and in last sc, turn.

Row 4: Ch 1, sc in first sc, *ch 1, sc in next ch-1 sp; rep from * to last 2 sc; ch 1, sk next sc, sc in last sc, turn.

Row 5: Ch 1, sc in first sc; *sc in next ch-1 sp, ch 1; rep from * to last ch-1 sp; sc in last ch 1 sp and in last sc, turn.

Rep rows 4 and 5 until armhole measures 4½ [5, 5¼, 6, 6¼] inches, ending with a WS row.

Fasten off and weave in all ends.

Place markers 10 [10, 11, 13, 15] sts in from sides for shoulders.

LEFT FRONT
Foundation row (RS): With A, ch 28 [32, 34, 38, 40]; sc in 2nd ch from hook; *ch 1, sk next ch, sc in next ch; rep from * across, turn. *(27 [31, 33, 37, 39] sts)*

Row 1: Ch 1, sc in first sc; *sc in next ch-1 sp, ch 1, sk next sc; rep from * to last ch-1 sp; sc in last ch 1 sp and in last sc, turn.

Row 2: Ch 1, sc in first sc, *ch 1,

* to last sc; sc in last sc, turn. (20 [24, 26, 30, 32] sts)

For Sizes 3 Months, 6 Months, 12 Months & 18 Months Only
Row 5: Ch 1, sc in first sc and in next ch-1 sp; *ch 1, sc in next ch-1 sp; rep from * to last 2 sts; sc dec in last 2 sc, turn. (19 [23, 25, 29] sts)

Row 6: Ch 1, sc dec in first 2 sts; *sc in next ch-1 sp, ch 1; rep from * to last sc, sc in last sc; turn. (18 [22, 24, 28] sts)

For Size 3 Months Only
Rows 7 & 8: Rep rows 5 and 6. (16 sts at end of row 6)

Continue with For All Sizes.

For Sizes 6 Months, 12 Months & 18 Months Only
Continue with For All Sizes.

For Size 24 Months Only
Continue with For All Sizes.

For All Sizes
Next row (RS): Ch 1, work in pattern to last 2 sts; sc dec in last 2 sc, turn. (15 [21, 23, 27, 31] sts)

Next row: Ch 1; work in pattern, turn.

[Work last 2 rows] 5 [11, 12, 14, 16] times. (10 [10, 11, 13, 15] sts at end of last row)

Next row: Ch 1, work in pattern, turn.

Rep last row until armhole measures same length as armhole on Back to shoulder, ending with a WS row.

Fasten off and weave in ends.

RIGHT FRONT
Work same as Left Front to Armhole Shaping, ending with a RS row.

sc in next ch-1 sp; rep from * to last 2 sc; ch 1, sk next sc, sc in last sc, turn.

Rows 3 & 4: Rep rows 1 and 2. At end of row 4, change to C by drawing lp through; cut A.

Rows 5 & 6: Rep rows 1 and 2. At end of row 6, change to A by drawing lp through; cut C.

Rows 7 & 8: Rep rows 1 and 2. At end of row 8, change to C; cut A.

Rows 9 & 10: Rep rows 1 and 2. At end of row 10, change to A; cut C.

Rows 11–14: [Work rows 1 and 2] twice. At end of row 14, change to B; cut A.

Rows 15–18: [Work rows 1 and 2] twice. At end of row 18, change to A; cut B.

Rep rows 11–18 until piece measures 5 [6½, 7¾, 8½, 9½] inches from beg, ending with a WS row. Continue with color rep of 4 rows A and 4 rows B.

ARMHOLE SHAPING
Row 1: Sl st in first 5 sts; ch 1; sc in next sc and in next ch-1 sp; *ch 1, sc in next ch-1 sp; rep from * last 2 sc; ch 1, sk next sc, sc in last sc. (22 [26, 28, 32, 34] sts)

Row 2: Ch 1, sc in first sc; *sc in next ch-1 sp, ch 1; rep from * to last sc; sc in in last sc, turn.

V-NECK SHAPING
Row 3 (RS): Ch 1, sc in first sc; *sc in next ch-1 sp, ch 1; rep from * to last ch-1 sp; sc in last ch-1 sp, **sc dec** (see Stitch Guide) in last 2 sc, turn. (21 [25, 27, 31, 33] sts)

Row 4: Ch 1, sc dec in first 2 sts; *sc in next ch-1 sp, ch 1; rep from

ARMHOLE SHAPING
Row 1 (WS): Sl st in first 5 sts; ch 1, work in pattern, turn. *(22 [26, 28, 32, 34] sts)*

V-NECK SHAPING
Next row (RS): Ch 1, sc dec in first 2 sts; work in pattern, turn.

Next row: Ch 1, work in pattern to last 2 sts; sc dec in last 2 sts, turn.

[Work last 2 rows] 2 [1, 1, 1, 0] time(s). *(16 [22, 24, 28, 32] sts at end of last row)*

Next row (RS): Ch 1, sc dec in first 2 sts; work in pattern, turn. *(15 [21, 23, 27, 31] sts)*

Next row: Ch 1, work in pattern, turn.

[Work last 2 rows] 5 [11, 12, 14, 16] times. *(10 [10, 11, 13, 15] sts at end of last row)*

Next row: Ch 1, work in pattern, turn.

Rep last row until armhole measures same length as armhole on Back to shoulder, ending with a WS row.

Fasten off and weave in ends.

SLEEVE
Make 2.
Foundation row (RS): With A, ch 34 [38, 38, 40, 40]; sc in 2nd ch from hook; *ch 1, sk next ch, sc in next ch; rep from * across, turn. *(33 [37, 37, 39, 39] sts)*

Row 1: Ch 1, sc in first sc; *sc in next ch-1 sp, ch 1, sk next sc; rep from * to last ch-1 sp; sc in last ch 1 sp and in last sc, turn.

Row 2: Ch 1, sc in first sc, *ch 1, sc in next ch-1 sp; rep from * to last 2 sc; ch 1, sk next sc, sc in last sc, turn.

Row 3: Ch 1, 2 sc in first sc; *sc in next ch-1 sp, ch 1; rep from *

to last ch-1 sp; sc in last ch-1 sp, 2 sc in last sc, turn. *(35 [39, 39, 41, 41] sts)*

Row 4: Ch 1, work in pattern; change to C by drawing lp through; cut A, turn.

Row 5: Ch 1, 2 sc in first st; work in pattern to last st; 2 sc in last st, turn. *(37 [41, 41, 43, 43] sts)*

For Sizes 3 Months & 6 Months Only
Row 6: Ch 1, work in pattern; change to A; cut C.

Row 7: Ch 1, 2 sc in first st; work in pattern to last st; 2 sc in last st, turn. *(39 [43] sts)*

Row 8: Ch 1, work in pattern, turn.

Row 9: Rep row 7. *(41 [45] sts at end of row)*

Rows 10 & 11: Rep rows 6 and 7. *(43 [47] sts at end of row)*

Row 12: Ch 1, work in pattern, turn.

Row 13: Rep row 7. *(45 [49] sts at end of row)*

Row 14: Ch 1, work in pattern; change to B; cut A.

Row 15: Rep row 7. *(47 [51] sts at end of row)*

Rows 16 & 17: Rep row 12.

Row 18: Ch 1, work in pattern; change to A; cut B.

Row 19: Rep row 7. *(49 [53] sts at end of row)*

Rows 20 & 21: Rep row 12.

Row 22: Ch 1, work in pattern; change to B; cut A.

Row 23: Rep row 7. *(51 [55] sts at end of row)*

Rows 24 & 25: Rep row 12.

Row 26: Ch 1, work in pattern; change to A; cut B.

Row 27: Rep row 7. *(53 [57] sts at end of row)*

Rows 28 & 29: Rep row 12.

Row 30: Ch 1, work in pattern; change to B; cut A.

Row 31: Rep row 7. *(55 [59] sts at end of row)*

Rows 32 & 33: Rep row 12.

Row 34: Ch 1, work in pattern; change to A; cut B.

Row 35: Rep row 7. *(57 [61] sts at end of row)*

For Size 3 Months Only
Rep row 12 until piece measures 6 inches from beg. Place 2nd set of markers. Continue with color rep of 4 rows A and 4 rows B.

Rep row 12 for additional 1 inch, ending with a WS row.

Fasten off and weave in ends.

Continue with Assembly.

For Size 6 Months Only
Rows 36 & 37: Rep row 12.

Row 38: Ch 1, work in pattern; change to B; cut A.

Row 39: Rep row 7. *(63 sts at end of row)*

Rep row 12 until piece measures 7½ inches from beg. Place 2nd set of markers. Continue with color rep of 4 rows A and 4 rows B.

Rep row 12 for additional 1 inch, ending with a WS row.

Fasten off and weave in ends.

Continue with Assembly.

For Sizes 12 Months, 18 Months & 24 Months Only
Row 6: Ch 1, work in pattern; change to A; cut C.

Row 7: Ch 1, 2 sc in first st; work in pattern to last st; 2 sc in last st, turn. *(43 [45, 45] sts)*

Row 8: Ch 1, work in pattern, turn.

Row 9: Rep row 7. *(45 [47, 47] sts at end of row)*

Rows 10 & 11: Rep rows 6 and 7. *(47 [49, 49] sts at end of row)*

Row 12: Ch 1, work in pattern, turn.

Row 13: Rep row 7. *(49 [51, 51] sts at end of row)*

Row 14: Ch 1, work in pattern; change to B; cut A.

Row 15: Rep row 7. *(51 [53, 53] sts at end of row)*

Row 16: Rep row 12.

Row 17: Rep row 7. *(53 [55, 55] sts at end of row)*

Row 18: Ch 1, work in pattern; change to A; cut B.

Row 19: Rep row 7. *(55 [57, 57] sts at end of row)*

Row 20: Rep row 12.

Row 21: Rep row 7. *(57 [59, 59] sts at end of row)*

Row 22: Ch 1, work in pattern; change to B; cut A.

Row 23: Rep row 7. *(59 [61, 61] sts at end of row)*

Rows 24 & 25: Rep row 12.

Row 26: Ch 1, work in pattern; change to A; cut B.

Row 27: Rep row 7. *(61 [63, 63] sts at end of row)*

Rows 28 & 29: Rep row 12.

Row 30: Ch 1, work in pattern; change to B; cut A.

Row 31: Rep row 7. *(63 [65, 65] sts at end of row)*

Rows 32 & 33: Rep row 12.

Row 34: Ch 1, work in pattern; change to A; cut B.

Row 35: Rep row 7. *(65 [67, 67] sts at end of row)*

Rows 36 & 37: Rep row 12.

Row 38: Ch 1, work in pattern; change to B; cut A.

Row 39: Rep row 7. *(67 [69, 69] sts at end of row)*

Rows 40 & 41: Rep row 12.

Row 42: Ch 1, work in pattern; change to A; cut B.

Row 43: Rep row 7. *(69 [71, 71] sts at end of row)*

For Size 12 Months Only
Rep row 12 until piece measures 8 inches from beg. Place 2nd set of markers. Continue with color rep of 4 rows A and 4 rows B.

Rep row 12 for additional 1 inch, ending with a WS row.

Fasten off and weave in ends.

Continue with Assembly.

For Sizes 18 Months & 24 Months Only
Rows 44 & 45: Rep row 12.

Row 46: Ch 1, work in pattern; change to B; cut A.

Row 47: Rep row 7. *(73 sts at end of row)*

Rows 48 & 49: Rep row 12.

Row 50: Ch 1, work in pattern; change to A; cut B.

Row 51: Rep row 7. *(75 sts at end of row)*

For Size 18 Months Only
Rep row 12 until piece measures 9 inches from beg. Place 2nd set of markers. Continue with color rep of 4 rows A and 4 rows B.

Rep row 12 for additional 1 inch, ending with a WS row.

Fasten off and weave in ends.

Continue with Assembly.

For Size 24 Months Only
Rows 52 & 53: Rep row 12.

Row 54: Ch 1, work in pattern; change to B; cut A.

Row 55: Rep row 7. *(77 sts at end of row)*

Rows 56 & 57: Rep row 12.

Row 58: Ch 1, work in pattern; change to A; cut B.

Row 59: Rep row 7. *(79 sts at end of row)*

Rep row 4 until piece measures 10 inches from beg. Place 2nd set of markers.

Rep row 4 for additional 1 inch, ending with a WS row.

Fasten off and weave in ends.

Continue with Assembly.

ASSEMBLY

With tapestry needle and matching yarn, sew shoulder seams. Sew in sleeves, placing rows above markers along sk sts of armholes of Fronts and Back, forming square armholes. Sew side and Sleeve seams.

RIGHT FRONT COLLAR

Row 1 (WS): With B, ch 3; sc in 2nd ch from hook and in next ch, turn. *(2 sc)*

Row 2: Ch 2, hdc in each sc, turn.

Row 3: Ch 2, hdc in first hdc, 2 hdc in next hdc, turn. *(3 hdc)*

Row 4: Ch 2, hdc in each, turn.

Row 5: Ch 2, hdc in each hdc to last hdc, 2 hdc in last hdc, turn. *(4 hdc)*

Rows 6–21 [6–25, 6–25, 6–29, 6–29]: [Work rows 4 and 5] 8 [10, 10, 12, 12] *times. (12 [14, 14, 16, 16] hdc at end of last row)*

Fasten off and weave in ends.

LEFT FRONT COLLAR

Row 1 (WS): With B, ch 3; sc in 2nd ch from hook and in next ch, turn. *(2 sc)*

Row 2 (RS): Ch 2, hdc in each sc, turn.

Row 3: Ch 2, 2 hdc in first hdc; hdc in next hdc, turn. *(3 hdc)*

Row 4: Ch 2, hdc in each hdc, turn.

Row 5: Ch 2, 2 hdc in first hdc, hdc in each rem hdc, turn.

Rows 6–21 [6–25, 6–25, 6–29, 6–29]: [Work rows 4 and 5] 8 [10, 10, 12, 12] times. *(12 [14, 14, 16, 16] hdc at end of last row)*

Row 22 [26, 26, 30, 30]: Ch 2,

hdc in next 12 [14, 14, 16, 16] hdc; hold WS of Back facing you; work 25 [28, 30, 35, 35] hdc across back neck edge; working across Right Front Collar extension, hdc in next 12 [14, 14, 16, 16] hdc, turn. *(49 [56, 58, 67, 67] hdc)*

Row 23 [27, 27, 31, 31]: Ch 2, hdc in each hdc, turn.

Rep last row until piece measures 3½ (3½, 4, 4, 5] inches from row 22 [26, 26, 30, 30], ending with a RS row. Fasten off.

FRONT TIES & COLLAR EDGING

Row 1: With B, ch 40; sc in 2nd ch from hook and in each rem sc—*tie made;* hold collar with RS facing you; working in ends of rows of left side of Collar, sc evenly spaced to last row of Collar; 3 sc in first hdc of last row—*corner made;* sc in each hdc to last hdc; 3 sc in last hdc—*corner made;* working in ends of rows of right side of collar, sc evenly spaced to row 1 of Right Front Collar; ch 40; sc in 2nd ch from hook and in each rem ch—*tie made.* Fasten off.

Row 2: Hold piece with RS facing you; join C with sl st in **back lp** *(see Stitch Guide)* of first sc; working in back lps only, sc in each sc and 3 sc in 2nd sc of each corner. Fasten off.

Row 3: With B, rep row 2.

Weave in all ends.

Sew Front Collar edges to V-Neck Shaping.

BUTTONHOLE EDGING

Row 1: Hold piece with RS facing you; join B with sl st in beg of V-Neck Shaping at Left Front; ch 1, sc in same sp, work 29 [37, 45, 49, 57] sc evenly spaced to beg ch; change to A, turn. *(30 [38, 46, 50, 58] sc)*

Row 2: Ch 1, sc in first 2 sc; *ch 2, sk next 2 sc—*Buttonhole made;* sc in next 4 [6, 8, 9, 11] sc; rep from * 3 times; ch 2, sk next 2 sc—*Buttonhole made;* sc in last 2 sc; change to B, turn.

Row 3: Ch 1, sc in each sc and 2 sc in each ch-2 sp.

Fasten off and weave in ends.

BUTTON BAND EDGING

Row 1: Hold piece with RS facing you; join B with sl st in end of foundation row of Right Front; ch 1, sc in same sp, work 29 [37, 45, 49, 57] sc evenly spaced to V-Neck Shaping; change to A, turn. *(30 [38, 46, 50, 58] sc)*

Row 2: Ch 1, sc in each sc; change to B, turn.

Row 3: Ch 1, sc in each sc.

Fasten off and weave in ends.

FINISHING

Step 1: With sewing needle and matching thread, sew 5 shank buttons to Right Front opposite Buttonholes.

Step 2: Referring to photo and with C, embroider anchor on Right Front, using chain st *(see page 44).*

Seaside Cardigan

Design by Nanette Seale

SKILL LEVEL ■■□□
EASY

FINISHED SIZES
Instructions given fit child's size 6 months; changes for 12, 18, and 24 months are in [].

FINISHED GARMENT MEASUREMENTS
Chest: 19 [20, 21, 22½] inches

MATERIALS
• Bernat Softee Baby light (light worsted) weight yarn (5 oz/455 yds/140g per ball):
  1 [2, 2, 2] ball(s) #30300 baby denim marl (A)
  1 ball #02002 pale blue (B)
• Size 10 crochet cotton:
  small amount light blue (C)
  small amount dark blue (D)
• Size I/9/5.5mm crochet hook or size needed to obtain gauge
• Size 7/1.65mm steel crochet hook (for fish)
• Tapestry needle
• 6 white ⅝-inch buttons
• Sewing needle and matching thread

GAUGE
Size I hook: 16 sc = 4 inches

Take time to check gauge.

Instructions

BODY
Row 1 (WS): With I hook and A, ch 77 [81, 85, 89]; working in **front lps** (see Stitch Guide) only, sc in 2nd ch from hook and in each rem ch, turn. (76 [80, 84, 88] sc)

Row 2 (RS): Ch 1, sc in first unused lp of beg ch and in front lp of first sc at same time; *sc in next unused lp of beg ch and in front lp of next sc at same time; rep from * across, turn.

Row 3: Ch 1, sc in first unused lp on 2nd row below and in front lp of first sc at same time; *sc in next unused lp on 2nd row below and in front lp of next sc at same time; rep from * across, turn.

Rows 4–47 [4–51, 4–55, 4–59]: Rep row 3.

RIGHT FRONT
Row 48 [52, 56, 60]: Ch 1, sc in first unused lp on 2nd row below and in front lp of first sc at same time; *sc in next unused lp on 2nd row below and in front lp of next sc at same time; rep from * 14 [15, 16, 17] times, turn, leaving rem sc unworked. (16 [17, 18, 19] sc)

Rows 49–59 [53–63, 57–69, 61–79]: Rep row 3.

NECK SHAPING
Note: *On following rows, work sc dec through unused lp indicated on 2nd row below and front lps of sc indicated on working row.*

Row 60 [64, 70, 80]: Ch 1, **sc dec** (see Stitch Guide) in first 2 sc; *sc in next unused lp on 2nd row below and in front lp of next sc at same time; rep from * across, turn. (15 [16, 17, 18] sc)

Row 61 [65, 71, 81]: Rep row 3.

Row 62 [66, 72, 82]: Ch 1, sc dec in first 2 sc; *sc in next unused lp on 2nd row below and in front lp of next sc at same time; rep from * across, turn. (14 [15, 16, 17] sc)

For Size 6 Months Only
Row 63: Ch 1, sc in first unused lp on 2nd row below and in front lp of first sc at same time; *sc in next unused lp on 2nd row below and in front lp of next sc at same time; rep from * to last 2 sc; sc dec, turn. (13 sc)

Row 64: Ch 1, sc dec in first 2 sc; *sc in next unused lp on 2nd row below and in front lp of next sc at same time; rep from * across, turn. (12 sc)

Row 65: Ch 1, sc in first unused lp on 2nd row below and in front lp of first sc at same time; *sc in next unused lp on 2nd row below and in front lp of next sc at same time; rep from * 7 times, turn, leaving rem sc unworked. (9 sc)

Row 66: Ch 1, sc in first unused lp on 2nd row below and through both lps of first sc at same time; *sc in next unused lp on 2nd row below and through both lps of next sc at same time; rep from * across.

Fasten off and weave in ends.

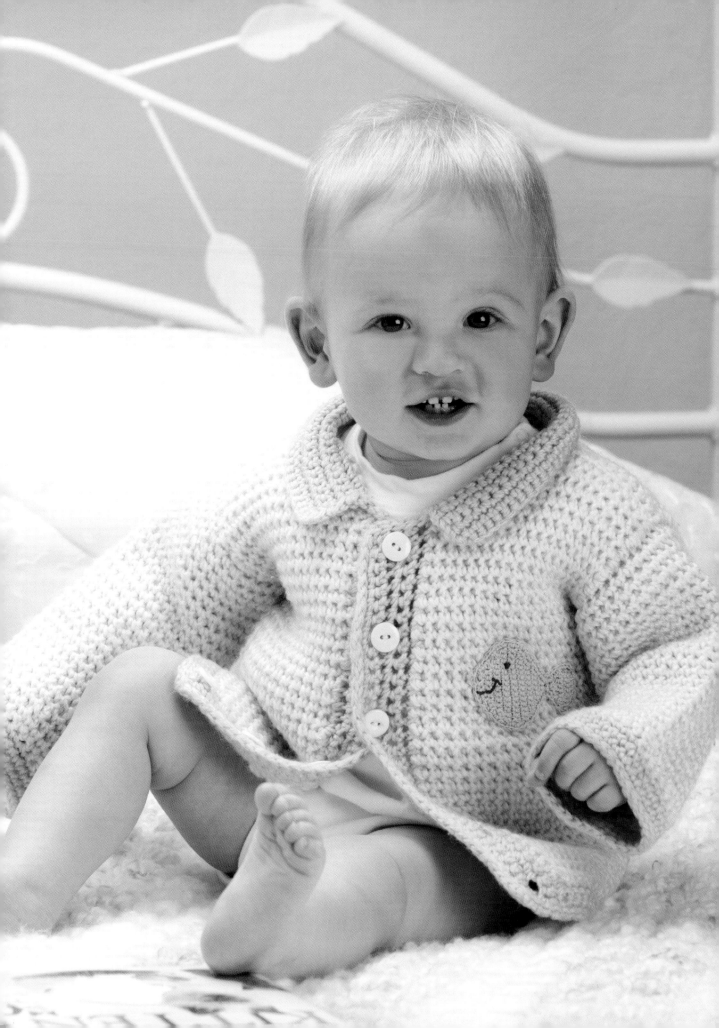

Continue with Back.

For Sizes 12, 18 & 24 Months Only
Row 67 [73, 83]: Rep row 3.

Row 68 [74, 84]: Ch 1, sc dec in first 2 sc; *sc in next unused lp on 2nd row below and in front lp of next sc at same time; rep from * across, turn. (14 [15, 16] sc)

Row 69 [75, 85]: Rep row 3.

Row 70 [76, 86]: Ch 1, sc dec in first 2 sc; *sc in next unused lp on 2nd row below and in front lp of next sc at same time; rep from * across, turn. (13 [14, 15] sc)

For Size 12 Months Only
Row 71: Ch 1, sc in first unused lp on 2nd row below and in front lp of first sc at same time; *sc in next unused lp on 2nd row below and in front lp of next sc at same time; rep from * 8 times, turn, leaving rem sc unworked. (10 sc)

Row 72: Ch 1, sc in first unused lp on 2nd row below and through both lps of first sc at same time; *sc in next unused lp on 2nd row

below and through both lps of next sc at same time; rep from * across.

Fasten off and weave in ends.

Continue with Back.

For Sizes 18 & 24 Months Only
Row 77 [87]: Rep row 3.

Row 78 [88]: Ch 1, sc dec in first 2 sc; *sc in next unused lp on 2nd row below and in front lp of next sc at same time; rep from * across, turn. (13 [14] sc)

For Size 18 Months Only
Row 79: Ch 1, sc in first unused lp on 2nd row below and in front lp of first sc at same time; *sc in next unused lp on 2nd row below and in front lp of next sc at same time; rep from * 8 times, turn, leaving rem sc unworked. (10 sc)

Row 80: Ch 1, sc in first unused lp on 2nd row below and through both lps of first sc at same time; *sc in next unused lp on 2nd row below and through both lps of next sc at same time; rep from * across.

Fasten off and weave in ends.

Continue with Back.

For Size 24 Months Only
Row 89: Rep row 3.

Row 90: Sl st in first 2 sc, ch 1; *sc in next unused lp on 2nd row below and in front lp of next sc at same time; rep from * 11 times, turn. (12 sc)

Row 91: Ch 1, sc in first unused lp on 2nd row below and through both lps of first sc at same time; *sc in next unused lp on 2nd row below and through both lps of next sc at same time; rep from * across.

Fasten off and weave in ends.

Continue with Back.

BACK
Row 48 [52, 56, 60]: Hold piece with RS facing you; sk next 4 sc on row 47 [51, 55, 59] from Right Front; join A with sl st in front lp of next sc, ch 1, sc in corresponding unused lp on 2nd row below and in same lp as joining; *sc in next unused lp on 2nd row below and in front lp of next sc at same time; rep from * 34 [36, 38, 40] times, turn, leaving rem sc unworked. (36 [38, 40, 42] sc)

Rows 49–63 [53–69, 57–77, 61–84]: Rep row 3.

For Size 6 Months Only

RIGHT SHOULDER
Row 64: Ch 1, sc in first unused lp on 2nd row below and in front lp of first sc at same time; *sc in next unused lp on 2nd row below and in front lp of next sc at same time; rep from * 13 times, turn, leaving rem sc unworked. (15 sc)

Row 65: Ch 1, sc dec in first 2 sc; *sc in next unused lp on 2nd row below and in front lp of next sc at same time; rep from * across, turn. *(14 sc)*

Row 66: Ch 1, sc in first unused lp on 2nd row below and in front lp of first sc at same time; *sc in next unused lp on 2nd row below and in front lp of next sc at same time; rep from * 9 times, turn, leaving rem sc unworked. *(11 sc)*

Note: *On following row, work sc dec through corresponding unused lps on 2nd row below and both lps of sc indicated.*

Row 67: Ch 1, sc dec in first 2 sc; sc dec in next 2 sc; *sc in next unused lp on 2nd row below and through both lps of next sc at same time; rep from * across. *(9 sc)*

Fasten off.

LEFT SHOULDER
Row 64: Hold Back with RS facing you; sk next 6 sc on row 63 from Right Shoulder; join A with sl st in front lp of next sc, ch 1, sc in corresponding unused lp on 2nd row below and in same lp as joining; *sc in next unused lp on 2nd row below and in front lp of next sc at same time; rep from * across, turn. *(15 sc)*

Row 65: Ch 1, sc in first unused lp on 2nd row below and in front lp of first sc at same time; *sc in next unused lp on 2nd row below and in front lp of next sc at same time; rep from * to last 2 sc; sc dec, turn. *(14 sc)*

Row 66: Sl st in first 3 sc, ch 1; *sc in next unused lp on 2nd row below and in front lp of next sc at same time; rep from * 10 times, turn. *(11 sc)*

Note: *On following row, work sc dec through corresponding unused lps on 2nd row below and both lps of sc indicated.*

Row 67: Ch 1, sc in first unused lp on 2nd row below and through both lps of first sc at same time; *sc in next unused lp on 2nd row below and through both lps of next sc at same time; rep from * 5 times; [sc dec in next 2 sc] twice. *(9 sc)*

Fasten off and weave in ends.

Continue with Left Front.

For Size 12 Months Only

RIGHT SHOULDER
Row 70: Ch 1, sc in first unused lp on 2nd row below and in front lp of first sc at same time; *sc in next unused lp on 2nd row below and in front lp of next sc at same time; rep from * 14 times, turn, leaving rem sc unworked. *(16 sc)*

Row 71: Ch 1, sc dec in first 2 sc; *sc in next unused lp on 2nd row below and in front lp of next sc at same time; rep from * across, turn. *(15 sc)*

Row 72: Ch 1, sc in first unused lp on 2nd row below and in front lp of first sc at same time; *sc in next unused lp on 2nd row below and in front lp of next sc at same time; rep from * 10 times, turn, leaving rem sc unworked. *(12 sc)*

Note: *On following row, work sc dec through corresponding unused lps on 2nd row below and both lps of sc indicated.*

Row 73: Ch 1, sc dec in first 2 sc; sc dec in next 2 sc; *sc in next unused lp on 2nd row below and through both lps of next sc at same time; rep from * across. *(10 sc)* Fasten off.

LEFT SHOULDER
Row 70: Hold Back with RS facing you; sk next 6 sc on row 69 from Right Shoulder; join A with sl st in front lp of next sc, ch 1, sc in corresponding unused lp on 2nd row below and in same lp as joining; *sc in next unused lp on 2nd row below and in front lp of next sc at same time; rep from * across, turn. *(16 sc)*

Row 71: Ch 1, sc in first unused lp on 2nd row below and in front lp of first sc at same time; *sc in next unused lp on 2nd row below and in front lp of next sc at same time; rep from * to last 2 sc; sc dec, turn. *(15 sc)*

Row 72: Sl st in first 3 sc, ch 1; *sc in next unused lp on 2nd row below and in front lp of next sc at same time; rep from * 11 times, turn. *(12 sc)*

Note: *On following row, work sc dec through corresponding unused lps on 2nd row below and both lps of sc indicated.*

Row 73: Ch 1, sc in first unused lp on 2nd row below and through both lps of first sc at same time; *sc in next unused lp on 2nd row below and through both lps of next sc at same time; rep from * 6 times; [sc dec in next 2 sc] twice. *(10 sc)*

Fasten off and weave in ends.

Continue with Left Front.

For Size 18 Months Only

RIGHT SHOULDER
Row 78: Ch 1, sc in first unused lp on 2nd row below and in front lp of first sc at same time; *sc in next unused lp on 2nd row below and in front lp of next sc at same time; rep from * 14 times, turn, leaving rem sc unworked.

Row 79: Ch 1, sc dec in first 2 sc; *sc in next unused lp on 2nd row below and in front lp of next sc at same time; rep from * across, turn. *(15 sc)*

Row 80: Ch 1, sc in first unused lp on 2nd row below and in front lp of first sc at same time; *sc in next unused lp on 2nd row below and in front lp of next sc at same time; rep from * 10 times, turn, leaving rem sc unworked. *(12 sc)*

Note: *On following row, work sc dec through corresponding unused lps on 2nd row below and both lps of sc indicated.*

Row 81: Ch 1, sc dec in first 2 sc; sc dec in next 2 sc; *sc in next unused lp on 2nd row below and through both lps of next sc at same time; rep from * across. *(10 sc)*

Fasten off.

LEFT SHOULDER

Row 78: Hold Back with RS facing you; sk next 8 sc on row 77 from Right Shoulder; join A with sl st in front lp of next sc, ch 1, sc in corresponding unused lp on 2nd row below and in same lp as joining; *sc in next unused lp on 2nd row below and in front lp of next sc at same time; rep from * across, turn. *(16 sc)*

Row 79: Ch 1, sc in first unused lp on 2nd row below and in front lp of first sc at same time; *sc in next unused lp on 2nd row below and in front lp of next sc at same time; rep from * to last 2 sc; sc dec, turn. *(15 sc)*

Row 80: Sl st in first 3 sc, ch 1; *sc in next unused lp on 2nd row below and in front lp of next sc at same time; rep from * 11 times, turn. *(12 sc)*

Note: *On following row, work sc dec through corresponding unused lps on 2nd row below and both lps of sc indicated.*

Row 81: Ch 1, sc in first unused lp on 2nd row below and through both lps of first sc at

same time; *sc in next unused lp on 2nd row below and through both lps of next sc at same time; rep from * 6 times; [sc dec in next 2 sc] twice. *(10 sc)*

Fasten off and weave in ends.

Continue with Left Front.

For Size 24 Months Only

RIGHT SHOULDER

Row 85: Ch 1, sc in first unused lp on 2nd row below and in front lp of first sc at same time; *sc in next unused lp on 2nd row below and in front lp of next sc at same time; rep from * 15 times, turn, leaving rem sc unworked. *(17 sc)*

Row 86: Ch 1, sc dec in first 2 sc; *sc in next unused lp on 2nd row below and in front lp of next sc at same time; rep from * across, turn. *(16 sc)*

Row 87: Ch 1, sc in first unused lp on 2nd row below and in front lp of first sc at same time; *sc in next unused lp on 2nd row below and in front lp of next sc at same time; rep from * to last 2 sc; sc dec, turn. *(15 sc)*

Row 88: Ch 1, sc dec in first 2 sc; *sc in next unused lp on 2nd row below and in front lp of next sc at same time; rep from * across, turn. *(14 sc)*

Row 89: Ch 1, sc in first unused lp on 2nd row below and in front lp of first sc at same time; *sc in next unused lp on 2nd row below and in front lp of next sc at same time; rep from * to last 2 sc; sc dec, turn. *(13 sc)*

Row 90: Rep row 3.

Row 91: Ch 1, sc dec in first 2 sc; *sc in next unused lp on 2nd row below and in front lp of next sc at same time; rep from * across, turn. *(12 sc)*

Row 92: Ch 1, sc in first unused lp on 2nd row below and through both lps of first sc at same time; *sc in next unused lp on 2nd row below and through both lps of next sc at same time; rep from * across. Fasten off.

LEFT SHOULDER

Row 85: Hold Back with RS facing you; sk next 8 sc on row 84 from Right Shoulder; join A with sl st in front lp of next sc, ch 1, sc in corresponding unused lp on 2nd row below and in same lp as joining; *sc in next unused lp on 2nd row below and in front lp of next sc at same time; rep from * across, turn. *(17 sc)*

Row 86: Ch 1, sc in first unused lp on 2nd row below and in front lp of first sc at same time; *sc in next unused lp on 2nd row below and in front lp of next sc at same time; rep from * to last 2 sc; sc dec, turn. *(16 sc)*

Row 87: Ch 1, sc dec in first 2 sc; *sc in next unused lp on 2nd row below and in front lp of next sc at same time; rep from * across, turn. *(15 sc)*

Row 88: Ch 1, sc in first unused lp on 2nd row below and in front lp of first sc at same time; *sc in next unused lp on 2nd row below and in front lp of next sc at same time; rep from * to last 2 sc; sc dec, turn. *(13 sc)*

Row 89: Ch 1, sc dec in first 2 sc; *sc in next unused lp on 2nd row below and in front lp of next sc at same time; rep from * across, turn. *(13 sc)*

Row 90: Rep row 3.

Row 91: Ch 1, sc dec in first 2 sc; *sc in next unused lp on 2nd row below and in front lp of next sc at same time; rep from * across, turn. *(12 sc)*

Row 92: Ch 1, sc in first unused lp on 2nd row below and through both lps of first sc at same time; *sc in next unused lp on 2nd row below and through both lps of next sc at same time; rep from * across.

Fasten off and weave in ends.

Continue with Left Front.

LEFT FRONT
Row 48 [52, 56, 60]: Hold piece with RS facing you; sk next 4 sc on row 47 [51, 55, 59] from Back; join A with sl st in front lp of next sc, ch 1, sc in corresponding unused lp on 2nd row below and in same lp as joining; *sc in next unused lp on 2nd row below and in front lp of next sc at same time; rep from * across, turn. *(16 [17, 18,19] sc)*

Rows 49–59 [53–63, 57–69, 61–79]: Rep row 3.

NECK SHAPING
Row 60 [64, 70, 80]: Ch 1, sc in first unused lp on 2nd row below and in front lp of first sc at same time; *sc in next unused lp on 2nd row below and in front lp of next sc at same time; rep from * to last 2 sc; sc dec, turn. *(15 [16, 17, 18] sc)*

Row 61 [65, 71, 81]: Rep row 3.

Row 62 [66, 72, 82]: Ch 1, sc in first unused lp on 2nd row below and in front lp of first sc at same time; *sc in next unused lp on 2nd row below and in front lp of next sc at same time; rep from * to last 2 sc; sc dec, turn. *(14 [15, 167, 17] sc)*

For Size 6 Months Only
Row 63: Ch 1, sc dec in first 2 sc; *sc in next unused lp on 2nd row below and in front lp of next sc at same time; rep from * across, turn. *(13 sc)*

Row 64: Ch 1, sc in first unused lp on 2nd row below and in

front lp of first sc at same time; *sc in next unused lp on 2nd row below and in front lp of next sc at same time; rep from * to last 2 sc; sc dec, turn. *(12 sc)*

Row 65: Sl st in first 3 sc, ch 1; *sc in next unused lp on 2nd row below and in front lp of next sc at same time; rep from * 8 times, turn. *(9 sc)*

Row 66: Ch 1, sc in first unused lp on 2nd row below and through both lps of first sc at same time; *sc in next unused lp on 2nd row below and through both lps of next sc at same time; rep from * across.

Fasten off and weave in ends.

Continue with Assembly.

For Sizes 12, 18 & 24 Months Only
Row 67 [73, 83]: Rep row 3.

Row 68 [74, 84]: Ch 1, sc in first unused lp on 2nd row below and in front lp of first sc at same time; *sc in next unused lp on 2nd row below and in front lp of next sc at same time; rep from * to last 2 sc; sc dec, turn. *(14 [15, 16] sc)*

Row 69 [75, 85]: Rep row 3.

Row 70 [76, 86]: Ch 1, sc in first unused lp on 2nd row below and in front lp of first sc at same time; *sc in next unused lp on 2nd row below and in front lp of next sc at same time; rep from * to last 2 sc; sc dec, turn. *(13 [14, 15] sc)*

For Size 12 Months Only
Row 71: Sl st in first 3 sc, ch 1; *sc in next unused lp on 2nd row below and in front lp of next sc at same time; rep from * 9 times, turn. *(10 sc)*

Row 72: Ch 1, sc in first unused lp on 2nd row below and through both lps of first sc at same time; *sc in next unused lp on 2nd row below and through both lps of next sc at same time; rep from * across.

Fasten off and weave in ends.

Continue with Assembly.

For Sizes 18 & 24 Months Only
Row 77 [87]: Rep row 3.

Row 78 [88]: Ch 1, sc in first unused lp on 2nd row below and in front lp of first sc at same time;

*sc in next unused lp on 2nd row below and in front lp of next sc at same time; rep from * to last 2 sc; sc dec, turn. *(13 [14] sc)*

For Size 18 Months Only
Row 79: Sl st in first 3 sc, ch 1; *sc in next unused lp on 2nd row below and in front lp of next sc at same time; rep from * 8 times, turn. *(10 sc)*

Row 80: Ch 1, sc in first unused lp on 2nd row below and through both lps of first sc at same time; *sc in next unused lp on 2nd row below and through both lps of next sc at same time; rep from * across.

Fasten off and weave in ends.

Continue with Assembly.

For Size 24 Months Only
Row 88: Ch 1, sc in first unused lp on 2nd row below and in front lp of first sc at same time; *sc in next unused lp on 2nd row below and in front lp of next sc at same time; rep from * to last 2 sc; sc dec, turn. *(14 sc)*

Row 89: Rep row 3.

Row 90: Sl st in first 2 sc, ch 1; *sc in next unused lp on 2nd row below and in front lp of next sc at same time; rep from * 11 times, turn. *(12 sc)*

Row 91: Ch 1, sc in first unused lp on 2nd row below and through both lps of first sc at same time; *sc in next unused lp on 2nd row below and through both lps of next sc at same time; rep from * across.

Fasten off and weave in ends.

Continue with Assembly.

ASSEMBLY
With tapestry needle and A, sew shoulder seams.

SLEEVES
Rnd 1: Hold piece with RS facing you, with I hook make slip knot on hook and join with sc in 1 underarm; work 30 [33, 39, 45] sc evenly spaced around armhole, join in first sc, turn. *(31 [34, 40, 46] sc)*

Rnd 2: Ch 1, working in front lps only, sc in each sc; join in first sc, turn.

Rnd 3: Ch 1, sc in first unused lp on 2nd row below and in front lp of first sc at same time; *sc in next unused lp on 2nd row below and in front lp of next sc at same time; rep from * around; join in first sc, turn.

Rnds 4–41 [4–47, 4–51, 4–54]: Rep rnd 3.

Rnd 42 [48, 52, 55]: Ch 1, sc in first unused lp on 2nd row below and through both lps of first sc at same time; *sc in next unused lp on 2nd row below and through both lps of next sc at same time; rep from * across.

Fasten off and weave in ends.

Rep for 2nd Sleeve.

BOTTOM EDGING
Row 1 (RS): Hold piece with RS facing you and beg ch at top; with B make slip knot on I hook and join with sc in unused lp of first ch; working in rem unused lps of beg ch, sc in each lp, turn. *(76 [80, 84, 88] sc)*

Row 2: Ch 1, sc in each sc, turn.

Row 3: Ch 1, sc in each sc.

RIGHT FRONT BAND
Row 1: Ch 1, working in ends of rows across right front, work 33 [35, 40, 44] sc evenly spaced to row 59 [63, 69, 79], turn. *(33 [35, 40, 44] sc)*

Row 2: Ch 1, sc in each sc, turn.

Rows 3–5: Rep row 2. Fasten off.

LEFT FRONT BAND
Row 1: Hold piece with RS facing you; with B make slip knot on hook and join with sc in end of row 59 [63, 69, 79]; working in ends of rows of left front, work 32 [34, 39, 43] sc evenly spaced to row 3 of Bottom Edging, turn. *(33 [35, 40, 44] sc)*

Row 2: Ch 1, sc in each sc, turn.

For Size 6 Months Only
Row 3: Ch 1, sc in first 2 sc; *ch 2—*button lp made*; sk next sc, sc in next 4 sc; rep from * 4 times; ch 2—*button lp made*; sk next sc, sc in last 3 sc, turn.

Continue with For All Sizes.

For Size 12 Months Only
Row 3: Ch 1, sc in first 2 sc; *ch 2—*button lp made*; sk next sc, sc in next 5 sc; rep from * 4 times; ch 2—*button lp made*; sk next sc, sc in last 2 sc, turn.

Continue with For All Sizes.

For Size 18 Months Only
Row 3: Ch 1, sc in first 2 sc; *ch 2—*button lp made*; sk next sc, sc in next 6 sc; rep from * 4 times; ch 2—*button lp made*; sk next sc, sc in last 2 sc, turn.

Continue with For All Sizes.

For Size 24 Months Only
Row 3: Ch 1, sc in first 2 sc; *ch 2—*button lp made*; sk next sc, sc in next 5 sc, ch 2—*button lp made*; sk next sc, sc in next 6 sc; rep from * twice; sc in last 3 sc, turn.

Continue with For All Sizes.

For All Sizes
Row 4: Ch 1, sc in each sc and in each ch-2 sp, turn.

Row 5: Ch 1, sc in each sc.

Fasten off and weave in ends.

COLLAR
Note: *Collar is not worked across either front band.*

Row 1: Hold piece with RS facing you; with B make slip knot on hook and join with sc in first unused row of neck edge from Right Front Band; working across neck edge, work 40 [44, 48, 52] sc evenly spaced to Left Front Band, turn. *(40 [44, 48, 52] sc)*

Row 2: Ch 1, sc in each sc, turn.

Row 3: Ch 1, sc in first 3 sc, 2 sc in next sc; *sc in next 3 sc, 2 sc in next sc; rep from * across, turn. *(50 [55, 60, 65] sc)*

Rows 4 & 5: Rep row 2.

Row 6: Ch 1, sc in first 4 sc, 2 sc in next sc; *sc in next 4 sc, 2 sc in next sc; rep from * across, turn. *(60 [66, 72, 78] sc)*

For Sizes 6 Months & 12 Months Only
Row 7: Ch 1, sc in each sc. Do not turn.

EDGING
Working around outer edge of Cardigan, sl st in end of each row and in each sc; join in first sl st.

Fasten off and weave in ends.

Continue with Sleeve Band.

For Sizes 18 Months & 24 Months Only
Row 7: Ch 1, sc in each sc, turn.

Row 8: Rep row 7.

Row 9: Ch 1, sc in each sc. Do not turn.

EDGING
Working around outer edge of Cardigan, sl st in end of each row and in each sc; join in first sl st.

Fasten off and weave in ends.

Continue with Sleeve Band.

SLEEVE BAND
Rnd 1: Hold piece with 1 Sleeve at top; with B make slip knot on hook and join with sc in first sc of last rnd of Sleeve; sc in each rem sc; join with sl st in first sc. *(31 [34, 40, 46] sc)*

Rnd 2: Ch 1, sc in each sc; join with sl st in first sc.

Rnd 3: Rep rnd 2.

Rnd 4: Sl st in each sc; join in joining sl st.

Fasten off and weave in ends.

Rep on rem Sleeve.

FISH
Row 1: With size 7 hook and C, ch 10; sc in 2nd ch from hook and in each rem ch, turn. *(9 sc)*

Row 2: Ch 1, sc dec in first 2 sc; sc in each sc to last 2 sc; sc dec in last 2 sc, turn. *(7 sc)*

Row 3: Rep row 2. *(5 sc at end of row)*

Row 4: Ch 1, sc dec in first 2 sc; sc in next sc, sc dec, turn. *(3 sc)*

Row 5: Ch 1, draw up lp in each sc, yo and draw through all 4 lps on hook, turn.

Row 6: Ch 1, 3 sc in st, turn. *(3 sc)*

Row 7: Ch 1, 2 sc in first sc; sc in next sc, 2 sc in last sc, turn. *(5 sc)*

Row 8: Ch 1, 2 sc in first sc; sc in each sc to last sc; 2 sc in last sc, turn. *(7 sc)*

Rows 9–12: Rep row 8. *(15 sc at end of last row)*

Row 13: Ch 1, sc in each sc; turn.

Rows 14–17: Rep row 13.

Row 18: Ch 1, sc dec in first 2 sc; sc in each sc to last 2 sc; sc dec, turn. *(13 sc)*

Rows 19–22: Rep row 18. *(5 sc at end of last row)*

Row 23: Ch 1, sc dec in first 2 sc; sc in next sc, sc dec. Do not turn. *(3 sc)*

EDGING
Ch 1, working in ends of rows and in unused lps of beg ch, 2 sc in end of row 23; sc in each row to row 16; 2 sc in end of row 16; sc in end of row 15, 2 sc in end of row 14; sc in end of each row to row 1; 3 sc in end of row 1; sc in unused lp of each ch of beg ch; working across next side, 3 sc in end of row 1; sc in each row to row 14; 2 sc in end of row 14; sc in end of row 15, 2 sc in end of row 16; sc in each row to row 23; 2 sc in end of row 23; join in first sc of row 23.

Fasten off, leaving a 12-inch end for sewing.

FINISHING
Step 1: With sewing needle and matching thread, sew buttons to Right Front Band.

Step 2: Referring to photo for placement and with D, embroider eye and mouth on Fish. Sew Fish to Left Front of cardigan.

Little Boy Blue

Design by Laura Gebhardt

SKILL LEVEL

FINISHED SIZES

Instructions given fit child's size 6 months; changes for 12, 18 and 24 months are in [ ].

FINISHED GARMENT MEASUREMENTS

Chest: 19 [20, 21, 22½] inches

Hat: 14 [14, 16, 16]-inch circumference

MATERIALS

• Red Heart Soft Baby light (light worsted) weight yarn (7 oz/575 yds/198g per skein):
  1 [2, 2, 2] skein(s) #7881 powder blue
• Size G/6/4mm crochet hook or sizes needed to obtain gauge
• Tapestry needle
• 4 blue shank buttons:
  ⅜ inch for sizes 6 and 12 months
  ½ inch for sizes 18 and 24 months

GAUGE

18 hdc = 4 inches

Take time to check gauge.

SPECIAL STITCHES

Front post double crochet (fpdc): Yo, insert hook from front to back to front around **post** *(see Stitch Guide)* of st indicated, draw lp through, [yo, draw through 2 lps on hook] twice.

Back post double crochet (bpdc): Yo, insert hook from back to front to back around **post** *(see Stitch Guide)* of st indicated, draw lp through, [yo, draw through 2 lps on hook] twice.

Instructions

SWEATER

BACK

Row 1 (RS): Ch 44 [46, 48, 52]; hdc in 3rd ch from hook *(beg 2 sk chs count as a hdc)* and in each rem ch, turn. *(43 [45, 47, 51] hdc)*

Row 2: Ch 2; *hdc in **back lp** *(see Stitch Guide)* of next hdc, hdc in **front lp** *(see Stitch Guide)* of next hdc, rep from * to last hdc and beg 2 sk chs, hdc in back lp of last hdc and in 2nd ch of beg 2 sk chs, turn.

Row 3: Ch 2; *hdc in back lp of next hdc, hdc in front lp of next hdc; rep from * to last hdc and turning ch-2; hdc in back lp of next hdc and in 2nd ch of turning ch-2, turn.

Rows 4–22 [4–24, 4–26, 4–28]: Rep row 3.

Fasten off and weave in ends.

LEFT FRONT

Row 1 (RS): Ch 28 [30, 30, 32]; hdc in 3rd ch from hook *(beg 2 sk chs count as a hdc)* and in each rem ch, turn. *(27 [29, 29, 31] hdc)*

Row 2: Ch 2; *hdc in back lp of next hdc, hdc in front lp of next hdc, rep from * to last hdc and

beg 2 sk chs, hdc in back lp of last hdc and in 2nd ch of beg 2 sk chs, turn.

Row 3: Ch 2; *hdc in back lp of next hdc, hdc in front lp of next hdc; rep from * to last hdc and turning ch-2; hdc in back lp of next hdc and in 2nd ch of turning ch-2, turn.

Row 4: Rep row 3.

Row 5: Ch 2, *hdc in back lp of next hdc, hdc in front lp of next hdc; rep from * 8 [9, 9, 10] times; ch 1—*buttonhole made;* sk next hdc, [hdc in front lp of next hdc, hdc in back lp of next hdc] twice; ch 1—*buttonhole made;* sk next hdc, hdc in back lp of next hdc and in 2nd ch of turning ch-2, turn.

Row 6: Ch 2, hdc in back lp of next hdc and in next ch; [hdc in back lp of next hdc, hdc in front lp of next hdc] twice; hdc in next ch and in front lp of next hdc; *hdc in back lp of next hdc, hdc in front lp of next hdc; rep from * to last hdc and turning ch-2; hdc in back lp of last hdc and in 2nd ch of turning ch-2.

Rows 7 & 8 [7 & 8, 7–10, 7–10]: Rep row 3.

Rows 9 & 10 [9 & 10, 11 & 12, 11 & 12]: Rep rows 5 and 6.

Row 11 [11, 13, 13]: Ch 2; *hdc in back lp of next hdc, hdc in front lp of next hdc; rep from * to last hdc and turning ch-2; **hdc dec**

(see Stitch Guide) in last hdc and in 2nd ch of turning ch-2, turn. *(26 [28, 28, 30] hdc)*

Row 12 [12, 14, 14]: Ch 1, hdc in front lp of next hdc; *hdc in back lp of next hdc, hdc in front lp of next hdc; rep from * to last hdc and turning ch-2; hdc in back lp of last hdc and in 2nd ch of turning ch-2, turn. *(25 [27, 27, 29] hdc)*

Rows 13–22 [13–24, 15–26, 15–26]: [Work last 2 rows] 5 [6, 6, 6] times. *(15 [15, 15, 17] hdc at end of last row)*

For Sizes 6, 12 & 18 Months Only
Fasten off and weave in ends.

Continue with Right Front.

For Size 24 Months Only
Rows 27 & 28: Rep row 3.

Fasten off and weave in ends.

Continue with Right Front.

RIGHT FRONT

Row 1 (RS): Ch 28 [30, 30, 32]; hdc in 3rd ch from hook *(beg 2 sk chs count as a hdc)* and in each rem ch, turn. *(27 [29, 29, 31] hdc)*

Row 2: Ch 2; *hdc in back lp of next hdc, hdc in front lp of next hdc, rep from * to last hdc and beg 2 sk chs, hdc in back lp of last hdc and in 2nd ch of beg 2 sk chs, turn.

Row 3: Ch 2; *hdc in back lp of next hdc, hdc in front lp of next hdc; rep from * to last hdc and turning ch-2; hdc in back lp of next hdc and in 2nd ch of turning ch-2, turn.

Rows 4–10 [4–10, 4–12, 4–12]: Rep row 3.

Row 11 [11, 13, 13]: Ch 1; *hdc in back lp of next hdc, hdc in front lp of next hdc; rep from * to last hdc and turning ch-2; hdc in back lp of next hdc and in 2nd ch of turning ch-2, turn. *(26 [28, 28, 30] hdc)*

Row 12 [12, 14, 14]: Ch 2; *hdc in back lp of next hdc, hdc in front lp of next hdc; rep from * to last 3 hdc; hdc in back lp of next hdc, hdc dec in last 2 hdc, turn. *(25 [27, 27, 29] hdc)*

Rows 13–22 [13–24, 15–26, 15–26]: [Work last 2 rows] 5 [6, 6, 6] times. *(15 [15, 15, 17] hdc at end of last row)*

For Sizes 6, 12 & 18 Months Only
Fasten off and weave in ends.

Continue with Sleeve.

For Size 24 Months Only
Rows 27 & 28: Rep row 3.

Fasten off and weave in ends.

Continue with Sleeve.

SLEEVE
Make 2.

Row 1: Ch 24 [24, 28, 28], hdc in 3rd ch from hook *(beg 2 sk chs count as a hdc)* and in each rem ch, turn. *(23 [23, 27, 27] hdc)*

Row 2: Ch 2; *hdc in back lp of next hdc, hdc in front lp of next hdc, rep from * to last hdc and beg 2 sk chs, hdc in back lp of last hdc and in 2nd ch of beg 2 sk chs, turn.

Row 3: Ch 2, hdc in first hdc; *hdc in back lp of next hdc, hdc in front lp of next hdc; rep from * to last hdc and turning ch-2; hdc in back lp of next hdc, 2 hdc in 2nd ch of turning ch-2, turn. *(25 [25, 29, 29] hdc)*

Row 4: Ch 2, hdc in front lp of next hdc; *hdc in back lp of next hdc, hdc in front lp of next hdc; rep from * to turning ch-2; hdc in 2nd ch of turning ch-2, turn.

Row 5: Ch 2, hdc in first hdc and in front lp of next hdc; *hdc in back lp of next hdc, hdc in front lp of next hdc; rep from * turning ch-2; 2 hdc in 2nd ch of turning ch-2, turn. *(27 [27, 29, 29] hdc)*

Row 6: Ch 2; *hdc in back lp of next hdc, hdc in front lp of next hdc; rep from * to last hdc and turning ch-2; hdc in back lp of last hdc, hdc in 2nd ch of turning ch-2, turn.

Row 7: Ch 2, hdc in first hdc; *hdc in back lp of next hdc, hdc in front lp of next hdc; rep from * to last hdc and turning ch-2; hdc in back lp of last hdc, 2 hdc in 2nd ch of turning ch-2, turn. *(29 [29, 33, 33] hdc)*

Row 8: Ch 2, hdc in front lp of next hdc; *hdc in back lp of next hdc, hdc in front lp of next hdc; rep from * to turning ch-2; hdc in 2nd ch of turning ch-2, turn.

Row 9: Ch 2, hdc in first hdc and in front lp of next hdc; *hdc in back lp of next hdc, hdc in front lp of next hdc; rep from * to turning ch-2; 2 hdc in 2nd ch of turning ch-2, turn. *(31 [31, 35, 35] hdc)*

Row 10: Ch 2; *hdc in back lp of next hdc, hdc in front lp of next hdc; rep from * to last hdc and turning ch-2; hdc in back lp of last hdc and in 2nd ch of turning ch-2, turn.

Row 11: Ch 2, hdc in first hdc, *hdc in back lp of next hdc, hdc in front lp of next hdc; rep from * to last hdc and turning ch-2; hdc in back lp of last hdc, 2 hdc in 2nd ch of turning ch-2, turn. *(33 [33, 37, 37] hdc)*

For Sizes 6 & 12 Months Only
Row 12: Ch 2, hdc in front lp of next hdc; *hdc in back lp of next hdc, hdc in front lp of next hdc; rep from * to turning ch-2; hdc 2nd ch of turning ch-2, turn.

Row 13: Ch 2, hdc in first hdc and in front lp of next hdc; *hdc in back lp of next hdc, hdc in front lp of next hdc; rep from * to turning ch-2; 2 hdc in 2nd ch of turning ch-2, turn. *(35 hdc)*

Row 14: Ch 2; *hdc in back lp of next hdc, hdc in front lp of next hdc; rep from * to last hdc and turning ch-2; hdc in back lp of last hdc and in 2nd ch of turning ch-2, turn.

Rows 15 & 16: Rep row 14.

Row 17: Ch 2, hdc in first hdc; *hdc in back lp of next hdc, hdc in front lp of next hdc; rep from * to last hdc and turning ch-2; hdc in back lp of last hdc, 2 hdc in 2nd ch of turning ch-2, turn. *(37 hdc)*

For Size 6 Months Only
Row 18: Ch 2, hdc in front lp of next hdc; *hdc in back lp of next hdc, hdc in front lp of next hdc; rep from * to turning ch-2; hdc in 2nd ch of turning ch-2.

Fasten off and weave in ends.

Continue with Assembly.

For Size 12 Months Only
Row 18: Ch 2, hdc in front lp of next hdc; *hdc in back lp of next hdc, hdc in front lp of next hdc; rep from * to turning ch-2; hdc in 2nd ch of turning ch-2.

Rows 19–21: Rep row 18.

Fasten off and weave in ends.

Continue with Assembly.

For Sizes 18 & 24 Months Only
Row 12: Ch 2, hdc in front lp of next hdc; *hdc in back lp of next hdc, hdc in front lp of next hdc; rep from * to turning ch-2; hdc 2nd ch of turning ch-2, turn.

Rows 13 & 14: Rep row 12.

Row 15: Ch 2, hdc in first hdc and in front lp of next hdc; *hdc in back lp of next hdc, hdc in front lp of next hdc; rep from * to turning ch-2; 2 hdc in 2nd ch of turning ch-2, turn. *(39 hdc)*

Row 16: Ch 2; *hdc in back lp of next hdc, hdc in front lp of next hdc; rep from * to last hdc and turning ch-2; hdc in back lp of last hdc and in 2nd ch of turning ch-2, turn.

Rows 17 & 18: Rep row 16.

Row 19: Ch 2, hdc in first hdc and in front lp of next hdc; *hdc in back lp of next hdc, hdc in front lp of next hdc; rep from * to last hdc and turning ch-2; hdc in back lp of last hdc, 2 hdc in 2nd ch of turning ch-2, turn. *(41 hdc)*

Row 20: Ch 2, hdc in front lp of next hdc; *hdc in back lp of next hdc, hdc in front lp of next hdc; rep from * to turning ch-2; hdc in 2nd ch of turning ch-2.

Rows 21 & 22: Rep row 20.

For Size 18 Months Only

Fasten off and weave in ends.

Continue with Assembly.

For Size 24 Months Only
Rows 23 & 24: Rep row 20.

Fasten off and weave in ends.

Continue with Assembly.

ASSEMBLY
Sew shoulder seams. Sew Sleeves in place and sew Sleeve and side seams.

SLEEVE EDGING
Rnd 1 (RS): Hold 1 Sleeve with RS facing you and beg ch at top; join yarn with sl st in first unused lp of beg ch to left of seam; ch 1, sc in same lp and in each rem unused lp; join with sl st in first sc.

Rnd 2: Ch 1, working from left to right, work **reverse sc** *(see Stitch Guide)* in each sc; join with sl st in first reverse sc.

Fasten off and weave in ends.

Rep on 2nd Sleeve.

BODY & NECK EDGING
Rnd 1: Hold piece with RS of Back facing you; join yarn in first hdc to left of right shoulder seam; ch 1, sc in same hdc and in each hdc across Back neck edge; sc evenly spaced down Left Front, across lower edge of body, up Right Front and neck edge to first sc; join with sl st in first sc.

Rnd 2: Ch 1, working from left to right, work reverse sc in each sc; join in first reverse sc.

Fasten off and weave in ends.

FINISHING
With sewing needle and matching thread, sew buttons on Right Front opposite buttonholes.

HAT

Rnd 1: Ch 3, 8 hdc in 3rd ch from hook *(beg 2 sk chs count as a hdc)*; join with sl st in 2nd ch of beg 2 sk chs. *(9 hdc)*

Rnd 2: Ch 2 *(counts as a hdc on this and following rnds)*, hdc in same hdc; 2 hdc in each rem hdc; join with sl st in 2nd ch of beg ch-2. *(18 hdc)*

Rnd 3: Ch 2, hdc in each hdc; join with sl st in 2nd ch of beg ch-2.

Rnd 4: Ch 2, 2 hdc in next hdc; *hdc in next hdc, 2 hdc in next hdc; rep from * around; join with sl st in 2nd ch of beg ch-2. *(27 hdc)*

Rnd 5: Rep rnd 3.

Rnd 6: Ch 2, hdc in next hdc, 2 hdc in next hdc; *hdc in next 2 hdc, 2 hdc in next hdc; rep from * around; join with sl st in 2nd ch of beg ch-2. *(36 hdc)*

Rnd 7: Rep rnd 3.

Rnd 8: Ch 2, hdc in next 2 hdc, 2 hdc in next hdc; *hdc in next 3 hdc, 2 hdc in next hdc; rep from * around; join with sl st in 2nd ch of beg ch-2. *(45 hdc)*

Rnds 9 & 10: Rep rnd 3.

Rnd 11: Ch 2, hdc in next 3 hdc, 2 hdc in next hdc; *hdc in next 4 hdc, 2 hdc in next hdc; rep from * around; join with sl st in 2nd ch of beg ch-2. *(54 hdc)*

Rnd 12: Rep rnd 3.

Rnd 13: Ch 2, hdc in next 4 hdc, 2 hdc in next hdc; *hdc in next 5 hdc, 2 hdc in next hdc; rep from * around; join with sl st in 2nd ch of beg ch-2. *(63 hdc)*

For Sizes 6 & 12 Months Only
Rnds 14 & 15: Rep rnd 3.

Rnd 16: Ch 2; ***fpdc** *(see Special Stitches)* around next hdc, **bpdc** *(see Special Stitches)* around next hdc; rep from * around; join with sl st in 2nd ch of beg ch-2.

Rnd 17: Ch 2; *fpdc in around next dc, bpdc around next dc; rep from * around; join with sl st in 2nd ch of beg ch-2.

Rnds 18–20: Rep rnd 17.

Rnd 21: Ch 1, working in **front lps** *(see Stitch Guide)* only, sc in same ch as joining and in each rem st; join with sl st in first sc.

Note: *Remainder of Hat is worked in rows.*

Row 1: Ch 2; *hdc in back lp of next sc, hdc in front lp of next sc; rep from * to last 2 sc; hdc in **back lp** *(see Stitch Guide)* of next sc and through both lps of last sc, turn.

Row 2: Ch 2; *hdc in back lp of next hdc, hdc in front lp of next hdc; rep from * to last hdc and turning ch-2; hdc in back lp of next hdc and in 2nd ch of turning ch-2, turn.

Rows 3–6: Rep row 2.

Row 7: Ch 1, working left to right, work **reverse sc** *(see Stitch Guide)* in each hdc and in 2nd ch of turning ch-2.

Fasten off, leaving an 8-inch end for sewing.

Continue with Finishing.

For Sizes 18 & 24 Months Only
Rnd 14: Rep rnd 3.

Rnd 15: Ch 2, hdc in next 5 hdc, 2 hdc in next hdc; *hdc in next 6 hdc, 2 hdc in next hdc; rep from * around; join with sl st in 2nd ch of beg ch-2. *(72 hdc)*

Rnds 16–18: Rep rnd 3.

Rnd 19: Ch 2; ***fpdc** *(see Special Stitches)* in around next hdc, **bpdc** *(see Special Stitches)* around next hdc; rep from * around; join with sl st in 2nd ch of beg ch-2.

Rnd 20: Ch 2; *fpdc in around next dc, bpdc around next dc; rep from * around; join with sl st in 2nd ch of beg ch-2.

Rnds 21–24: Rep rnd 20.

Rnd 25: Ch 1, working in **front lps** *(see Stitch Guide)* only, sc in same ch as joining and in each rem st; join with sl st in first sc.

Note: *Remainder of Hat is worked in rows.*

Row 1: Ch 2; *hdc in **back lp** *(see Stitch Guide)* of next sc, hdc in front lp of next sc; rep from * to last 2 sc; hdc in back lp of next sc and through both lps of last sc, turn.

Row 2: Ch 2; *hdc in back lp of next hdc, hdc in front lp of next hdc; rep from * to last hdc and turning ch-2; hdc in back lp of next hdc and in 2nd ch of turning ch-2, turn.

Rows 3–8: Rep row 2.

Row 9: Ch 1, working left to right, work **reverse sc** *(see Stitch Guide)* in each hdc and in 2nd ch of turning ch-2.

Fasten off, leaving an 8-inch end for sewing.

Continue with Finishing.

FINISHING
With tapestry needle and long end, sew back seam of Hat cuff. Fold cuff up at rnd 21 [25].

Cherub Christening

Heavenly designs for baby's christening
day. Here you'll find an outfit for baby
boy and another for baby girl in sizes
3 months to 24 months plus an
afghan wrap for your little angel.

Gift From Heaven Christening Ensemble

Design by Joyce Nordstrom

SKILL LEVEL

INTERMEDIATE

FINISHED SIZES

Instructions given for Jacket and Shorts fit size 3 months; changes for 6, 12, 18 and 24 months are in [ ].

Instructions given for Hat fit size 3–6 months; changes for 9–12 months are in [ ].

Instructions given for Booties fit size 3–6 months.

FINISHED GARMENT MEASUREMENTS

Chest: 19 [20, 21, 22, 23] inches

Afghan: approximately 36 x 36 inches

MATERIALS

• Lion Brand Babysoft light (DK) weight yarn (5 oz/459 yds/141g per skein):
   6 skeins #100 white
• Size F/5/3.75mm crochet hook or size needed to obtain gauge (for jacket, shorts, booties and hat)
• Size G/6/4mm crochet hook or size needed to obtain gauge (for afghan)
• Tapestry needle
• 8 [8, 8, 8, 8] white ⅝-inch shank buttons
• 2 white ¾-inch shank buttons
• Sewing needle and white thread

GAUGE

Size F hook: 16 hdc = 4 inches
Size G hook: Motif = 5 inches

Take time to check gauge.

Instructions

JACKET

Note: *Jacket Back, Fronts and Sleeves are worked lengthwise and in* **back lps** *(see Stittch Guide) only.*

BACK

Foundation row (RS): Ch 46 [48, 50, 52, 54]; hdc in 3rd ch from hook and in each rem ch, turn. *(44 [46, 48, 50, 52] hdc)*

Row 1: Ch 2, hdc in each hdc, turn.

Rep row 1 until piece measures 9½ [10, 10½, 11, 11½] inches from beg. Fasten off.

RIGHT FRONT

Foundation row (RS): Beg at neck edge, ch 31 [33, 35, 37, 39]; hdc in 3rd ch from hook and in each rem ch, turn. *(29 [31, 33, 35, 37] hdc)*

Row 1: Ch 2, hdc in each hdc to last hdc; 2 hdc in last hdc, turn. *(30 [32, 34, 36, 38] hdc)*

Row 2: Ch 2, 2 hdc in first hdc; hdc in each rem hdc, turn. *(31 [33, 35, 37, 39] hdc)*

Row 3: Ch 2, hdc in each hdc to last hdc; 2 hdc in last hdc, turn. *(32 [34, 36, 38, 40] hdc)*

Rows 4–9 [4–11, 4–13, 4–15, 4–17]: [Work rows 2 and 3] 3 [4, 5, 6, 7] times. *(38 [40, 42, 44, 46] hdc at end of last row)*

RIGHT SHOULDER

Row 1: Ch 8; hdc in 3rd ch from hook, in next 5 chs, and in each hdc, turn. *(44 [46, 48, 50, 52] hdc)*

Row 2: Ch 2, hdc in each hdc, turn.

Rep row 2 until piece measures 5¼ [5½, 5¾, 6, 6¼] inches from beg. Fasten off.

LEFT FRONT

Foundation row (RS): Ch 31 [33, 35, 37, 39]; hdc in 3rd ch from hook and in each rem ch, turn. *(29 [31, 33, 35, 37] hdc)*

Row 1: Ch 2, hdc in first hdc and in next hdc; *ch 1, sk next hdc—buttonhole made; hdc in next 7 hdc; rep from * twice; ch 1, sk next hdc—buttonhole made; hdc in each rem hdc, turn. *(30 [32, 34, 36, 38] sts)*

Row 2: Ch 2, hdc in each hdc and in each ch-1 sp to last hdc; 2 hdc in last hdc, turn. *(31 [33, 35, 37, 39] hdc)*

Row 3: Ch 2, 2 hdc in first hdc; hdc in each rem hdc, turn. *(31 [33, 35, 37, 39] hdc)*

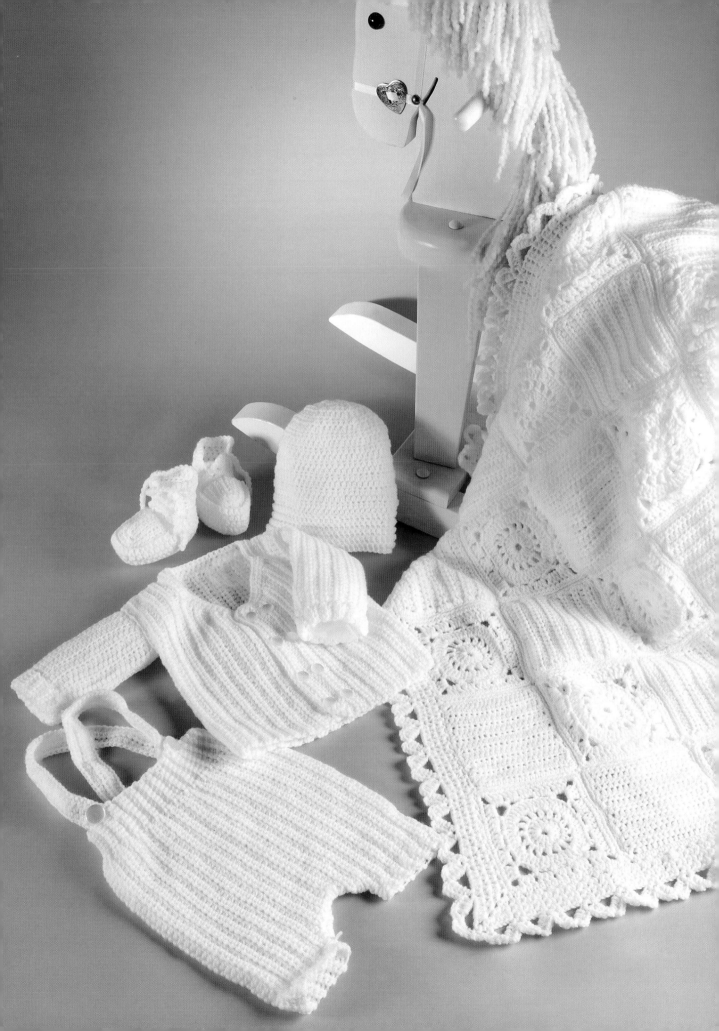

Rows 4–9 [4–11, 4–13, 4–15, 4–17]: [Work rows 2 and 3] 3 [4, 5, 6, 7] times. *(38 [40, 42, 44, 46] hdc at end of last row)*

LEFT SHOULDER
Row 1: Ch 8; hdc in 3rd ch from hook, in next 5 chs, and in each hdc, turn. *(44 [46, 48, 50, 52] hdc)*

Row 2: Ch 2, hdc in each hdc, turn.

Rep row 2 until piece measures 5¼ [5½, 5¾, 6, 6¼] inches from beg.

Fasten off and weave in ends.

SLEEVE
MAKE 2.
Foundation row: Ch 30 [32, 36, 38, 40]; hdc in 3rd ch from hook and in each rem ch to last 5 chs; sc in last 5 chs, turn. *(23 [25, 29, 31, 33] hdc)*

Row 1: Ch 1, sc in first 5 sc, hdc in each hdc, turn.

Row 2: Ch 2, hdc in each hdc, sc in each sc, turn.

Rep rows 1 and 2 until piece measures 7¼ [7¾, 8¼, 8¾, 9¼] inches from beg.

Fasten off and weave in ends.

ASSEMBLY
Sew shoulder seams, matching shoulders of fronts to shoulder edge of back and leaving center of back unsewn for back of neck.

EDGING
Row 1: Hold Jacket with RS facing you; join yarn at lower edge of Right Front; sc evenly up Right Front; 3 sc at neck edge corner; sc evenly around neck edge, across back, down Left Front neck edge; 3 sc at neck edge corner; sc evenly down Left Front, taking care to keep edges flat, turn.

Note: *For buttonholes on Edging,*

mark sc on row 1 to correspond to buttonholes on Left Front.

Row 2: Ch 2, [hdc in each sc to first marked sc; ch 1—*buttonhole made*; sk marked sc] 4 times; hdc in each sc to 2nd sc of next corner; 3 hdc in 2nd sc; hdc in each sc to 2nd sc of next corner; 3 hdc in 2nd sc; hdc in each rem sc, turn.

Row 3: Ch 1, sc in each hdc to 2nd hdc of next corner; 3 sc in 2nd hdc; sc in each hdc to 2nd hdc of next corner; 3 sc in 2nd sc; sc in each rem hdc and in each ch-1 sp.

Fasten off and weave in ends.

FINISHING
Sew buttons to Right Front matching buttonholes on Left Front.

SHORTS
Note: *Shorts are worked in 1 piece from back seam to back seam and in* **back lps** *(see Stitch Guide) only.*

LEFT LEG
Row 1: Ch 40 [42, 44, 46, 48]; hdc in 3rd ch from hook and in next 29 [31, 33, 35, 37] chs, sc in last 8 chs, turn. *(38 [40, 42, 44, 46] sts)*

Row 2: Ch 1, sc in first 8 sc, hdc in each hdc to last hdc; 2 hdc in last hdc, turn. *(39 [41, 43, 45, 47] sts)*

Row 3: Ch 2, 2 hdc in first hdc; hdc in each hdc; sc in each sc, turn. *(40 [42, 44, 46, 48] sts)*

Row 4: Ch 1, sc in first 8 sc, hdc in each hdc to last hdc, 3 hdc in last hdc, turn. *(42 [44, 46, 48, 50] sts)*

Row 5: Ch 5, sc in 2nd ch from hook and next 2 chs, hdc in next ch and in each rem hdc, sc in each sc, turn. *(46 [48, 50, 52, 54] sts)*

Row 6: Ch 1, sc in first 8 sc, hdc in each hdc to last 3 hdc; sc in last 3 hdc, turn.

Row 7: Ch 1, sc in first 3 sc; hdc in each hdc, sc in each sc, turn.

Rep rows 6 and 7 until piece measures 8½ [8¾, 9, 9¼, 9¾] from beg.

WAISTBAND
Row 1: Ch 1, sc in first 8 sc, hdc each hdc to last 4 sts, turn, leaving rem sts unworked. *(42 [44, 46, 48, 50] sts)*

Row 2: Ch 2, hdc first hdc, [yo, draw up lp in next hdc] 3 times, yo and draw through all 7 lps on hook; hdc in each rem hdc, sc in each sc, turn. *(40 [42, 44, 46, 48] sts)*

Row 3: Ch 1, sc in first 8 sc, hdc in each hdc to last 2 hdc; **hdc dec** *(see Stitch Guide)* in last 2 hdc, turn. *(39 [41, 43, 45, 47] sts)*

Row 4: Ch 2, hdc dec in first 2 hdc; hdc in each rem hdc, sc in each sc, turn. *(38 [40 42, 44, 46] sts)*

Row 5: Ch 1, sc in first 8 sc, hdc in each hdc, turn.

RIGHT LEG
Row 1: Ch 2, hdc in each hdc, sc in each sc, turn.

Row 2: Ch 1, sc in first 8 sc, hdc in each hdc to last hdc; 2 hdc in last hdc, turn. *(39 [41, 43, 45, 47] sts)*

Row 3: Ch 2, 2 hdc in first hdc; hdc in each hdc; sc in each sc, turn. *(40 [42, 44, 46, 48] sts)*

Row 4: Ch 1, sc in first 8 sc, hdc in each hdc to last hdc, 3 hdc in last hdc, turn. *(42 [44, 46, 48, 50] sts)*

Row 5: Ch 5, sc in 2nd ch from hook and next 2 chs, hdc in next ch and in each rem hdc, sc in each sc, turn. *(46 [48, 50, 52, 54] sts)*

Row 6: Ch 1, sc in first 8 sc, hdc in each hdc to last 3 hdc; sc in last 3 hdc, turn.

Row 7: Ch 1, sc in first 3 sc; hdc in each hdc, sc in each sc, turn.

Rep rows 6 and 7 until piece measures 8½ [8¾, 9, 9¼, 9¾] from beg.

WAISTBAND
Row 1: Ch 1, sc in first 8 sc, hdc each hdc to last 4 sts, turn, leaving rem sts unworked. *(42 [44, 46, 48, 50] sts)*

Row 2: Ch 2, hdc first hdc, [yo, draw up lp in next hdc] 3 times, yo and draw through all 7 lps on hook; hdc in each rem hdc, sc in each sc, turn. *(40 [42, 44, 46, 48] sts)*

Row 3: Ch 1, sc in first 8 sc, hdc in each hdc to last 2 hdc; hdc dec in last 2 hdc, turn. *(39 [41, 43, 45, 47] sts)*

Row 4: Ch 2, hdc dec in first 2 hdc; hdc in each rem hdc, sc in each sc, turn. *(38 [40, 42, 44, 46] sts)*

Row 5: Ch 1, sc in first 8 sc, hdc in each hdc.

Fasten off and weave in ends.

ASSEMBLY
Folding piece in half, sew beg ch of Left Leg to last short row of Right Leg to form back seam. Refold and sew inseams from end of 1 Leg to end of other Leg.

BUTTON LOOPS
Join yarn with sl st in approximate right front of Waistband; ch 4, sk next 2 ribs of Waistband, sc in next rib. Fasten off and weave in ends.

Rep for other Button Lp on left side of front.

SUSPENDER
MAKE 2.
Row 1: Ch 54 [58, 62, 66, 70]; hdc in 3rd ch from hook and in each rem ch, turn. *(52 [56, 60, 64, 68] hdc)*

Row 2: Ch 2, hdc in each hdc, turn.

Row 3: Ch 2, hdc in each hdc.

Fasten off and weave in ends.

FINISHING
Step 1: Sew 1 end of each Suspender to back of Shorts.

Step 2: Sew buttons in place at opposite ends of Suspenders.

HAT
BORDER
Row 1 (RS): Ch 57 [61]; sc in 2nd ch from hook and in each rem ch, turn. *(56 [60] sc)*

Row 2: Ch 1, working in **back lps** *(see Stitch Guide)* only, sc in each sc, turn.

Rep row 2 until piece measures 2½ inches from beg.

CROWN
Row 1: Ch 2, working in back lps only, hdc in each sc, turn

Row 2: Ch 2, hdc in each hdc, turn.

Rep row 2 until piece measures 5½ inches from beg.

SHAPE TOP
Row 1: Ch 2, hdc in first 3 hdc, **hdc dec** *(see Stitch Guide)* in next 2 hdc; *hdc in next 3 sts, hdc dec in next 2 hdc; rep from * across, turn. *(40 [50] hdc)*

Row 2: Ch 2, *hdc in next 5 hdc, hdc dec in next 2 hdc; rep from * to last 5 [1] hdc; hdc in each hdc, turn. *(35 [43] hdc)*

Row 3: Ch 2, hdc in first 4 hdc, hdc dec; *hdc in next 4 hdc, hdc dec; rep from * to last 5 [1] hdc; hdc in each hdc, turn. *(30 [36] hdc)*

Row 4: Ch 2, hdc in first 3 hdc, hdc dec; *hdc in next 3 hdc, hdc dec; rep from * to last 0 [1] hdc; hdc in each hdc, turn. *(24 [29] hdc)*

Row 5: Ch 2, hdc in first 2 hdc, hdc dec; *hdc in next 2 hdc, hdc dec; rep from * to last 0 [1] hdc; hdc in each hdc, turn. *(18 [22] hdc)*

Row 6: Ch 2, hdc in first hdc, hdc dec; *hdc in next hdc, hdc dec; rep from * to last 0 [1] hdc; hdc in each hdc, turn. *(12 [15] hdc)*

Fasten off, leaving a 15-inch end for sewing back seam.

FINISHING
Draw up all rem sts tightly and carefully sew back seam.

BOOTIE
Make 2.

SOLE
Rnd 1: Ch 13; sc in 2nd ch from hook *(mark for heel)*; 2 sc in next ch; sc in next 8 chs, 2 sc in next ch; sc in last ch *(mark for toe)*; working on opposite side in unused lps of beg ch, 2 sc in next lp; sc in next 8 lps, 2 sc in

next lp; join with sl st in **back lp** *(see Stitch Guide)* first sc. *(26 sc)*

Note: *Mark end of rnds.*

Rnd 2: Ch 1, sc in same lp as joining; working in back lps only, 2 sc in next sc; sc in next 10 sc, 2 sc in next sc; sc in next sc, 2 sc in next sc; sc in next 10 sc, 2 sc in next sc; join with sl st in back lp of first sc. *(30 sc)*

Rnd 3: Ch 1, sc in same lp as joining; working in back lps only, 2 sc in next sc; sc in next 12 sc, 2 sc in next sc; sc in next sc, 2 sc in next sc; sc in next 12 sc, 2 sc in next sc; join with sl st in back lp of first sc. *(34 sc)*

Rnd 4: Ch 1, sc in same lp as joining; working in back lps only, 2 sc in next sc; sc in next 14 sc, 2 sc in next sc; sc in next sc, 2 sc in next sc; sc in next 14 sc, 2 sc in next sc; join with sl st in back lp of first sc. *(38 sc)*

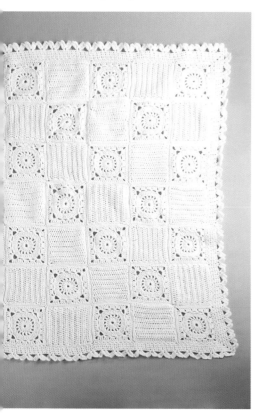

Rnd 5: Ch 1, sc in same lp as joining; working in back lps only, 2 sc in next sc; sc in next 16 sc, 2 sc in next sc; sc in next sc, 2 sc in next sc; sc in next 16 sc, 2 sc in next sc; join with sl st in back lp of first sc. *(42 sc)*

FOOT
Rnd 1: Ch 2, hdc in same lp as joining; working in back lps only, hdc in each rem sc; join in 2nd ch of beg ch-2.

Rnd 2: Ch 2, hdc in each hdc; join with sl st in 2nd ch of beg ch-2.

Rnd 3: Rep rnd 2.

Fasten off and weave in ends.

CUFF
Note: *Mark center of heel.*

Row 1 (WS): Hold piece with WS of heel end at top; join yarn in 8th hdc to right of center of heel; ch 2, hdc in same hdc and in next 15 hdc, turn, leaving rem hdc unworked. *(16 hdc)*

Row 2 (RS): Ch 2, hdc in first hdc; hdc dec in next 2 hdc; hdc to last 3 sts; hdc dec in next 2 hdc; hdc in last st, turn. *(14 hdc)*

Row 3: Rep row 2. *(12 hdc)*

Row 4: Ch 2, hdc in each hdc, turn.

Row 5: Ch 2, hdc in each hdc.

Fasten off and weave in ends.

EDGING
Row 1 (RS): Hold piece with RS facing you; join yarn in row 1 of Cuff; work 8 sc evenly spaced to corner; 3 sc in corner; sc in each st around back; 3 sc in corner; 8 sc to end of row 1 of Cuff, turn.

Row 2: Ch 1, sc in first sc, [ch 1, sk next sc, sc in next 2 sc] twice; ch 1, sk next sc, sc in next sc, 3 sc in

center sc of corner; sc in each sc of back; 3 sc in center sc of corner; sc in next sc, [ch 1, sk next sc, sc in next 2 sc] twice; ch 1, sk next sc, sc in last sc. Fasten off.

TONGUE
Rnd 1: Ch 13; sc in 2nd ch from hook *(mark for heel)*; 2 sc in next ch; sc in next 8 chs, 2 sc in next ch; sc in last ch *(mark for toe)*; working on opposite side in unused lps of beg ch, 2 sc in next lp; sc in next 8 lps, 2 sc in next lp; join with sl st in back lp of first sc. *(26 sc)*

Note: *Mark end of rnds.*

Rnd 2: Ch 1, sc in same lp as joining; working in back lps only, 2 sc in next sc; sc in next 10 sc, 2 sc in next sc; sc in next sc, 2 sc in next sc; sc in next 10 sc, 2 sc in next sc; join with sl st in back lp of first sc. *(30 sc)*

Rnd 3: Ch 1, sc in same lp as joining; working in back lps only, 2 sc in next sc; sc in next 12 sc, 2 sc in next sc; sc in next sc, 2 sc in next sc; sc in next 12 sc, 2 sc in next sc; join with sl st in back lp of first sc. *(34 sc)*

Rnd 4: Ch 1, sc in same lp as joining; working in back lps only, 2 sc in next sc; sc in next 14 sc, 2 sc in next sc; sc in next sc, 2 sc in next sc; sc in next 14 sc, 2 sc in next sc; join with sl st in back lp of first sc. *(38 sc)*

Rnd 5: Ch 1, sc in same lp as joining; working in back lps only, 2 sc in next sc; sc in next 16 sc, 2 sc in next sc; sc in next sc, 2 sc in next sc; sc in next 16 sc, 2 sc in next sc; join with sl st in back lp of first sc. *(42 sc)*

Fasten off and weave in ends.

TIE
MAKE 2.
With 2 strands held tog, ch 75.

Fasten off and weave in ends.

ASSEMBLY
Pin center of toe of Tongue to center of toe of Foot. Matching sts from center to each side of Foot, pin sts tog. Working through double thickness, work sc evenly around other side and around end of tongue; join with sl st to first sc. Fasten off.

FINISHING
Weave 1 Tie through row 2 of each Bootie.

AFGHAN
PLAIN MOTIF
MAKE 24.
Foundation row (RS): Ch 21; hdc in 3rd ch from hook and in each rem ch, turn. *(19 hdc)*

Row 1: Ch 2, hdc in each hdc, turn.

Rep row 1 until piece measures 5 inches from beg.

EDGING
Ch 1, sc evenly around Motif, working [sc, ch 1, sc] in each corner and 17 sc along each side; join in first sc.

Fasten off and weave in all ends.

CIRCLE MOTIF
MAKE 25.
Rnd 1 (RS): Ch 5; join with sl st to form a ring; ch 3 *(counts as a dc)*, 15 dc in ring; join with sl st in 3rd ch of beg ch-3. *(16 dc)*

Rnd 2: Ch 4 *(counts as a dc and a ch-1 sp)*, in each dc work (dc, ch 1); join with sl st in 3rd ch of beg ch-4. *(16 ch-1 sps)*

Rnd 3: Ch 3 *(counts as a dc)*, 2 dc in next ch-1 sp; [dc in next dc, 2 dc in next ch-1 sp] 5 times; join with sl st in 3rd ch of beg ch-3. *(48 dc)*

Rnd 4: Ch 1, sc in same ch as

joining; *ch 5, sk next 2 dc, sc in next dc; [ch 3, sk next 2 dc, sc in next dc] 3 times; rep from * twice; ch 5, sk next 2 dc, sc in next dc; [ch 3, sk next 2 dc, sc in next dc] twice; ch 3, sk next 2 dc; join with sl st in first sc.

Rnd 5: Sl st in next ch-5 sp; ch 3 *(counts as a dc)*, 2 dc in same sp; *3 dc in each of next 3 ch-3 sps; in next ch-5 sp work (3 dc, ch 3, 3 dc)—*corner made*; rep from * twice; 3 dc in each of next 3 ch-3 sps; 3 dc in same sp as beg ch-3 made; ch 1; join with hdc in 3rd ch of beg ch-3.

Row 6: Ch 1, 2 sc in sp formed by joining hdc; *sc in next 15 dc, in next ch-3 sp work (2 sc, ch 1, 2 sc)—*corner made*; rep from * twice; sc in next 15 dc, 2 sc in same sp as beg 2 sc made; ch 1; join with sl st in first sc.

Fasten off and weave in ends.

FINISHING
Referring to diagram for placement, sew Motifs tog.

BORDER
Rnd 1: Join yarn in any corner ch-1 sp; ch 1, in same sp work (sc, ch 2, sc); *ch 1, sk next st, sc in next st; rep from * around, working (sc, ch 2, sc) in each rem corner ch-1 sp; join with sl st in first sc.

Rnd 2: Sl st in next ch-1 sp; ch 2 *(counts as a hdc on this and following rnds)*, hdc in same sp; 2 hdc in each rem ch-1 sp and in each corner ch-2 sp work (2 hdc, ch 2, 2 hdc); join with sl st in 2nd ch of beg ch-2.

Rnd 3: Sl st in next hdc; ch 2, hdc in same hdc; *sk next hdc, 2 hdc in next hdc; rep from * around, working (2 hdc, ch 2, 2 hdc) in each corner ch-2 sp; join with sl st in 2nd ch of beg ch-2.

Rnd 4: Rep rnd 3. Fasten off.

Rnd 5: Join yarn with sl st in any corner ch-2 sp; ch 1, in same sp work (sc, ch 3, sc); [ch 6, sk next 5 hdc, sc in next hdc, ch 3, sk next hdc, sc in next hdc; rep from * around, adjusting reps so in each rem corner ch-2 sp work (sc, ch 3, sc); join with sl st in first sc.

Rnd 6: *Sl st in next ch-3 sp, in next ch-6 sp work (3 dc, ch 3, sl st, ch 3, 3 dc); rep from * around; join with sl st in first sl st.

Fasten off and weave in ends.

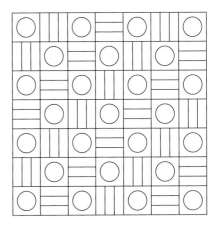

Assembly Diagram

MOTIF KEY
▦ Plain Motif
◎ Circle Motif

Blessed Darling Christening Set

Design by Svetlana Avrakh

SKILL LEVEL

INTERMEDIATE

FINISHED SIZES

Instructions given for Gown fit size 3 months; changes for 6, 12 and 24 months are in [ ].

FINISHED GARMENT MEASUREMENTS

Chest: 18 [19, 21, 23½] inches

Headband: One size

Afghan: approximately 32 x 32 inches

MATERIALS

- Bernat Baby super fine (fingering) weight yarn (1¾ oz/286 yds/50g per skein):
  4 [4, 5, 6] skeins #21008 antique white
- Size F/5/3.75mm crochet hook or size needed to obtain gauge
- Tapestry needle
- 4 yds ⅛-inch-wide off-white satin ribbon
- 4 [4, 5, 5] ⅜-inch matching buttons
- Sewing needle and matching thread

GAUGE

26 sts = 4 inches

Take time to check gauge.

SPECIAL STITCH

V-stitch (V-st): In st indicated work (dc, ch 1, dc).

Instructions

GOWN
BODY
Foundation row (RS): Ch 116 [124, 136, 152]; sc in 2nd ch from hook; *ch 1, sk next ch, sc in next ch; rep from * across, turn. *(115 [123, 135, 151] sts)*

Row 1: Ch 1, sc in first sc; *sc in next ch-1 sp, ch 1, sk next sc; rep from * to last 2 sts; sc in next ch-1 sp and in last sc, turn.

Row 2: Ch 1, sc in first sc; *ch 1, sk next sc, sc in next ch-1 sp; rep from * to last sc; sc in last sc, turn.

Rep rows 1 and 2 until piece measures 2 [2½, 3, 3½] inches from beg, ending with a WS row.

FOR SIZES 3 & 6 MONTHS ONLY

ARMHOLE SHAPING

LEFT BACK
Row 1: Ch 1, sc in first sc; *ch 1, sc in next ch-1 sp; rep from * 11 [12] times; sc in next sc, turn, leaving rem sts unworked. *(26 [28] sts)*

Row 2: Ch 1, **sc dec** *(see Stitch Guide)* in first 2 sts; *sc in next ch-1 sp, ch 1; rep from * to last ch-1 sp and last sc; sc in last ch-1 sp and in last sc, turn. *(25 [27] sts)*

Row 3: Ch 1, sc in first sc; *ch 1, sc in next ch-1 sp; rep from * to last 2 sts; sc dec in last 2 sts, turn. *(24 [26] sts)*

Row 4: Ch 1, sc in first sc; *ch 1, sc in next ch-1 sp; rep from * to last sc; sc in last sc, turn.

Rep row 4 until armhole measures 4¾ [5] inches from beg, ending with WS row. Fasten off.

FRONT
Row 1 (RS): Hold piece with RS facing you; sk next 6 sts from Left Back; join yarn with sl st in next st; ch 1, sc in same st; *ch 1, sc in next ch-1 sp; rep from * 24 [26] times, turn, leaving rem sts unworked. *(51 [55] sts)*

Row 2: Ch 1; sc dec in first 2 sc; *ch 1, sc in next ch-1 sp; rep from * to last 3 sts; ch 1, sk next sc, sc dec in last 2 sts; turn. *(49 [53] sts)*

Row 3: Rep row 2. *(47 [51] sts)*

Row 4: Ch 1, sc in first sc; *sc in next ch-1 sp, ch 1; rep from * to last 2 sts; sc in next ch-1 sp and in last sc, turn.

Row 5: Ch 1, sc in first sc; *ch 1, sc in next ch-1 sp; rep from * to last sc; sc in last sc, turn.

Rep rows 4 and 5 until armhole measures 12 rows less than Left Back, ending with a WS row.

NECK SHAPING & LEFT FRONT SHOULDER
Row 1: Ch 1, sc in first sc; *sc in next ch-1 sp, ch 1; rep from * 5 [6] times; sc in next ch-1 sp, sc dec in next 2 sts, turn, leaving rem sts unworked. *(15 [16] sts)*

Row 2: Ch 1, sc dec in first 2 sc; work in pattern across, turn. *(14 [15] sts)*

Row 3: Ch 1, work in pattern to last 2 sts; sc dec in last 2 sts, turn.

Rows 4–7: [Work rows 2 and 3] twice. *(9 [10] sts at end of row 7)*

Continue in pattern until armhole measures same length as Back, ending with a WS row. Fasten off.

NECK SHAPING & RIGHT FRONT SHOULDER
Row 1: Hold piece with RS facing you; sk next 15 [17] sts from Front; join yarn with sl st in next st; ch 1, sc dec in same st and next st; work in pattern across, turn.

Row 2: Ch 1, work in pattern to last 2 sts, sc dec in last 2 sts, turn.

Row 3: Ch 1, sc dec in first 2 sts; work in pattern across, turn,

Rows 4–7: [Work rows 2 and 3] twice. *(9 [10] sts at end of row 7)*

Continue in pattern until armhole measures same length as Back, ending with a WS row. Fasten off.

RIGHT BACK
Row 1: Hold piece with RS facing you; sk next 6 unworked sts from Right Front Shoulder, join yarn with sl st in next st; ch 1, sc in same st; work in pattern across; turn..

Work same as Left Back, reversing all shaping.

Continue with Skirt.

FOR SIZES 12 & 24 MONTHS ONLY

ARMHOLE SHAPING

LEFT BACK
Row 1: Ch 1, sc in first sc; *ch 1, sc in next ch-1 sp; rep from * 14

[16] times, turn, leaving rem sts unworked. *(31 [35] sts)*

Row 2: Ch 1, **sc dec** *(see Stitch Guide)* in first 2 sts; *ch 1, sc in next ch-1 sp; rep from * to last sc; sc in last sc, turn. *(30 [34] sts)*

Row 3: Ch 1, sc in first sc; *ch 1, sc in next ch-1 sp; rep from * to last 3 sts; ch 1, sk next sc, sc dec in last 2 sts, turn. *(29 [33] sts)*

Row 4: Ch 1, sc in first sc; *sc in next ch-1 sp, ch 1; rep from * to last 2 sts; sc in next ch-1 sp and in last sc, turn.

Row 5: Ch 1, sc in first sc; *ch 1, sc in next ch-1 sp; rep from * to last sc; sc in last sc, turn.

Rep rows 4 and 5 until armhole measures 5½ [6½] inches from beg, ending with a WS row.

Fasten off.

FRONT
Row 1: Hold piece with RS facing you; sk next 6 sts from Left Back; join yarn with sl st in next st; ch 1, sc in same st; *ch 1, sc in next ch-1 sp; rep from * 24 [26] times, turn, leaving rem sts unworked. *(51 [55] sts)*

Row 2: Ch 1; sc dec in first 2 sc; work in pattern to last 2 sts; sc dec in last 2 sts; turn. *(49 [53] sts)*

Row 3: Rep row 2. *(47 [51, 57, 65] sts)*

Continue in pattern until armhole measures 12 rows less than Back, ending with a WS row.

NECK SHAPING & LEFT FRONT SHOULDER
Row 1: Ch 1, sc in first sc; *sc in next ch-1 sp, ch 1; rep from * 7 [8] times; sc in next ch-1 sp, sc dec in next 2 sts, turn, leaving rem sts unworked. *(19 [22] sts)*

Row 2: Ch 1, sc dec in first 2

sc; work in pattern across, turn. *(14 [15] sts)*

Row 3: Ch 1, work in pattern to last 2 sts; sc dec in last 2 sts, turn.

Rows 4–7 [4–9]: [Work rows 2 and 3] 2 [3] times. *(13 [14] sts at end of last row)*

Continue in pattern until armhole measures same length as Back, ending with a WS row. Fasten off.

NECK SHAPING & RIGHT FRONT SHOULDER
Row 1: Hold piece with RS facing you; sk next 17 [19] sts from Front; join yarn with sl st in next st; ch 1, sc dec in same st and next st; work in pattern across, turn.

Row 2: Ch 1, work in pattern to last 2 sts, sc dec in last 2 sts, turn.

Row 3: Ch 1, sc dec in first 2 sts; work in pattern across, turn,

Rows 4–7 [4–9]: [Work rows 2 and 3] 2 [3] times. *(13 [14] sts at end of last row)*

Continue in pattern until armhole measures same length as Back, ending with a WS row. Fasten off.

RIGHT BACK
Row 1: Hold piece with RS facing you; sk next 6 unworked sts from Right Front, join yarn with sl st in next st; ch 1, sc in same st; work in pattern across; turn.

Work same as Left Back, reversing all shaping.

Continue with Skirt.

SKIRT
Row 1 (RS): Hold piece with RS facing you and beg ch at top; join yarn with sl st in first unused lp of beg ch; ch 4, working in rem unused lps, dc in next lp; *ch 3, sk next 3 lps, in next lp work (sc, ch 4,

sc, ch 5, sc, ch 4, sc); ch 3, sk next 3 lps, in next lp work **V-st** *(see Special Stitch)*; rep from * to last lp, turn, leaving last lp unworked.

Row 2: Sl st next ch-1 sp; ch 5, in same sp work (sc, ch 4, sc); *ch 3, V-st in next ch-5 sp; ch 3, in ch-1 of next V-st work (sc, ch 4, sc, ch 5, sc, ch 4, sc); rep from * to last V-st; ch 3, in ch-1 sp of last V-st work (sc, ch 5, sc, ch 1, dc), turn.

Row 3: Ch 4 *(counts as a dc and a ch-1 sp)*, dc in next ch-1 sp; *ch 3, in ch-1 sp of next V-st work (sc, ch 4, sc, ch 5, sc, ch 4, sc); ch 3, V-st in next ch-5 sp; rep from * to last ch-5 sp; V-st in last ch-5 sp, turn.

Rep rows 2 and 3 until piece measures 17 inches from beg, ending with a WS row.

Fasten off and weave in ends.

SLEEVE
MAKE 2.
Foundation row (RS): Ch 48 [48, 54, 54]; sc in 2nd ch from hook; *ch 1, sk next ch, sc in next ch; rep from * across, turn. *(47 [47, 53, 53] sts)*

Row 1: Ch 1, sc in first sc; *sc in next ch-1 sp, ch 1, sk next sc; rep from * to last 2 sts; sc in last ch-1 sp and in last sc, turn.

Row 2: Ch 1, sc in first sc; *ch 1, sk next sc, sc in next ch-1 sp; rep from * to last sc; sc in last sc, turn.

Rep rows 1 and 2 until piece measures 2 [2½, 3, 3½] inches, ending with a WS row.

SHAPE TOP
Row 1: Sl st in first 4 sts; ch 1, sc in same st as last sl st made; work in pattern to last 3 sts, turn, leaving rem sts unworked. *(41 [43, 45, 47] sts)*

Row 2: Ch 1, work in pattern across, turn.

Row 3: Ch 1, sc dec in first 2 sts; work in pattern to last 2 sts; sc dec in last 2 sts, turn.

Rows 4–12 [4–18, 4–14, 4–26]: [Work rows 2 and 3] 4 [7, 5, 11] times. *(31 [27, 33, 23] sts at end of last row)*

Next row: Ch 1, work in pattern across, turn.

Next row: Ch 1, sc dec in first 2 sts; work in pattern to last 2 sts; sc dec in last 2 sts, turn. *(29 [25, 31, 21] sts)*

Rep last row 9 [7, 10, 5] times. *(11 sts at end of last row)*

Fasten off and weave in ends.

FINISHING
Sew shoulder seams. Sew Sleeve seams and sew in Sleeves. Sew Skirt seam.

SLEEVE EDGING
Row 1 (RS): Hold 1 Sleeve with

RS facing you and beg ch at top; join yarn with sl st in first unused lp of beg ch; ch 4, dc in same lp; *ch 3, working in rem unused lps, sk next 3 lps, in next lp work (sc, ch 4, sc, ch 5, sc, ch 4, sc); ch 3, sk next 3 lps, V-st in next lp; rep from * to last 6 [6, 4, 4] lps; ch 3, sk next 2 lps, in next lp work (sc, ch 4, sc, ch 5, sc, ch 4, sc); ch 3; join with sl st in 3rd ch of beg ch-4.

Fasten off and weave in all ends.

Rep on 2nd Sleeve.

BUTTONHOLE BAND
Row 1: Hold piece with RS of body facing you; join yarn with sl st at top of Right Back opening; ch 1, sc in same sp; work 37 [39, 44, 48] sc down back opening to beg of Skirt, turn.

Row 2: Ch 1, sc in first 4 [6, 5, 5] sc; *ch 1—*Buttonhole made*; sk next sc, sc in next 9 [9, 8, 9] sc; rep from * to last 3 sc; ch 1, sk next sc, sc in

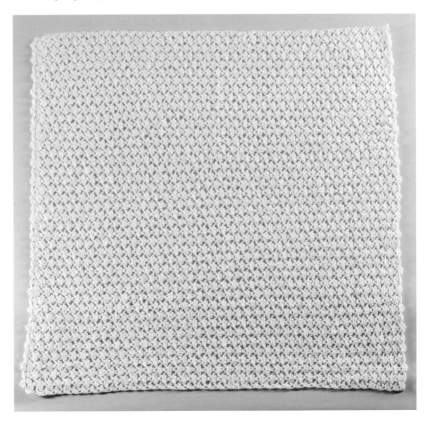

last 2 sc, turn.

Row 3: Ch 1, sc in each st.

Fasten off and weave in ends.

BUTTONBAND
Row 1: Hold piece with RS of body facing you; join yarn with sl st at lower edge of Left Back opening; ch 1, sc in same sp; work 37 [39, 44, 48] sc to top of neck edge, turn.

Row 2: Ch 1, sc in each sc, turn.

Row 3: Ch 1, sc in each sc.

Fasten off and weave in ends.

NECK EDGING
Row 1 (RS): Hold piece with RS of body facing you; join yarn with sl st at top of back opening; ch 1, work 13 [13, 13, 16] sc along Left Back neck edge, 13 sc down Left Front neck edge, 13 [13, 13, 14] sc across Front neck edge, 13 sc up Right Front neck edge, 13 [13, 13, 16] sc along Right Back neck edge, turn. (65 [65, 65, 73] sc)

Row 2: Ch 1, sc in each sc, turn.

Row 3: Ch 4, dc in first sc; *ch 3, sk next 3 sc, in next sc work (sc, ch 4, sc, ch 5, sc, ch 4, sc); ch 3, sk next 3 sc, V-st in next sc; rep from * across.

Fasten off and weave in ends.

FINISHING
Step 1: With sewing needle and matching thread, sew buttons opposite buttonholes.

Step 2: Thread length of ribbon through first row of body. Tie in bow at front. Thread length of ribbon through last row before edging of Sleeves. Tie in bow at sides. Thread length of ribbon through first row of neck edging. Secure ends at back

opening. Make small bow and sew at neck edge.

HEADBAND

CENTER
Row 1 (RS): Ch 94; sc in 2nd ch from hook and in each rem ch, turn. *(93 sc)*

Row 2: Ch 1, sc in first sc; *ch 1, sk next sc, sc in next sc; rep from * across, turn.

Row 3: Ch 1, sc in each st. Do not turn.

CENTER
Working across next side in ends of rows, sl st in end of row 3 and row 2, in end of row 2 work (sc, ch 5, sc, ch 4, sc); ch 3, sk next row, working across next side in unused lps of beg ch, V-st in first lp; *ch 3, sk next 3 lps, in next lp work (sc, ch 4, sc, ch 5, sc, ch 4, sc); ch 3, sk next 3 lps, V-st in next lp; rep from * across; working across next side in ends of rows, ch 3, sk first row, in end of next row work (sc, ch 4, sc, ch 5, sc, ch 4, sc); sk next row; working across row 3, V-st in first sc; *ch 3, sk next 3 sc, in next sc work (sc, ch 4, sc, ch 5, sc, ch 4, sc); ch 3, sk next 3 sc, V-st in next sc; rep from * across; ch 3; join with sl st in first sc.

Fasten off and weave in ends.

FINISHING
Cut a piece of ribbon 20 inches longer then length of Headband. Weave ribbon through ch-1 sps of row 2. Tack ends of ribbon to Headband, leaving 10 inches at each side for ties.

BLANKET
Row 1 (RS): Ch 165; dc in 5th ch from hook *(beg 4 sk chs count as a dc and a ch-1 sp)*; *ch 3, sk next 3 chs, in next ch work (sc, ch 4, sc, ch 5, sc, ch 4, sc); ch 3, sk next 3 chs, in next

st work **V-st** *(see Special Stitch)*; rep from * across, turn.

Row 2: Sl st in next ch-1 sp; ch 5, in same sp work (sc, ch 4, sc); *ch 3, V-st in next ch-5 sp; ch 3, in ch-1 sp of next V-st work (sc, ch 4, sc, ch 5, sc, ch 4, sc); rep from * to sp formed by beg 4 sk chs; ch 3, in sp formed by beg 4 sk chs work (sc, ch 5, sc, ch 1, dc), turn.

Row 3: Ch 4 *(counts as dc and a ch-1 sp)*, dc in first ch-1 sp; *ch 3, in ch-1 sp of next V-st work (sc, ch 4, sc, ch 5, sc, ch 4, sc); ch 3, V-st in next ch-5 sp; rep from * to last ch-5 sp; V-st in last ch-5 sp, turn.

Rep rows 2 and 3 until piece measures 32 inches from beg, ending with a WS row. Fasten off.

BOTTOM EDGE
Hold piece with RS facing you and beg ch at top; join yarn with sl st in first unused lp of beg ch; ch 4, dc in same lp; working in rem unused lps of beg ch; *ch 3, sk next 3 lps, in next lp work (sc, ch 4, sc, ch 5, sc, ch 4, sc); ch 3, sk next 3 lps, V-st in next lp; rep from * across.

Fasten off and weave in all ends.

Toddler Town

Clothes for active toddlers to wear out into the world. Garments sized 2 to 4 designed for any time of the year from cool summer styles to cozy winter wear.

Flower Child Cardigan

Design by Shelia Leslie

SKILL LEVEL
EASY

FINISHED SIZES
Instructions given fit child's size
2T; changes for 3T and 4T are in [ ].

**FINISHED GARMENT
MEASUREMENTS**
Chest: 24 [26, 28] inches

MATERIALS
• Bernat Baby Coordinates
light (DK) weight yarn (6
oz/471 yds/170g per ball):
   2 skeins #09412 sweet pink
• Size F/5/3.75 crochet hook or
size needed to obtain gauge
(for sizes 2T and 3T)
• Size G/6/4mm crochet hook or
size needed to obtain gauge
(for size 4T)
• Tapestry needle
• 3 [3, 4] 15mm matching daisy
buttons
• Sewing needle and matching
thread

GAUGE
Size F hook: 5 sc = 1 inch
Size G hook: 4½ sc = 1 inch

Take time to check gauge.

Instructions

Note: *For sizes 2T and 3T, use F
hook; for size 4T, use G hook.*

LEFT FRONT
Row 1 (RS): Ch 28 [30, 30]; sc in
2nd ch from hook and in each
rem ch, turn. *(27 [29, 29] sc)*

Row 2: Ch 1, dc in first sc; *ch 1,
sk next sc, dc in next sc; rep from *
across, turn. *(13 [14, 14] ch-1 sps)*

Row 3: Ch 1, dc in first dc; *ch 1, dc
in next dc, rep from * across, turn.

Row(s) 4 [4 & 5], [4–6]: Rep row 3.

Row 5 [6, 7]: Ch 1, sc in first dc, in
each ch-1 sp and in each rem dc,
turn. *(27 [29, 29] sc)*

Row 6 [7, 8]: Ch 1, sc in each sc, turn.

Rows 7–32 [8–36, 9–42]: Rep
row 6 [7, 8].

Row 33 [37, 43]: Ch 1, sc in each st
to last 2 sc; **sc dec** *(see Stitch Guide)*
in last 2 sc, turn. *(26 [28, 28] sc)*

Row 34 [38, 44]: Ch 1, sc dec in
first 2 sc; sc in each rem sc, turn.
(25 [27, 27] sc)

Rows 35–40 [39–46, 45–52]: Rep
rows 33 and 34 [37 and 38, 43 and
44] 3 [4, 4] times. *(19 [19, 19] sc)*

Rows 41–52 [47–58, 53–66]:
Rep row 6 [7, 8].

Row 53 [59, 67]: Ch 1, sc in each sc.

Fasten off and weave in ends.

RIGHT FRONT
Rows 1–32 [1–36, 1–42]: Rep
rows 1–32 [1–36, 1–42] of Left Front.

Row 33 [37, 43]: Ch 1, sc dec in
first 2 sc; sc in each rem sc, turn.
(26 [28, 28] sc)

Row 34 [38, 44]: Ch 1, sc in each
sc to last 2 sc; sc dec in last 2 sc,
turn. *(25 [27, 27] sc)*

Rows 35–40 [39–46, 45–52]: Rep
rows 33 and 34 [37 and 38, 43 and
44] 3 [4, 4] times. *(19 [19, 19] sc)*

Rows 41–52 [47–58, 53–66]:
Rep row 6 [7, 8].

Row 53 [59, 67]: Ch 1, sc in each sc.

Fasten off and weave in ends.

BACK
Row 1: Ch 58 [62, 62]; sc in 2nd
ch from hook and in each rem ch,
turn. *(57 [61, 61] sc)*

Row 2: Ch 1, dc in first sc; *ch 1,
sk next sc, dc in next sc; rep from *
across, turn. *(28 [30, 30] ch-1 sps)*

Row 3: Ch 1, dc in first dc; *ch 1, dc
in next dc, rep from * across, turn.

Row(s) 4 [4 & 5], [4–6]: Rep row 3.

Row 5 [6, 7]: Ch 1, sc in first dc, in
each ch-1 sp and in each rem dc,
turn. *(57 [61, 61] sc)*

Row 6 [7, 8]: Ch 1, sc in each sc, turn.

Rows 7–47 [8–53, 9–61]: Rep
row 6 [7, 8].

LEFT SHOULDER
Row 48 [54, 62]: Ch 1, sc in next
22 [23, 23] sc; sc dec in next 2 sc,
turn, leaving rem sc unworked. *(23
[24, 24] sc)*

Row 49 [55, 63]: Ch 1, sc dec in first 2 sc; sc in each rem sc, turn. *(22 [23, 23] sc)*

Row 50 [56, 64]: Ch 1, sc in each sc to last 2 sc; sc dec in last 2 sc, turn. *(21 [22, 22] sc)*

Row 51 [57, 65]: Ch 1, sc dec in first 2 sc; sc in each rem sc, turn. *(20 [21, 21] sc)*

Row 52 [58, 66]: Ch 1, sc in each sc to last 2 sc; sc dec in last 2 sc, turn. *(19 [20, 20] sc)*

FOR SIZE 2T ONLY
Row 53: Ch 1, sc in each sc. Fasten off.

Continue with Right Shoulder.

FOR SIZES 3T & 4T ONLY
Row 59 [67]: Ch 1, sc dec in first 2 sc; sc in each rem sc. *(19 [19] sc)*

Fasten off.

Continue with Right Shoulder.

RIGHT SHOULDER
Row 48 [54, 62]: Hold piece with WS facing you; sk next 9 [11, 11] sc on row 48 [54, 62] from Left Shoulder; join yarn with sl st in next st; sc dec in same st as joining and in next st; sc in each rem sc, turn. *(23 [24, 24] sc)*

Row 49 [55, 63]: Ch 1, sc in each sc to last 2 sc; sc dec in last sc, turn. *(22 [23, 23] sc)*

Row 50 [56, 64]: Ch 1, sc dec in first 2 sc; sc in each rem sc, turn. *(21 [22, 22] sc)*

Row 51 [57, 65]: Ch 1, sc in each sc to last 2 sc; sc dec in last 2 sc, turn. *(20 [21, 21] sc)*

Row 52 [58, 66]: Ch 1, sc dec in first 2 sc; sc in each rem sc, turn. *(19 [20, 20] sc)*

FOR SIZE 2T ONLY
Row 53: Ch 1, sc in each sc. Fasten off and weave in ends.

Continue with Sleeve.

FOR SIZES 3T & 4T ONLY
Row 59 [67]: Ch 1, sc in each sc to last 2 sc; sc dec. *(19 [19] sc)*

Fasten off and weave in ends.

Continue with Sleeve.

SLEEVE
MAKE 2.
Row 1 (RS): Ch 30 [32, 32]; sc in 2nd ch from hook and in each rem ch, turn. *(29 [31, 31] sc)*

Row 2: Ch 1, dc in first sc; *ch 1, sk next sc, dc in next sc; rep from * across, turn. *(14 [15, 15] ch-1 sps)*

Row 3: Ch 1, dc in first dc; *ch 1, dc in next dc, rep from * across, turn.

FOR SIZES 2T & 3T ONLY
Row 4: Ch 1, sc in first dc; *sc in next ch-1 sp, sc in next dc, rep from * across, turn. *(29 [31] sc)*

Row 5: Ch 1, 2 sc in first sc; sc in each sc to last sc; 2 sc in last sc, turn. *(31 [33] sc)*

Row 6: Ch 1, sc in each sc, turn.

Row 7: Rep row 6.

Rows 8–28: [Work rows 5–7] 7 times. *(45 [47] sc at end of row 28)*

Row 29: Rep row 5. *(47 [49] sc)*

Rows 30–38: Rep row 6.

Row 39: Ch 1, sc in each sc.

Fasten off and weave in ends.

Continue with Assembly.

FOR SIZE 4T ONLY
Row 4: Rep row 3.

Row 5: Ch 1, sc in first dc; *sc in next ch-1 sp, sc in next dc, rep from * across, turn. *(31 sc)*

Row 6: Ch 1, 2 sc in first sc; sc in each sc to last sc; 2 sc in last sc, turn. *(33 sc)*

Row 7: Ch 1, sc in each sc, turn.

Row 8: Rep row 7.

Rows 9–29: [Work rows 6–8] 7 times. *(47 sc at end of row 29)*

Row 30: Rep row 6. *(49 sc)*

Rows 31 & 32: Rep row 7.

Row 33: Rep row 6. *(51 sc)*

Rows 34 & 35: Rep row 7.

Row 36: Rep row 6. *(53 sc)*

Rows 37–44: Rep row 7.

Row 45: Ch 1, sc in each sc.

Fasten off and weave in ends.

Continue with Assembly.

ASSEMBLY
With RS tog, sew Fronts to Back at shoulders. Matching centers of Sleeves to shoulder seams, sew Sleeves in. Sew side and Sleeve seams.

EDGINGS
SLEEVE EDGING
Rnd 1: Hold 1 Sleeve with beg ch at top; join yarn with sl st in seam; ch 1, sc in same sp; working in unused lps of beg ch, work 27 sc evenly spaced; join with sl st in first sc. *(30 sc)*

Rnd 2: Ch 3 *(counts as a dc)*, 4 dc in same sc; sk next 2 sc, sc in next sc; *sk next 2 sc, 5 dc in next sc; sk next 2 sc, sc in next sc; rep from * to last 2 sc; sk last 2 sc; join with sl st in 3rd ch of beg ch-3.

Fasten off and weave in ends

FRONT, BOTTOM, & NECK EDGING
Rnd 1: Hold Cardigan with WS facing you; join yarn with sl st in first row of Left Front; ch 1, sc in same sp; working up Left Front edge, 29 [35, 43] sc to neck shaping; work 24 [24, 26] sc around neck edge to shoulder seam; work 6 sc across Left Back Shoulder neck edge; working across Back, work 2 sc in first st; sc in next 7 [9, 9] sts, 2 sc in next st; work 6 sc across Right Back Shoulder neck edge; work 24 [24, 26] sc around neck edge to beg of neck shaping on Right Front; work 29 [35, 42] sc to first row of Right Front; 3 sc in first row; working across bottom edge, work 28 [29, 29] sc across Right Front, 58 [63, 63] sc across Back, and 28 [29, 29] sc across Left Front; 2 sc in same sp as first sc; join with sl st in first sc, turn. *(249 [270, 288] sc)*

FOR SIZE 2T ONLY
Rnd 2: Ch 1, sl st in next sc, ch 3 *(counts as a dc)*, 4 dc in same sc; sk next 2 sc, sc in next sc, [sk next 2 sc, 5 dc in next sc; sk next 2 sc, sc in next sc] 4 times; sk next 3 sc, 5 dc in next sc; sk next 2 sc, sc in next sc, [sk next 2 sc, 5 dc in next sc; sk next 2 sc, sc in next sc] 9 times; sk next 3 sc, 5 dc in next sc; sk next 2 sc, sc in next sc, [sk next

2 sc, 5 dc in next sc; sk next 2 sc, sc in next sc] 3 times; sk next 2 sc, 5 dc in next sc; sk next sc, sc in next sc, sk next 2 sc, 5 dc in next sc; sk next 2 sc, sc in next sc; *sk next sc, in next sc work (3 dc, ch 2, 2 dc)—*buttonhole made*; sk next 2 sc, sc in next sc, sk next 2 sc, 5 dc in next sc; sk next 2 sc, sc in next sc; rep from * twice; [sk next 2 sc, 5 dc in next sc; sk next 2 sc, sc in next sc] 10 times; [sk next sc, 5 dc in next sc; sk next 2 sc, sc in next sc, sk next 2 sc, 5 dc in next sc; sk next 2 sc, sc in next sc] twice; sk next sc, 5 dc in next sc; sk next sc, sc in next sc, sk next 2 sc, 5 dc in next sc; sk next sc, sc in next sc; join with sl st in 3rd ch of beg ch-3.

Fasten off and weave in ends.

Continue with Finishing.

FOR SIZE 3T ONLY
Rnd 2: Ch 1, sl st in next sc, ch 3 *(counts as a dc)*, 4 dc in same sc; sk next 2 sc, sc in next sc, [sk next 2 sc, 5 dc in next sc; sk next 2 sc, sc in next sc] 5 times; sk next sc, 5 dc in next sc; sk next 2 sc, sc in next sc, [sk next 2 sc, 5 dc in next sc; sk next 2 sc, sc in next sc] 8 times; sk next sc, 5 dc in next sc; sk next 2 sc, sc in next sc, [sk next 2 sc, 5 dc in next sc; sk next 2 sc, sc in next sc] 7 times; *sk next 2 sc, in next sc work (3 dc, ch 2, 2 dc)—*buttonhole made*; sk next 2 sc, sc in next sc, sk next 2 sc, 5 dc in next sc; sk next 2 sc, sc in next sc; rep from * twice; [sk next 2 sc, 5 dc in next sc; sk next 2 sc, sc in next sc] 3 times; sk next sc, 5 dc in next sc; sk next 2 sc, sc in next sc, [sk next 2 sc, 5 dc in next sc; sk next 2 sc, sc

in next sc] twice; sk next sc, 5 dc in next sc; sk next 2 sc, sc in next sc, [sk next 2 sc, 5 dc in next sc; sk next 2 sc, sc in next sc] 10 times; join with sl st in 3rd ch of beg ch-3.

Fasten off and weave in ends.

Continue with Finishing.

FOR SIZE 4T ONLY
Rnd 2: Ch 1, sl st in next sc, ch 3 *(counts as a dc)*, 4 dc in same sc; sk next 2 sc, sc in next sc, [sk next 2 sc, 5 dc in next sc; sk next 2 sc, sc in next sc] 5 times; sk next sc, 5 dc in next sc; sk next 2 sc, sc in next sc, [sk next 2 sc, 5 dc in next sc; sk next 2 sc, sc in next sc] 8 times; sk next sc, 5 dc in next sc; sk next 2 sc, sc in next sc, [sk next 2 sc, 5 dc in next sc; sk next 2 sc, sc in next sc] 7 times; *sk next 2 sc, in next sc work (3 dc, ch 2, 2 dc)—*buttonhole made*; sk next 2 sc, sc in next sc, sk next sc, 5 dc in next sc; sk next 2 sc, sc in next sc; rep from * 3 times; [sk next 2 sc, 5

dc in next sc; sk next 2 sc, sc in next sc] 12 times; [sk next sc, 5 dc in next sc; sk next 2 sc, sc in next sc, sk next 2 sc, 5 dc in next sc; sk next 2 sc, sc in next sc] 3 times; sk next sc, 5 dc in next sc; sk next 2 sc, sc in next sc; join with sl st in 3rd ch of beg ch-3.

Fasten off and weave in ends.

Continue with Finishing.

FINISHING
With sewing needle and matching thread, sew buttons to Left Front on 5-dc groups opposite buttonholes.

Out 'n About Jacket & Purse

Design by Joyce Nordstrom

SKILL LEVEL

INTERMEDIATE

FINISHED SIZES
Instructions given fit child's size 2T; changes for 3T and 4T are in [ ].

FINISHED GARMENT MEASUREMENTS
Chest: 24 [25, 26] inches

Purse: 7 inches wide x 6 inch tall excluding handles

MATERIALS
• Red Heart Soft Baby fine (sport) weight yarn (7 oz/575 yds/198g per skein):
   2 skeins #7001 white *(A)*
   1 skein #7624 lime *(B)*
• Size G/6/4mm crochet hook or size needed to obtain gauge
• Tapestry needle

GAUGE
In pattern: 18 hdc = 4 inches

Take time to check gauge.

SPECIAL STITCHES
Shell: In st indicated work (hdc, ch 1, hdc, ch 1, hdc).

V-stitch (V-st): In st indicated work (hdc, ch 1, hdc).

Instructions

JACKET
Note: *Jacket is worked lengthwise.*

RIGHT FRONT
Row 1 (WS): With A, ch 50; sc in 2nd ch from hook; *sk next 2 chs, in next ch work **shell** *(see Special Stitches)*; sk next 2 chs, sc in next ch; rep from * 7 times; in last ch work **V-st** *(see Special Stitches)*, turn.

Row 2 (RS): Ch 1, sc in first hdc; *shell in next sc, sk next hdc and next ch-1 sp; sc in next hdc; rep from * to last sc; V-st in last sc, turn.

Row 3: Ch 1, sc in first hdc; *shell in next sc, sk next hdc and next ch-1 sp; sc in next hdc; rep from * to last sc; shell in last sc, turn.

Row 4: Ch 6, sc in 2nd ch from hook, sk next 2 chs, shell in next ch; sk next 2 chs, sk next hdc and next ch-1 sp, sc in next hdc; *shell in next sc; sk next hdc and next ch-1 sp, sc in next hdc; rep from * to last sc; V-st in last sc, turn.

Rows 5–8: [Work rows 3 and 4] twice.

Rep row 2 until piece measures 5 [5½, 6] inches from beg.

Fasten off and weave in ends.

BACK
Row 1: With A, ch 71; sc in 2nd ch from hook; *sk next 2 chs, in next ch work shell; sk next 2 chs, sc in next ch; rep from * 10 times; in last ch work V-st, turn.

Row 2: Ch 1, sc in first hdc; *shell in next sc, sk next hdc and next ch-1 sp; sc in next hdc; rep from * 10 times; V-st in last sc, turn.

Rep row 2 until piece measures 11 [11½, 12] inches from beg.

Fasten off and weave in ends.

LEFT FRONT
Row 1 (WS): With A, ch 71; sc in 2nd ch from hook; *sk next 2 chs, in next ch work shell; sk next 2 chs, sc in next ch; rep from * 10 times; in last ch work V-st, turn.

Row 2 (RS): Ch 1, sc in first hdc, sk next ch-1 and next hdc; *shell in next sc, sk next hdc and next ch-1 sp, sc in next hdc; rep from * 10 times; V-st in last sc, turn.

Rep row 2 until piece measures 5 [5½, 6] inches from beg, ending with a RS row.

NECK SHAPING
Row 1 (WS): Ch 1, sc in first hdc; *shell in next sc, sk next hdc and next ch-1 sp, sc in next hdc; rep from * 9 times; sk next hdc and next ch-1 sp, sc in next hdc, turn, leaving rem sts unworked.

Row 2 (RS): Ch 2, sk next hdc and next ch-1 sp, sc in next hdc; *shell in next sc; sk next hdc and next ch-1 sp, sc in next hdc; rep from * to last sc; V-st in last sc, turn.

Row 3: Ch 1, sc in first hdc; *shell in next sc, sk next hdc and next ch-1 sp, sc in next hdc; rep from * 8 times; sk next hdc and next ch-1 sp, sc in next hdc, turn.

Row 4: Rep row 2.

Row 5: Ch 1, sc in first hdc; *shell in next sc, sk next hdc and next ch-1 sp, sc in next hdc; rep from * 8 times; sk next hdc and next ch-1 sp, sc in next hdc, V-st in next sc, turn.

Row 6: Ch 1, sc in first hdc; *shell in next sc, sk next hdc and next ch-1 sp; sc in next hdc; rep from * to last sc; shell in last sc, turn.

Row 7: Ch 1, sc in first hdc; *shell in next sc, sk next hdc and next ch-1 sp; sc in next hdc; rep from * to last sc; V-st in last sc.

Fasten off and weave in ends.

SLEEVE
MAKE 2.
Foundation row (RS): With A, ch 35; sc in 2nd ch from hook; *sk next 2 chs, in next ch work shell; sk next 2 chs, sc in next ch; rep from * 4 times; sk next 2 chs, V-st in last ch, turn.

Row 1: Ch 1, sc in first hdc; *shell in next sc, sk next hdc and next ch-1 sp; sc in next hdc; rep from * to last sc; V-st in last sc, turn.

Row 2: Rep row 1.

Row 3: Ch 1, sc in first hdc; *shell in next sc, sk next hdc and next ch-1 sp; sc in next hdc; rep from * to last sc; in last sc work (V-st, hdc), turn.

Row 4: Ch 2, hdc in first hdc, sc in next hdc; *shell in next sc, sk next hdc and next ch-1 sp; sc in next hdc; rep from * to last sc; in last sc work (V-st, hdc), turn.

Row 5: Ch 2, hdc in first hdc, sc in next hdc; *shell in next sc, sk next hdc and next ch-1 sp; sc in next hdc; rep from * to last sc; V-st in last sc; hdc in last hdc, turn.

Row 6: Rep row 5.

Row 7: Ch 2, 2 hdc in first hdc; sc in next hdc; *shell in next sc, sk next hdc and next ch-1 sp; sc in next hdc; rep from * to last sc; V-st in last sc; 2 hdc in last hdc, turn.

Row 8: Ch 2, hdc in first 2 hdc, sc in next hdc; *shell in next sc, sk next hdc and next ch-1 sp; sc in next hdc; rep from * to last sc; V-st in last sc; hdc in last 2 hdc, turn.

Row 9: Rep row 8.

Row 10: Ch 2, 2 hdc in first hdc; hdc in next hdc, sc in next hdc; *shell in next sc, sk next hdc and next ch-1 sp; sc in next hdc; rep from * to last sc; V-st in last sc; hdc in next hdc, 2 hdc in last hdc, turn.

Row 11: Ch 2, hdc in first 3 hdc, sc in next hdc; *shell in next sc, sk next hdc and next ch-1 sp; sc in next hdc; rep from * to last sc; V-st in last sc; hdc in last 3 hdc, turn.

Row 12: Rep row 11.

Row 13: Ch 2, 2 hdc in first hdc; hdc in next 2 hdc, sc in next hdc; *shell in next sc, sk next hdc and next ch-1 sp; sc in next hdc; rep from * to last sc; V-st in last sc; hdc in next 2 hdc, 2 hdc in last hdc, turn.

Row 14: Ch 2, hdc in first 4 hdc, sc in next hdc; *shell in next sc, sk next hdc and next ch-1 sp; sc in next hdc; rep from * to last sc; V-st in last sc; hdc in last 4 hdc, turn.

Row 15: Rep row 14.

Row 16: Ch 2, 2 hdc in first hdc; hdc in next 3 hdc, sc in next hdc; *shell in next sc, sk next hdc and next ch-1 sp; sc in next hdc; rep from * to last sc; V-st in last sc; hdc in next 3 hdc, 2 hdc in last hdc, turn.

Row 17: Ch 2, hdc in first 5 hdc, sc in next hdc; *shell in next sc, sk next hdc and next ch-1 sp; sc in next hdc; rep from * to last sc; V-st in last sc; hdc in last 5 hdc, turn.

Row 18: Rep row 17.

Row 19: Ch 2, 2 hdc in first hdc; hdc in next 4 hdc, sc in next hdc; *shell in next sc, sk next hdc and next ch-1 sp; sc in next hdc; rep from * to last sc; V-st in last sc; hdc in next 4 hdc, 2 hdc in last hdc, turn.

FOR SIZE 2T ONLY
Continue with For All Sizes.

FOR SIZES 3T & 4T ONLY
Row 20: Ch 2, hdc in first 6 hdc, sc in next hdc; *shell in next sc, sk next hdc and next ch-1 sp; sc in next hdc; rep from * to last sc; V-st in last sc; hdc in last 6 hdc, turn.

Row 21: Rep row 20.

Row 22: Ch 2, 2 hdc in first hdc; hdc in next 5 hdc, sc in next hdc; *shell in next sc, sk next hdc and next ch-1 sp; sc in next hdc; rep from * to last sc; V-st in last sc; hdc in next 5 hdc, 2 hdc in last hdc, turn.

Row 23: Ch 2, hdc in first 7 hdc, sc in next hdc; *shell in next sc, sk next hdc and next ch-1 sp; sc in next hdc; rep from * to last sc; V-st in last sc; hdc in last 6 hdc, turn.

Row 24: Rep row 23.

Row 25: Ch 2, 2 hdc in first hdc; hdc in next 6 hdc, sc in next hdc; *shell in next sc, sk next hdc and next ch-1 sp; sc in next hdc; rep from * to last sc; V-st in last sc; hdc in next 6 hdc, 2 hdc in last hdc, turn.

FOR SIZE 3T ONLY
Continue with For All Sizes.

FOR SIZE 4T ONLY
Row 26: Ch 2, hdc in first 8 hdc, sc in next hdc; *shell in next sc, sk next hdc and next ch-1 sp; sc in next hdc; rep from * to last sc; V-st in last sc; hdc in last 8 hdc, turn.

Row 27: Rep row 26.

Row 28: Ch 2, 2 hdc in first hdc; hdc in next 7 hdc, sc in next hdc; *shell in next sc, sk next hdc and next ch-1 sp; sc in next hdc; rep from * to last sc; V-st in last sc; hdc in next 7 hdc, 2 hdc in last hdc, turn.

Row 29: Ch 2, hdc in first 9 hdc, sc in next hdc; *shell in next sc, sk next hdc and next ch-1 sp; sc in next hdc; rep from * to last sc; V-st in last sc; hdc in last 8 hdc, turn.

Row 30: Rep row 29.

Row 31: Ch 2, 2 hdc in first hdc; hdc in next 8 hdc, sc in next hdc; *shell in next sc, sk next hdc and next ch-1 sp; sc in next hdc; rep from * to last

sc; V-st in last sc; hdc in next 8 hdc, 2 hdc in last hdc, turn.

Continue with For All Sizes.

FOR ALL SIZES
Row 20 [26, 32]: Ch 2, hdc in first 6 [8, 10] hdc, sc in next hdc; *shell in next sc, sk next hdc and next ch-1 sp; sc in next hdc; rep from * to last sc; V-st in last sc; hdc in last 6 [8, 10] hdc, turn.

Rep last row until piece measures 8 [9, 10] inches from beg.

Fasten off and weave in ends.

ASSEMBLY
Sew shoulder seams. Matching centers of Sleeves to shoulder seams, sew in Sleeves. Sew side seams.

JACKET EDGING
Rnd 1: Hold Jacket with RS facing you; join A with sl st in 1 side seam; ch 1, sc in same sp; sc evenly around outside edge of Jacket, working 3 sc at each corner; join with sl st in first sc.

Rnd 2: Ch 2, working in **back lps** *(see Stitch Guide)* only, hdc in each sc and 3 hdc in 2nd sc of each corner; join with sl st in 2nd ch of beg ch-2.

continued on page 172

Day in the Sun Dress & Bag

Design by Joyce Nordstrom

SKILL LEVEL
INTERMEDIATE

FINISHED SIZES
Instructions given fit child's size 2T; changes for 3T and 4T are in [ ].

FINISHED GARMENT MEASUREMENTS
Chest: 24 [25, 26] inches

Bag: 6 inches wide x 7 inches tall

MATERIALS
- Red Heart Soft Baby fine (sport) weight yarn
  (solids: 7 oz/575 yds/198g per skein; prints: 6 oz/430 yds/170g per skein):
  2 skeins #8889 laddie print *(A)*
  1 skein #7001 white *(B)*
  1 skein #7624 lime *(C)*
- Size G/6/4mm crochet hook or size needed to obtain gauge
- Tapestry needle
- 2 white ½-inch shank buttons
- ½ yd ½-inch-wide elastic buttons
- Sewing needle and matching thread

GAUGE
16 hdc = 4 inches

Take time to check gauge.

SPECIAL STITCHES
Shell: In st indicated work (hdc, ch 1, hdc, ch 1, hdc).

V-stitch (V-st): In st indicated work (hdc, ch 1, hdc).

Instructions

DRESS
SKIRT
Foundation row: Starting at waist edge with A, ch 47 [49, 51]; sc in 2nd ch from hook and in next 9 chs, hdc in next 6 chs, dc in each rem ch, turn. *(46 [48, 50] sts)*

Note: *Work following rows in* **back lps** *(see Stitch Guide) only.*

Row 1: Ch 3, dc in next 30 [32, 34] dc, hdc in next 6 hdc, sc in last 10 sc, turn.

Row 2: Ch 1, sc in first 10 sc, hdc in next 6 hdc, dc in each dc, turn.

Rep rows 1 and 2 until piece

measures 11 [11½, 12] inches from beg, ending with a WS row.

FRONT PANEL
Row 1: Ch 3, dc in next 30 [32, 34] dc, hdc in next 6 hdc, sc in next 5 sc, turn, leaving rem sc unworked.

Row 2: Ch 16 [17, 18]; sc in 2nd ch from hook, in next 14 [15, 16] chs, in next 5 sc, hdc in next 6 hdc, dc in each dc, turn. *(56 [58, 60] sts)*

Row 3: Ch 3, dc in first 30 [32, 34] dc, hdc in next 6 hdc, sc in each sc, turn.

Row 4: Ch 1, sc in first 2 sc, ch 1—*buttonhole made;* sk next sc, sc in 17 [18, 19] sc, hdc in next 6 hdc, dc in each dc, turn.

Row 5: Ch 3, dc in first 30 [32, 34] dc, hdc in next 6 hdc, sc in each sc, turn.

Row 6: Ch 1, sc in each st, turn.

Row 7: Ch 1, sc in each sc, turn.

Rows 8 & 9: Rep row 7.

Row 10 (WS): Ch 1, working through both lps, sc in first sc; [sk next 2 sts, **shell** (see Special Stitches) in next st; sk next 2 sts, sc in next st] 9 times; in next st work **V-st** (see Special Stitches); hdc in rem 0 [1, 2] sts, turn.

Row 11: Ch 1, sc in 0 [1, 2] st(s), sc in next hdc, sk next ch-1 sp and next hdc; *shell in sc, sk next hdc and next ch-1 sp, sc in next hdc; rep from * to last sc; V-st in last sc, turn.

Row 12: Ch 1, sc in first sc, [shell in next sc, sk next hdc and next ch-1 sp, sc in next hdc] 9 times; V-st in next st; hdc in rem 0 [1, 2] st(s), turn.

Rows 13–18: [Work row 11 and 12] 3 times.

Row 19: Ch 1, sc in each st, turn.

Note: *Work rem rows in back lps only.*

Rows 20–22: Rep row 19.

Row 23: Ch 3, dc in first 30 [32, 34] dc, hdc in next 6 hdc, sc in each sc, turn.

Row 24: Ch 1, sc in first 2 sc, ch 1—buttonhole made; sk next sc, sc in 17 [18, 19] sc, hdc in next 6 hdc, dc in each dc, turn.

Row 25: Ch 3, dc in first 30 [32, 34] dc, hdc in next 6 hdc, sc in each sc and in ch-1 sp, turn.

Row 26: Ch 1, sc in first 20 [21, 22] sc, hdc in next 6 hdc, dc in each dc, turn.

Row 27: Ch 3, dc in first 30 [32, 34] dc, hdc in next 6 hdc, sc in each sc. Fasten off.

Row 28: Hold piece with WS facing you; with A, ch 5, sk first 15 [16, 17] sc on row 27, sc in next 5 sc, hdc in next 6 hdc, dc in each dc, turn.

Row 29: Ch 3, dc in first 30 [32, 34] dc, hdc in next 6 hdc, sc in each sc and in each ch of beg ch-5, turn.

Row 30: Ch 1, sc in first 10 sc, hdc in next 6 hdc, dc in each dc, turn.

Row 31: Ch 3, dc in first 30 [32, 34] dc, hdc in next 6 hdc, sc in each sc, turn.

Rep rows 30 and 31 until piece measures 20 [21, 22] inches from beg when slightly stretched at waistband edge, ending with a WS row.

Fasten off and weave in all ends.

STRAPS
Row 1 (RS): With A, ch 64 [66, 68]; sc in 2nd ch from hook and in each rem ch, turn.

Row 2: Ch 1, sc in each sc, turn.

Rows 3–6: Rep row 2. Fasten off.

EDGING
Rnd 1 (RS): Hold piece with RS facing you and row 6 at top; join B with sl st in first sc in upper right-hand corner; ch 1, 3 sc in same sc—corner made; sc in each sc to last sc; 3 sc in last sc; working across next side in ends of rows, sc in each row; working across next side in unused lps of beg ch, 3 sc in first lp—corner made; sc in each lp to last lp; 3 sc in last lp—corner made; working across next side in ends of rows, sc in each row; join with sl st in first sc. Fasten off.

Rnd 2: Hold piece with WS facing you; join C with sl st in front lp of any sc; ch 1, sc in same lp; working in **front lps** (see Stitch Guide) only, *sl st in next sc, sc in next sc; rep from * around; join with sl st in first sc.

Fasten off and weave in all ends.

ASSEMBLY
Hold pieces with RS facing you; sew edge of last row of Skirt to edge of beg ch of Skirt.

TOP EDGING
Row 1 (RS): Hold Dress with RS facing you and Skirt to right; join B with sl st in first unworked sc on row 27; ch 1, sc in same sc and in each sc to last sc; 3 sc in last sc—corner made; working across next side in ends of rows, sc in each row; working in unused lps of turning ch, 3 sc in first lp—corner made; sc in each rem lp. Fasten off.

Row 2: Hold piece with WS facing you; join C with sl st in front lp of first sc of previous row; ch 1, sc in same lp; working in front lps only, *sl st in next sc, sc in next sc; rep from * across.

Fasten off and weave in ends.

SKIRT EDGING
Rnd 1 (RS): Hold Dress with RS facing you and lower edge at top; join B with sl st in seam; ch 1, sc in same sp; working in ends of rows, sc evenly around; join with sl st in first sc. Fasten off.

Rnd 2 (WS): Hold piece with WS facing you; join C with sl st in front lp of same sc as joining of previous rnd; ch 1, sc in same lp; working in front lps only, *sl st in next sc, sc in next sc; rep from * around; join in first sc.

FINISHING
Step 1: Cut 13 [14, 15]-inch piece of elastic. Fold waistband in half over elastic; tack top edge to

bottom edge. Tack ends of elastic and waistband securely to sides of front panel.

Step 2: Sew 1 short end of each Strap to waistband at back. Sew 1 button to opposite end of each Strap.

BAG
Row 1: With C, ch 26; hdc in 3rd ch from hook and in each rem ch, turn. *(24 hdc)*

Row 2: Ch 2, hdc in each hdc, turn.

Rep row 2 until piece measures 13 inches from beg.

Fasten off and weave in ends.

ASSEMBLY
Fold piece in half with RS tog. Sew end of row 13 to beg ch forming side seam. Sew across 1 open end, forming bottom seam of Bag.

TOP EDGING
Rnd 1: Hold piece with opening at top; ch 1, sc in side seam; working in ends of rows, sc evenly around; join with sl st in **back lp** *(see Stitch Guide)* of first sc.

Rnd 2: Ch 2 *(counts as a hdc on this and following rnd)*, working in back lps only, hdc in next sc; *ch 1, sk next sc, hdc in next 2 sc; rep from * around, adjusting last rep as necessary to end with ch-1; join with sl st in 2nd ch of beg ch-2.

Rnd 3: Ch 2; working in back lps only, *ch 1, hdc in next st; rep from * around; join with sl st in 2nd ch of beg ch-2. Fasten off.

Rnd 4: Hold piece with WS facing you; join B in front lp of any sc; ch 1, sc in same sc; working in front lps only, *sl st in next st, sc in next st; rep from * around; join with sl st in first sc.

Fasten off and weave in all ends.

TIE
MAKE 2.
With B, ch 80; sl st in 2nd ch from hook and in each rem ch.

Fasten off and weave in ends.

LARGE FLOWER
MAKE 2.
With B, ch 4; join to form ring; [ch 2, hdc in ring, ch 2, sl st in ring] 6 times.

Fasten off and weave in ends.

SMALL FLOWER
MAKE 2.

With B, ch 4; join to form ring; [ch 2, hdc in ring, ch 2, sl st in ring] 5 times.

Fasten off and weave in ends.

FINISHING
Step 1: Beg and ending at 1 side seam, weave 1 Tie through ch-1 sps of rnd 2. Tie ends in knot. Rep with other Tie, beg and ending at fold side.

Step 2: Sew Flowers to Bag, having 3 Flowers on front and 1 Flower on back.

Sassy-Style Sweater

Design by Tammy Hildebrand

SKILL LEVEL ■■□□ EASY

FINISHED SIZES
Instructions given fit child's size 2; changes for 4 and 6 are in [ ].

FINISHED GARMENT MEASUREMENTS
Chest: 22½ [24½, 26½] inches

MATERIALS
- Patons Lacette fine (sport) weight yarn (1¾ oz/235 yds/50g per ball):
  2 [3, 3] balls #30422 lilac lace
- Size H/8/5mm crochet hook or size needed to obtain gauge
- Tapestry needle

GAUGE
With 2 strands held tog and in pattern: 7 sc and 6 ch-1 sps = 4 inches

Take time to check gauge.

Instructions

Note: *Sweater is made with 2 strands held tog.*

FRONT
MAKE 2.
Row 1 (RS): Ch 4; sc in 2nd ch from hook, ch 1, sk next ch, sc in last ch, turn. *(2 sc)*

Row 2: Ch 3 *(counts as a hdc and a ch-1 sp on this and following rows)*, hdc in next sc, turn. *(2 hdc)*

Row 3: Ch 1, in first hdc work [sc, ch 1] twice; sc in sp formed by turning ch-3, ch 1, sc in 2nd ch of turning ch-3, turn. *(4 sc)*

Row 4: Ch 3, hdc in next sc, ch 1, sk next sc, hdc in last sc, turn. *(3 hdc)*

Row 5: Ch 1, in first hdc work [sc, ch 1] twice; sc in next ch-1 sp, ch 1, sc in next hdc, ch 1, sc in 2nd ch of turning ch-3, turn. *(5 sc)*

Row 6: Ch 3, [hdc in next sc, ch 1] twice; sk next sc, hdc in last sc, turn. *(4 hdc)*

Row 7: Ch 1, in first hdc work [sc, ch 1] twice; sc in next ch-1 sp, ch 1, [sc in next hdc, ch 1] twice; sc in 2nd ch of turning ch-3, turn. *(6 sc)*

Row 8: Ch 3, [hdc in next sc, ch 1] 3 times; sk next sc, hdc in last sc, turn. *(5 hdc)*

Row 9: Ch 1, in first hdc work [sc, ch 1] twice; sc in next ch-1 sp, ch 1, [sc in next hdc, ch 1] 3 times; sc in 2nd ch of turning ch-3, turn. *(7 sc)*

Row 10: Ch 3, [hdc in next sc, ch 1] 4 times; sk next sc, hdc in last sc, turn. *(6 hdc)*

FOR SIZE 2 ONLY
Continue with For All Sizes.

FOR SIZES 4 & 6 ONLY
Row 11: Ch 1, in first hdc work [sc, ch 1] twice; sc in next ch-1 sp, ch 1, [sc in next hdc, ch 1] 4 times; sc in 2nd ch of turning ch-2, turn. *(8 sc)*

Row 12: Ch 3, [hdc in next sc, ch 1] 5 times; sk next sc, hdc in last sc, turn. *(7 hdc)*

FOR SIZE 4 ONLY
Continue with For All Sizes.

FOR SIZE 6 ONLY
Row 13: Ch 1, in first hdc work [sc, ch 1] twice; sc in next ch-1 sp, ch 1, [sc in next hdc, ch 1] 5 times; sc in 2nd ch of turning ch-3, turn. *(9 sc)*

Row 14: Ch 3, [hdc in next sc, ch 1] 6 times; sk next sc, hdc in last sc, turn. *(8 hdc)*

Continue with For All Sizes.

FOR ALL SIZES
Row 11 [13, 15]: Ch 1, sl st in next ch-1 sp, ch 1, sc in same sp and in next hdc; [ch 1, sc in next hdc] 3 [4, 5] times; ch 1, sc in 2nd ch of turning ch-3, turn. *(6 [7, 8] sc)*

Row 12 [14, 16]: Ch 3, hdc in next sc, [ch 1, hdc in next sc] 3 [4, 5] times, turn, leaving last sc unworked. *(5 [6, 7] hdc)*

Row 13 [15, 17]: Ch 1, sl st in next ch-1 sp, ch 1, sc in same sp and in next hdc; [ch 1, sc in next hdc] 2 [3, 4] times; ch 1, sc in 2nd ch of turning ch-3, turn. *(5 [6, 7] sc)*

Row 14 [16, 18]: Ch 3, hdc in next sc, [ch 1, hdc in next sc] 2 [3, 4] times, turn, leaving last sc unworked. *(4 [5, 6] hdc)*

Row 15 [17, 19]: Ch 1, sc in first hdc, [ch 1, sc in next hdc] 2 [3, 4]

times; ch 1, sc in 2nd ch of turning ch-3. *(4 [5, 6] sc)*

Fasten off, leaving a 12-inch end for sewing.

BACK
Row 1 (RS): Ch 38 [42, 46]; sc in 2nd ch from hook; *ch 1, sk next ch, sc in next ch; rep from * across, turn. *(19 [21, 23] sc)*

Row 2: Ch 3 *(counts as a hdc and a ch-1 sp on this and following rows)*, hdc in next sc; *ch 1, hdc in next sc; rep from * across, turn. *(19 [21, 23] hdc)*

Row 3: Ch 1, sc in first hdc; *ch 1, sc in next hdc; rep from * to turning ch-3; ch 1, sc in 2nd ch of turning ch-3, turn.

Rows 4–15 [4–17, 4–19]: [Work rows 2 and 3] 6 [7, 8] times. Fasten off and weave in ends.

ASSEMBLY
Hold 1 Front and Back with RS tog and Front on top; carefully matching hdc on last row of Front to first 6 [7, 8] hdc from right-hand edge of Back, sew Front to Back forming shoulder seam. Sew 2nd Front to Back, matching sts on Front to last 6 [7, 8] sts from left-hand edge of Back. Beg at lower edge, sew rows 1–5 of sides for side seams.

EDGING
Rnd 1 (RS): Hold piece with RS of Back facing you; make slip knot on hook and join with sc in first unworked st on Back from right shoulder seam; loosely sc in each st across Back; working in ends of rows of left Front, work sc in each sc row and 2 sc in each hdc

row; working in unused lps of beg chs at lower edge, sc in each lp; working in end of rows of right Front, work sc in each sc row and 2 sc in each hdc row; join with sl st in joining sc. *(93 [103, 113] sc)*

Rnd 2: Ch 1, sc in same sc as joining and in each rem sc; join with sl st in first sc.

Rnds 3–5: Rep rnd 2.

Rnd 6: Ch 1, in same sc as joining work (sc, ch 3, sc); insert hook in next 2 sts, yo and draw through all 3 lps on hook; *in next st work (sc, ch 3, sc), sl st in next st; rep from * around; join with sl st in first sc.

Fasten off and weave in ends.

SLEEVES
Rnd 1 (RS): Make slip knot on hook and join with sc in 1 underarm seam; ch 1, working in ends of rows of armhole opening, sc in next row; *ch 1, sk next row, sc in next row; rep from * to shoulder seam; ch 1, sc in seam;

**ch 1, sk next row, sc in next row, rep from ** to joining sc; join with sl st in joining sc, turn.

Rnd 2: Ch 3; *dc in next st, ch 1; rep from * around; join with sl st in 2nd ch of beg ch-3, turn.

Rnd 3: Ch 1, sc in same ch as joining; ch 1; *sc in next st, ch 1; rep from * around; join with sl st in first sc, turn.

Rnd 4–15 [4–21, 4–25]: [Work rnds 2 and 3] 6 [9, 11] times.

Rnd 16 [22, 26]: Rep rnd 2.

Rnd 17 (23, 27): Sl st in next ch-1 sp, ch 1, in same ch-1 sp work (sc, ch 3, sc); sl st around **post** *(see Stitch Guide)* of next hdc; *in next ch-1 sp work (sc, ch 3, sc); sl st around post of next hdc; rep from * around; join with sl st in first sc. Fasten off and weave in ends.

Color-Play Sweater & Beanie

Design by Tammy Hildebrand

SKILL LEVEL

EASY

FINISHED SIZES
Instructions given fit child's size 2; changes for 4 and 6 are in [ ].

FINISHED GARMENT MEASUREMENTS
Chest: 23 [25, 27] inches

Hat: 16 [16½, 17] inches in circumference

MATERIALS
- Caron Simply Soft Brites medium (worsted) weight yarn (6 oz/330 yds/170g per skein):
  - 1 [1, 1] skein #9604 watermelon *(A)*
  - 1 [1, 1] skein #9605 mango *(B)*
  - 1 [1, 1] skein #9607 limelight *(C)*
  - 1 [1, 1] skein #9606 lemonade *(D)*
  - 1 [1, 1] skein #9608 blue mint *(E)*
- Caron Simply Soft medium (worsted) weight yarn (6 oz/330 yds/170g per skein):
  - 1 [1, 1] skein #9747 iris *(F)*
  - 1 [1, 1] skein #9748 rubine red *(G)*
- Size I/9/5.5mm crochet hook or size needed to obtain gauge
- Tapestry needle

GAUGE
In pattern: 13 sts = 4 inches

Take time to check gauge.

SPECIAL STITCH
Front post double crochet (fpdc): Yo, insert hook from front to back to front around post *(see Stitch Guide)* of st indicated, draw lp

through, [yo, draw through 2 lps on hook] twice; yo and draw through all 3 lps on hook.

Instructions

SWEATER
BODY
Rnd 1 (RS): Starting at lower edge with A, ch 74 [80, 86]; join with sl st to form ring; ch 3 *(counts as a dc)*, dc in each rem ch; join with sl st in 3rd ch of beg ch-3. *(74 [80, 86] dc)*

Fasten off.

Rnd 2: With B make slip knot on hook and join with sc in same ch as joining of rnd 1; **fpdc** *(see Special Stitch)* around next dc; *sc in next dc, fpdc around next dc; rep from * around; join with sl st in joining sc. *(74 [80, 86] sts)*

Fasten off.

Rnd 3: With C make slip knot on hook and join with sc in same sc as joining of previous rnd; fpdc around next fpdc; *sc in next sc, fpdc around next fpdc; rep from * around; join with sl st in joining sc. Fasten off.

Rnd 4: With F, rep rnd 3.

Rnd 5: With D, rep rnd 3.

Rnd 6: With G, rep rnd 3.

Rnd 7: With E, rep rnd 3.

Rnd 8: With A, rep rnd 3.

FOR SIZE 2 ONLY
Rnds 9–14: Rep rnds 3–8.

Rnd 15: With B, rep rnd 3.

Rnds 16–18: Rep rnds 3–5.

Continue with Front.

FOR SIZE 4 ONLY
Rnds 9–20: [Work rnds 3–8] twice.

Rnd 21: With B, rep rnd 3.

Rnds 22–24: Rep rnds 3–5.

Continue with Front.

FOR SIZE 6 ONLY
Rnds 9–26: [Work rnds 3–8] 3 times.

Rnd 27: With B, rep rnd 3.

Rnds 28–30: Rep rnds 3–5.

Continue with Front.

FRONT
Row 1: Hold piece with RS facing you; with G make slip knot on hook and join with sc in same ch as joining of last rnd; [fpdc around next fpdc, sc in next sc] 17 [18, 19] times. *(35 [37, 39] sts)*

Fasten off.

Row 2: Hold piece with RS facing you; with E make slip knot on hook and join with sc in joining sc of last row; [fpdc in around next fpdc, sc in next sc] 17 [18, 19] times. Fasten off.

FOR SIZE 2 ONLY
Row 3: With A, rep row 2.

Row 4: With B, rep row 2.

Row 5: With C, rep row 2.

Row 6: With F, rep row 2.

Row 7: With D, rep row 2.

Row 8: With G, rep row 2.

Row 9: With E, rep row 2.

Rows 10–12: Rep rows 3–5.

Continue with Back.

FOR SIZE 4 ONLY
Row 3: With A, rep row 2.

Row 4: With B, rep row 2.

Row 5: With C, rep row 2.

Row 6: With F, rep row 2.

Row 7: With D, rep row 2.

Row 8: With G, rep row 2.

Row 9: With E, rep row 2.

Rows 10–16: Rep rows 3–9.

Continue with Back.

FOR SIZE 6 ONLY
Row 3: With A, rep row 2.

Row 4: With B, rep row 2.

Row 5: With C, rep row 2.

Row 6: With F, rep row 2.

Row 7: With D, rep row 2.

Row 8: With G, rep row 2.

Row 9: With E, rep row 2.

Rows 10–16: Rep rows 3–9.

Rows 17–20: Rep rows 3–6.

Continue with Back.

BACK
Row 1: Hold piece with RS facing you; sk next 2 [4, 4] sts on Body from front; join G with sl st in next fpdc; ch 3 *(counts as a dc)*, [sc in next sc, fpdc around next fpdc] 17 [17, 19] times. *(35 [35, 39] sts)*

Fasten off, leaving rem sts unworked.

Row 2: Hold piece with RS facing you; with E make slip knot on hook and join with sc in joining sc of last row; [fpdc in around next fpdc, sc in next sc] 17 [17, 19] times. Fasten off.

Rows 3–12: Rep rows 3–12 of Front.

Continue with Assembly.

FOR SIZE 4 ONLY
Rows 3–16: Rep rows 3–16 of Front.

Continue with Assembly.

FOR SIZE 6 ONLY
Rows 3–20: Rep rows 3–20 of Front.

Continue with Assembly.

ASSEMBLY
Hold Front and Back with WS tog; for shoulder seams, beg from armhole edges, sew 10 [10, 11] sts for each shoulder seam, leaving 30 [30, 34] sts unsewn for neck opening.

COLLAR
Rnd 1 (RS): Hold Sweater with RS facing you; with next color in sequence make slip knot on hook and join with sc in any st of neck opening; sc in each rem sc of neck opening; join with sl st in joining sc. [30 (30, 34) sc]

Rnd 2: Ch 1, sc in same sc as joining and in each rem sc; join with sl st in first sc.

Rnd 3: Rep rnd 2.

Fasten off and weave in all ends.

SLEEVES
Rnd 1: Join A with sl st in first unworked st of 1 underarm section; ch 3 *(counts as a dc)*, dc in next 1 [3, 3] st(s), working in ends of rows around armhole, dc in each row; join with sl st in 3rd ch of beg ch-3. *(26 [36, 40] dc)*

Fasten off.

Rnd 2: With B make slip knot

on hook and join with sc in same ch as joining of rnd 1; fpdc around next dc; *sc in next dc, fpdc around next dc; rep from * around; join with sl st in joining sc. *(26 [36, 40] sts)*

Fasten off.

Rnds 3–24 [3–29, 3–32]: Working in same color sequence as Body, rep rnd 2.

EDGING
Rnd 1: With next color in sequence make slip knot on hook and join with sc in any st;

sc in next st, ***sc dec** (see Stitch Guide)* in next 2 sts; rep from * around; join with sl st in joining sc. *(14 [19, 21] sc)*

Rnd 2: Ch 1, sc in same sc and in each rem sc; join with sl st in first sc.

Rnd 3: Ch 1, sl st in each rem sc; join with sl st in joining sl st.

Fasten off and weave in all ends.

Rep on rem armhole opening.

continued on page 173

Floral Mary Janes

Design by Nazanin S. Fard

FINISHED SIZE
Fits 3–4 year old

FINISHED GARMENT MEASUREMENT
Approximately 6½ inches long

MATERIALS
- Bernat Berella "4" medium (worsted) weight yarn (3½ oz/195 yds/100g per ball):
  - 1 ball #08814 pale antique rose
- Size H/8/5mm crochet hook or size needed to obtain gauge
- Tapestry needle
- Stitch markers
- 2 rose ⅜-inch buttons
- Sewing needle and matching thread

GAUGE
15 dc = 4 inches

Take time to check gauge.

Instructions

RIGHT SHOE
Rnd 1 (RS): Ch 18; dc in 4th ch from hook (*beg 3 sk chs count as a dc*), [dc in next ch, 2 dc in next ch] 7 times; dc in next ch, 5 dc in last ch—*front of shoe made*; working in unused lps on opposite side of beg ch, [dc in next lp, 2 dc in next lp] 7 times; join with sl st in 3rd ch of beg ch-18. *(48 dc)*

Note: *Remainder of shoe is worked in continuous rnds. Do not join unless specified, mark beg of rnds.*

Rnd 2: Dc in next dc, 2 dc in next dc; dc in next 22 dc, 3 dc in next dc; dc in next 22 dc, 2 dc in last dc. *(52 dc)*

Rnd 3: Dc in each dc.

Rnd 4: Dc in next 10 dc, [**dc dec** (*see Stitch Guide*) in next 2 dc] 17 times; dc in last 9 dc.

Rnd 5: Dc in next 14 dc, [dc dec] 4 times; dc in last 14 dc.

Rnd 6: Sc in next 11 dc, ch 19, sc in 5th ch from hook—*button lp made*; sc in each rem ch and in each rem dc; join with sl st in first sc.

Fasten off and weave in ends.

LEFT SHOE
Rnds 1–5: Rep rnds 1–5 of Right Shoe.

Rnd 6: Sc in next 21 dc, ch 19, sc in 5th ch from hook—*button lp made*; sc in each rem ch and in each rem dc; join with sl st in first sc.

Fasten off and weave in all ends.

FLOWER

MAKE 2.
Rnd 1 (RS): Make slip knot, leaving a 6-inch end; [ch 4, sl st in ring] 5 times; pull end to tighten ring.

Rnd 2: In each ch-4 sp work (sc, hdc, dc, hdc, sc); join with sl st in first sc.

Fasten off and weave in ends.

FINISHING
Step 1: With sewing needle and matching thread, sew 1 button opposite button lp on each Shoe.

Step 2: Referring to photo for placement, sew 1 Flower to front of each Shoe.

Cute-as-a-Bug Footies

Design by Nazanin S. Fard

SKILL LEVEL ■■□□
EASY

FINISHED SIZE
Fits 2–3 year old

FINISHED GARMENT MEASUREMENT
Approximately 6 inches long

MATERIALS
- Bernat Berella "4" medium (worsted) weight yarn (3½ oz/195 yds/100g per ball):
  1 ball #08940 natural
- Size H/8/5mm crochet hook or size needed to obtain gauge
- Tapestry needle
- 4 ladybug ¾-inch buttons from Favorite Findings, Blumenthal Lansing Co.
- Sewing needle and matching thread

GAUGE
15 dc = 4 inches

Take time to check gauge.

Instructions

FOOTIE
MAKE 2.
Note: Footie is worked in continuous rnds. Do not join unless specified; mark beg of rnds.

Rnd 1 (RS): Ch 40; join with sl st to form ring; ch 1, sc in same ch as joining and in each rem ch. *(39 sc)*

Rnd 2: Dc in next 15 sc, 2 dc in next sc; dc in next 2 sc, 2 dc in next sc; dc in next sc, 2 dc in next sc; dc in next 2 sc, 2 dc in next sc; dc in next 15 sc. *(43 dc)*

Rnd 3: Dc in next 20 dc, 2 dc in next dc; dc in next dc, 2 dc in next dc; dc in next 20 dc. *(45 dc)*

Rnd 4: Dc in each dc.

Rnd 5: Dc in next dc; [**dc dec** *(see Stitch Guide)* in next 2 dc] 22 times; join with sl st in first dc.

Fasten off, leaving a 6-inch end for sewing. Weave in other end.

FINISHING
Step 1: With tapestry needle and long ends, sew sole seams.

Step 2: Referring to photo for placement and with sewing needle and matching thread, sew 2 buttons to top of each Footie.

I'm So Beautiful Jacket

Design by Melanie Mays

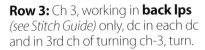

SKILL LEVEL

EASY

FINISHED SIZES

Instructions given fit child's size 2T; changes for 3T and 4T are in [ ].

FINISHED GARMENT MEASUREMENTS

Chest: 24 [25, 26] inches

MATERIALS

- Caron Simply Soft Brites medium (worsted) weight yarn (6 oz/330 yds/170g per skein): 2 [2, 3] skeins #9604 watermelon
- Size G/6/4.25mm crochet hook or size needed to obtain gauge
- Tapestry needle

GAUGE

16 dc = 4 inches

Take time to check gauge.

Instructions

Note: *Back, Fronts and Sleeves are worked lengthwise.*

BACK

Row 1 (RS): Ch 38 [42, 46]; dc in 4th ch from hook *(beg 3 sk chs count as a dc)* and in each rem ch, turn. *(36 [40, 44] dc)*

Row 2: Ch 3 *(counts as a dc on this and following rows)*, working in **front lps** *(see Stitch Guide)* only, dc in each dc and in 3rd ch of beg 3 sk chs, turn.

Row 3: Ch 3, working in **back lps** *(see Stitch Guide)* only, dc in each dc and in 3rd ch of turning ch-3, turn.

Row 4: Ch 3, working in front lps only, dc in each dc and in 3rd ch of turning ch-3, turn.

Row 5: Ch 3, working in back lps only, dc in each dc and in 3rd ch of turning ch-3, turn.

Rows 6–21 [6–23, 6–25]: [Work rows 4 and 5] 8 [9, 10] times.

Fasten off and weave in ends.

FRONT
MAKE 2.

Row 1 (RS): Ch 38 [42, 46]; dc in 4th ch from hook *(beg 3 sk chs count as a dc)* and in each rem ch, turn. *(36 [40, 44] dc)*

Do not turn.

Row 2: Ch 7, working left to right in front lps only of row 1, sk first dc, sl st in next dc; *ch 7, sl st in next dc; rep from * to beg 3 sk chs; ch 7, sl st in 3rd ch of beg 3 sk chs. Do not turn.

Row 3: Ch 3 *(counts as a dc on this and following rows)*, sk beg ch-3 of row 1, working in back lps only, dc in each dc. Do not turn.

Row 4: Ch 7, working left to right in front lps only of row 3, sk first

dc, sl st in next dc; *ch 7, sl st in next dc; rep from * to beg ch-3; ch 7, sl st in 3rd ch of beg ch-3. Do not turn.

Row 5: Ch 3, sk beg ch-3 of row 3, working in back lps only, dc in each dc. Do not turn.

Row 6: Ch 7, working left to right in front lps only of row 5, sk first dc, sl st in next dc; *ch 7, sl st in next dc; rep from * to beg ch-3; ch 7, sl st in 3rd ch of beg ch-3. Do not turn.

Row 7: Ch 3, sk beg ch-3 of row 5, working in back lps only, dc in each dc, turn.

Row 8: Ch 3, working in front lps only, dc in each rem dc and in 3rd ch of turning ch-3, turn.

Row 9: Ch 3, working in back lps only, dc in each rem dc and in 3rd ch of turning ch-3, turn.

FOR SIZE 2T ONLY
Rows 10–13: [Work rows 8 and 9] twice.

Row 14: Rep row 8.

Fasten off and weave in ends.

Continue with Sleeve.

FOR SIZE 3T ONLY
Rows 10–15: [Work rows 8 and 9] 3 times.

Fasten off and weave in ends.

Continue with Sleeve.

FOR SIZE 4T ONLY
Rows 10–15: [Work rows 8 and 9] 3 times.

Row 16: Rep row 8.

Fasten off and weave in ends.

Continue with Sleeve.

SLEEVE
Make 2.
Row 1 (RS): Ch 34 [38, 42]; dc in 4th ch from hook *(beg 3 sk chs count as a dc)* and in each rem ch. *(32 [36, 40] dc)* Do not turn.

Row 2: Ch 7, working left to right in front lps only of row 1, sk first dc, sl st in next dc; *ch 7, sl st in next dc; rep from * to beg 3 sk chs; ch 7, sl st in 3rd ch of beg 3 sk chs. Do not turn.

Row 3: Ch 3 *(counts as a dc on this and following rows)*, sk first dc of row 1, working in back lps only, dc in each dc. Do not turn.

Row 4: Ch 7, working left to right in front lps only of row 3, sk first dc, sl st in next dc; *ch 7, sl st in next dc; rep from * to beg ch-3; ch 7, sl st in 3rd ch of beg ch-3. Do not turn.

Row 5: Ch 3, sk beg ch-3 of row 3, working in back lps only, dc in each dc. Do not turn.

Row 6: Ch 7, working left to right in front lps only of row 5, sk first dc, sl st in next dc; *ch 7, sl st in next dc; rep from * to beg ch-3; ch 7, sl st in 3rd ch of beg ch-3. Do not turn.

Row 7: Ch 3, sk beg ch-3 of row 5, working in back lps only, dc in each dc, turn.

Row 8: Ch 3, working in front lps only, dc in each rem dc and in 3rd ch of turning ch-3, turn.

Row 9: Ch 3, working in back lps only, dc in each rem dc and in 3rd ch of turning ch-3, turn.

FOR SIZE 2T ONLY
Rows 10–15: [Work rows 8 and 9] 3 times.

Row 16: Rep row 8.

Fasten off and weave in ends.

Continue with Assembly.

FOR SIZE 3T ONLY
Rows 10–17: [Work rows 8 and 9] 4 times.

Fasten off and weave in ends.

Continue with Assembly.

FOR SIZE 4T ONLY
Rows 10–17: [Work rows 8 and 9] 4 times.

Row 18: Rep row 8.

Fasten off and weave in ends.

Continue with Assembly.

ASSEMBLY
Turn pieces so sts are horizontal instead of vertical. To join Fronts to Back, hold WS of 1 Front with ruffles to left facing WS of Back. Working through both pieces at same time, join yarn with sl st in end of first row at armhole edge; working in ends of rows, sl st in each row to first ruffle row. Fasten off. Hold rem Front with ruffles to right facing WS of Back. Sew shoulder seam in same manner. Matching centers of Sleeves to shoulder seams, and beg and ending at underarm, sl st Sleeves to armhole openings. Sl st Sleeve seams and side seams.

BOTTOM EDGING
Row 1 (RS): Ch 87 [95, 103]; dc in 4th ch from hook *(beg 3 sk chs count as a dc)* and in each rem ch. *(85 [93, 101] dc)* Do not turn.

Row 2: Ch 7, working left to right in front lps only of row 1, sk first dc, sl st in next dc; *ch 7, sl st in next dc; rep from * to beg 3 sk chs; ch 7, sl st in 3rd ch of beg 3 sk chs. Do not turn.

Row 3: Ch 3 *(counts as a dc on this and following rows)*, sk first dc of row 1, working in back lps only, dc in each dc. Do not turn.

Row 4: Ch 7, working left to right in front lps only of row 3, sk first dc, sl st in next dc; *ch 7, sl st in next dc; rep from * to beg ch-3; ch 7, sl st in 3rd ch of beg ch-3. Do not turn.

Row 5: Ch 3, sk beg ch-3 of row 3, working in back lps only, dc in each dc. Do not turn.

Row 6: Ch 7, working left to right in front lps only of row 5, sk first dc, sl st in next dc; *ch 7, sl st in next dc; rep from * to beg ch-3; ch 7, sl st in 3rd ch of beg ch-3. Do not turn.

Place Jacket with RS of Back facing you; spread sides of Jacket out flat. Place row 6 of Edging along bottom edge, easing to fit. Working in ends of rows of Jacket and sts on Edging, sl st evenly across.

Fasten off and weave in ends.

COLLAR
Row 1: Hold Jacket with RS facing you; join yarn with sl st in end of first row at neck edge of Right Front; sc in same sp; working around neck edge to last row of Left Front, work 33 sc evenly spaced. Do not turn.

Row 2: Ch 7, working left to right in front lps only of row 1, sk first sc, sl st in next sc; *ch 7, sl st in next sc; rep from * across. Do not turn.

Row 3: Ch 1, working in back lps only of sc of row 1, sc in each sc. Do not turn.

Row 4: Ch 7, working left to right in front lps only of row 3, sk first sc, sl st in next sc; *ch 7, sl st in next sc; rep from * across. Do not turn.

continued on page 173

Pink Marshmallow Hoodie

Design by Ann E. Smith

SKILL LEVEL
EASY

FINISHED SIZES
Instructions given fit child's size 2T; changes for 3T and 4T are in [ ].

FINISHED GARMENT MEASUREMENTS
Chest: 26 [28, 30] inches

MATERIALS
- Moda Dea Dream medium (worsted) weight yarn (1¾ oz/93 yds/50g per ball):
  6 [7, 8] balls #3701 waterlily
- Size G/6/4mm crochet hook or size needed to obtain gauge
- Tapestry needle
- 3 matching ¾-inch buttons
- 2½ x 3½-inch piece of cardboard

GAUGE
15 sts = 4 inches

Take time to check gauge

SPECIAL STITCH
Loop stitch (lp st): In front lp of st indicated work (sl st, ch 3, sl st).

Instructions

BACK
Row 1 (RS): Ch 50 [54, 58]; sc in 2nd ch from hook and in each rem ch, turn. *(49 [53, 57] sc)*

Row 2: Ch 1, sc in each sc; turn.

Row 3: Ch 1, sc in first 6 [2, 4] sc; ***lp st** (see Special Stitch) in next sc; sc in next 5 sc; rep from * to last 7

[3, 5] sc; lp st in next sc, sc in last 6 [2, 4] sc, turn.

Row 4: Ch 1, sc in each sc and in each unused lp, turn.

Rows 5–10: Rep row 2.

Row 11: Ch 1, sc in first 3 [5, 1] sc; *lp st in next sc; sc in next 5 sc; rep from * to last 4 [6, 2] sc; lp st in next sc, sc in last 3 [5, 1] sc, turn.

Rows 12–18: Rep rows 4–10.

Rep rows 3–18 until piece measures 4½ [5½, 6½] inches from beg, ending with a WS row.

ARMHOLE SHAPING
Next row: Sl st in first 7 [8, 8] sts, work in pattern as established to last 7 [8, 8] sts, turn, leaving rem sts unworked. *(35 [37, 41] sts)*

Continue in pattern as established until piece measures 9½ [11, 12½] inches from beg.

Fasten off and weave in ends.

RIGHT FRONT
Row 1: Ch 23 [25, 27]; sc in 2nd ch from hook and in each rem ch, turn. *(22 [24, 26] sc)*

Row 2: Ch 1, sc in each sc, turn.

Row 3: Ch 1, sc in first 2 [6, 5] sc; *lp st in next sc; sc in next 5 sc; rep from * to last 2 [6, 3] sc; lp st in next sc; sc in last 1 [5, 2] sc, turn.

Row 4: Ch 1, sc in each sc and in

each unused lp, turn.

Rows 5–10: Rep row 2.

Row 11: Ch 1, sc in first 5 [3, 2] sc; *lp st in next sc; sc in next 5 sc; rep from * to last 5 [3, 6] sc; lp st in next sc; sc in last 4 [2, 5] sc, turn.

Row 12: Ch 1, sc in each sc and in each unused lp, turn.

Rows 13–18: Rep row 2.

Rep rows 3–18 until piece measures 4½ (5½, 6½] inches from beg, ending with a WS row.

ARMHOLE SHAPING
Next row: Ch 1, work in pattern as established to last 7 [8, 8] sts, turn, leaving rem sts unworked. *(15 [16, 18] sts)*

Continue in pattern as established until piece measures 7½ [9, 10½] inches from beg, ending with a WS row.

NECK SHAPING
Row 1: Ch 1, **sc dec** *(see Stitch Guide)* in first 2 sts; work in pattern across, turn. *(14 [15, 17] sts)*

Row 2: Ch 1, work in pattern to last 2 sts; sc dec in last 2 sts, turn. (13 [14, 16] sts)

Row 3: Ch 1, sc dec in first 2 sts; work in pattern across, turn. (12 [13, 15] sts)

Rows 4 & 5: Rep rows 2 and 3. (10 [11, 13] sts at end of row 5)

FOR SIZES 2T & 3T ONLY
Continue with For All Sizes.

FOR SIZE 4T ONLY
Row 6: Rep row 2. *(12 sts)*

Continue with For All Sizes.

FOR ALL SIZES
Continue in pattern as established until piece measures same length as Back.

Fasten off and weave in ends.

LEFT FRONT
Row 1: Ch 23 [25, 27]; sc in 2nd ch from hook and in each rem ch, turn. *(22 [24, 26] sc)*

Row 2: Ch 1, sc in each sc, turn.

Row 3: Ch 1, sc in first 1 [5, 2] sc; *lp st in next sc; sc in next 5 sc; rep from * to last 3 [7, 6] sc; lp st in next sc; sc in last 2 [6, 5] sc, turn.

Row 4: Ch 1, sc in each sc and in each unused lp, turn.

Rows 5–10: Rep row 2.

Row 11: Ch 1, sc in first 4 [2, 5] sc; *lp st in next sc; sc in next 5 sc; rep from * to last 6 [4, 3] sc; lp st in next sc; sc in last 5 [3, 2] sc, turn.

Row 12: Ch 1, sc in each sc and in each unused lp, turn.

Rows 13–18: Rep row 2.

ARMHOLE SHAPING
Next row: Ch 1, sl st in first 7 [8, 8] sts; work in pattern as established across, turn. *(15 [16, 18] sts)*

Continue in pattern as established until piece measures 7½ [9, 10½] inches from beg, ending with a WS row.

NECK SHAPING
Row 1: Ch 1, work in pattern across to last 2 sts; **sc dec** *(see*

Stitch Guide) in last 2 sts, turn. *(14 [15, 17] sts)*

Row 2: Ch 1, sc dec in first 2 sts, work in pattern across, turn. (13 [14, 16] sts)

Row 3: Ch 1, work in pattern to last 2 sts; sc dec in last 2 sts, turn. (12 [13, 15] sts)

Rows 4 & 5: Rep rows 2 and 3. (10 [11, 13] sts at end of row 5)

FOR SIZES 2T & 3T ONLY
Continue with For All Sizes.

FOR SIZE 4T ONLY
Row 6: Rep row 2. *(12 sts)*

Continue with For All Sizes.

FOR ALL SIZES
Continue in pattern as established until piece measures same length as Back.

Fasten off and weave in ends.

SLEEVE
MAKE 2.
Row 1 (RS): Ch 26; sc in 2nd ch from hook and in each rem ch, turn. *(25 sc)*

Row 2: Ch 1, sc in each sc, turn.

Row 3: Ch 1, sc in first 3 sc; *lp st in next sc; sc in next 5 sc; rep from * to last 4 sc; lp st in next sc; sc in last 3 sc, turn.

Row 4: Ch 1, sc in each sc and in each unused lp, turn.

Rows 5–8: Rep row 2.

Row 9: Ch 1, sc in first sc, 2 sc in next sc; sc in each sc to last 2 sc; 2 sc in next sc; sc in last sc, turn. *(27 sc)*

Row 10: Ch 1, sc in each sc, turn.

Row 11: Ch 1, sc in first sc; *lp st in next sc; sc in next 5 sc; rep from * to last 2 sc; lp st in next sc; sc in last sc, turn.

Row 12: Ch 1, sc in each sc and in each unused lp, turn.

Row 13: Ch 1, sc in first sc, 2 sc in next sc; sc in each sc to last 2 sc; 2 sc in next sc; sc in last sc, turn. *(29 sc)*

Continue to work in pattern as established, inc 1 st at each end of every 4th row 4 [6, 8] times. *(37 [41, 45] sts at end of last row)*

Continue to work in pattern as established on 37 [41, 45] sts until piece measures 10 [11½, 12½] inches from beg.

Fasten off and weave in ends.

HOOD
Row 1 (RS): Ch 76; sc in 2nd ch from hook and in each rem ch, turn. *(75 sc)*

Row 2: Ch 1, sc in each sc, turn.

FOR SIZES 2T & 3T ONLY
Continue with For All Sizes.

FOR SIZE 4T ONLY
Rows 3 & 4: Rep row 2.

Continue with For All Sizes.

FOR ALL SIZES
Row 3 [3, 5]: Ch 1, sc in first sc; *lp st in next sc; sc in 5 sc; rep from * to last 2 sc; lp st in next sc; sc in last sc, turn.

Row 4 [4, 6]: Ch 1, sc in each sc and in each unused lp, turn.

Rows 5–10 [5–10, 7–12]: Rep row 2.

Row 11 [11, 13]: Ch 1, sc in first 4 sc; *lp st in next sc; sc in 5 sc; rep from * to last 5 sc; lp st in next sc; sc in last 4 sc, turn.

Rows 12–18 [12–18, 14–20]: Rep rows 4–10 [4–10, 6–12].

Rows 19–27 [19–27, 21–29]: Rep rows 3–11 [3–11, 5–13].

Fasten off and weave in ends.

ASSEMBLY
Hold Hood with WS facing you; fold beg ch in half to form back seam; beg at fold, sl st across side.

FINISHING
Sew shoulder seams. Sew in Sleeves, sewing sk sts of armholes to Sleeve sides to form square armholes. Sew Sleeve seams and side seams.

BORDER
Row 1: Hold piece with RS facing you; join yarn with sl st in first Neck Shaping row on Left Front; ch 1, sc in same row and in each row across Left Front edge to last row; 3 sc in last row—*corner made;* working across lower edge in unused lp of beg chs, sc in each lp; working in ends of rows of Right Front, 3 sc in first row—*corner made;* sc in each rem row to first Neck Shaping row; turn.

Row 2: Ch 3 *(counts as a dc)*, dc in each sc and 3 dc in 2nd dc of each corner; turn.

Row 3: Ch 1, sc in each dc and in 3rd ch of turning ch-3 and 3 sc in 2nd dc of each corner.

Row 4: Ch 1, working left to right, work **reverse sc** *(see Stitch Guide)* in each sc.

Fasten off and weave in ends.

ASSEMBLY
Hold piece and Hood with RS tog, matching back seam of Hood to center of back neck and Hood sides ending at 2nd row of Right Front Border and Left Front Border. Sew pieces tog across neck edge.

FINISHING
Step 1: Sew first button to Left Front ½ inch from top of neckband. Sew rem buttons 2¼ inches apart. For buttonholes, push buttons between corresponding 2 dc on Right Front.

Step 2: For pompom, wrap yarn around cardboard 50 times. Remove lps from cardboard and tie separate strand tightly around center of lps. Cut lps and trim to form pompom. Sew to point of Hood.

Get-Up 'n Go Shirt

Design by Joyce Nordstrom

SKILL LEVEL
INTERMEDIATE

FINISHED SIZES
Instructions given fit child's size 2T; changes for 3T and 4T are in [ ].

FINISHED GARMENT MEASUREMENTS
Chest: 20 [21, 22] inches

MATERIALS
Red Heart Soft Baby fine (sport) weight yarn (7 oz/575 yds/198g per skein):
    1 skein #7624 lime *(A)*
    2 yds #7001 white *(B)*
• Size G/6/4mm crochet hook or size needed to obtain gauge
• Tapestry needle

GAUGE
In pattern: 16 hdc = 4 inches

Take time to check gauge.

Instructions

FRONT
LEFT SLEEVE
Foundation row (RS): With A, ch 17 [18, 19]; hdc in 3rd ch from hook and in each rem ch, turn. *(15 [16, 17] hdc)*

Note: *Mark right edge as shoulder. Turning ch-2 does not count as a st. Work in **back lps** (see Stitch Guide) only.*

Row 1: Ch 2, hdc in each hdc, turn.

Row 2: Ch 2, hdc in each hdc to last hdc; 2 hdc in last hdc, turn. *(16 [17, 18] hdc)*

Row 3: Ch 2, 2 hdc in first hdc; hdc in each rem hdc, turn. *(17 [18, 19] hdc)*

Row 4: Ch 2, hdc in each hdc to last hdc; 2 hdc last hdc, turn. *(18 [19, 20] hdc)*

Row 5: Ch 2, 2 hdc in first hdc, hdc in each rem hdc, turn. *(19 [20, 21] hdc)*

Row 6: Ch 2, hdc in each hdc to last hdc; 2 hdc in last hdc, turn. *(20 [21, 22] hdc)*

LEFT SHOULDER SHAPING
Row 7: Ch 27 [29, 31], sc in 2nd ch from hook and in next 2 chs, hdc in each rem ch, and in each hdc, turn. *(46 [49, 52] sts)*

Row 8: Ch 2, hdc in each hdc to last 3 sc; sc in each sc, turn.

Row 9: Ch 1, sc in first 3 sc, hdc in each hdc, turn.

Rep rows 8 and 9 until piece measures 3 [3½, 4] inches from row 7, ending with RS row.

NECK SHAPING
Next row: Ch 1, sc in first 3 sc, hdc in next 35 [38, 40] hdc, turn, leaving rem sts unworked.

Rep rows 8 and 9 until piece measures 7½ [8, 8½] inches from row 7.

RIGHT SHOULDER SHAPING
Row 1 (RS): Ch 10 [10, 11]; hdc in 3rd ch from hook, in next 7 [7, 10] chs, and in each hdc; sc in last 3 sc, turn. *(46 [49, 52] sts)*

Row 2: Ch 1, sc in first 3 sc, hdc in each hdc, turn.

Row 3: Ch 2, hdc in each hdc to last 3 sc; sc in each sc, turn.

Rep rows 2 and 3 until piece measures 10½ [11, 11½] inches from row 7, ending with a WS row.

RIGHT SLEEVE
Row 1: Ch 2, hdc in next 19 [20, 21] hdc, **hdc dec** *(see Stitch Guide)* in next 2 sts, turn, leaving rem sts unworked. *(20 [21, 22] hdc)*

Row 2: Ch 2, hdc dec in first 2 hdc; hdc in each rem hdc, turn. *(19 [20, 21] hdc)*

Row 3: Ch 2, hdc in each hdc to last 2 hdc; hdc dec in last 2 hdc, turn. *(18 [19, 20] hdc)*

Rows 4 & 5: Rep rows 2 and 3. *(16 [17, 18] hdc at end of row 5)*

Row 6: Rep row 2. *(15 [16, 17] hdc)*

Row 7: Ch 2, hdc in each hdc, turn.

Row 8: Ch 2, hdc in each hdc.

Fasten off and weave in ends.

BACK
RIGHT SLEEVE
Foundation row (RS): With A, ch 17 [18, 19]; hdc in 3rd ch from hook and in each rem ch, turn. *(15 [16, 17] hdc)*

Note: *Mark right edge as shoulder. Turning ch-2 does not count as a st. Work in back lps only.*

Row 1: Ch 2, hdc in each hdc, turn.

Row 2: Ch 2, hdc in each hdc to last hdc; 2 hdc in last hdc, turn. *(16 [17, 18] hdc)*

Row 3: Ch 2, 2 hdc in first hdc; hdc in each rem hdc, turn. *(17 [18, 19] hdc)*

Row 4: Ch 2, hdc in each hdc to last hdc; 2 hdc last hdc, turn. *(18 [19, 20] hdc)*

Row 5: Ch 2, 2 hdc in first hdc, hdc in each rem hdc, turn. *(19 [20, 21] hdc)*

Row 6: Ch 2, hdc in each hdc to last hdc; 2 hdc in last hdc, turn. *(20 [21, 22] hdc)*

BODY
Row 7: Ch 27 [29, 31], sc in 2nd ch from hook and in next 2 chs, hdc in each rem ch, and in each hdc, turn. *(46 [49, 52] sts)*

Row 8: Ch 2, hdc in each hdc to last 3 sc; sc in each sc, turn.

Row 9: Ch 1, sc in first 3 sc, hdc in each hdc, turn.

Rep rows 8 and 9 until piece measures 10½ [11, 11½] inches from row 7, ending with RS row.

LEFT SLEEVE
Row 1: Ch 2, hdc in next 19 [20, 21] hdc, hdc dec in next 2 sts, turn, leaving rem sts unworked. *(20 [21, 22] hdc)*

Row 2: Ch 2, hdc dec in first 2 hdc; hdc in each rem hdc, turn. *(19 [20, 21] hdc)*

Row 3: Ch 2, hdc in each hdc to last 2 hdc; hdc dec in last 2 hdc, turn. *(18 [19, 20] hdc)*

Rows 4 & 5: Rep rows 2 and 3. *(16 [17, 18] hdc at end of row 5)*

Row 6: Rep row 2. *(15 [16, 17] hdc)*

Row 7: Ch 2, hdc in each hdc, turn.

Row 8: Ch 2, hdc in each hdc.

Fasten off and weave in ends.

ASSEMBLY
Sew shoulder and underarm seams.

EDGINGS
NECK EDGING
Rnd 1 (RS): Hold Shirt with RS facing you; join A with sl st in 1 shoulder seam; ch 1, sc in same sp; sc evenly around neck edge; join with sl st in first sc.

Rnd 2: Ch 2, hdc in same sc as joining, working in back lps only, hdc in each rem hdc; join with sl st in 2nd ch of beg ch-2.

Rnd 3: Ch 1, sc in same ch as joining; working in back lps only, sc in each rem hdc; join with sl st in first sc. Fasten off.

Rnd 4: Hold Shirt with WS facing you; join B in **front lp** *(see Stitch Guide)* of any sc; working in front lps only; *sc in next sc, sl st in next sc; rep from * around; join in first sc.

Fasten off and weave in all ends.

SLEEVE EDGING
Rnd 1 (RS): Hold 1 Sleeve with RS facing you; join A with sl st in 1 seam; ch 1, sc in same sp; sc evenly around Sleeve edge; join with sl st in first sc.

Rnd 2: Ch 2, hdc in same sc as joining, working in back lps only, hdc in each rem sc; join with sl st in 2nd ch of beg ch-2.

Rnd 3: Ch 1, sc in same ch as joining; working in back lps only, sc in each rem hdc; join with sl st in first sc. Fasten off.

Rnd 4: Hold Sleeve with WS facing you; join B in front lp of any sc; working in front lps only; *sc in next sc, sl st in next sc; rep from *

around; join in first sc.

Fasten off and weave in all ends.

Rep on rem Sleeve.

Rnd 3: Ch 1, working in back lps only, sc in each hdc and 3 sc in 2nd hdc of each corner; join with sl st in first sc. Fasten off.

Rnd 4: Hold piece with WS facing you; join B with sl st in **front lp** *(see Stitch Guide)* of any sc; ch 1, sc in same lp; working in front lps only, *sc in next sc, sl st in next sc; rep from * around; join with sl st in first sc.

Fasten off and weave in all ends.

SLEEVE EDGING
Rnd 1: Hold 1 Sleeve with RS facing you; join A with sl st in 1 seam; ch 1, sc in same sp; sc evenly around Sleeve edge; join with sl st in first sc.

Rnd 2: Ch 2, working in back lps only, hdc in each sc; join with sl st in 2nd ch of beg ch-2.

Rnd 3: Ch 1, working in back lps only, sc in each hdc; join with sl st in first sc. Fasten off.

Rnd 4: Hold piece with WS facing you; join B with sl st in front lp of any sc; ch 1, sc in same lp; working in front lps only, *sc in next sc, sl st in next sc; rep from * around; join with sl st in first sc.

Fasten off and weave in all ends.

SMALL FLOWER
MAKE 11.
With B, ch 4; join to form ring; [ch 2, hdc in ring, ch 2, sl st in ring] 5 times.

Fasten off and weave in ends.

TIES
Hold Jacket with RS facing you; join B with sl st at top corner of 1 Front; ch 35; sc in 2nd ch from hook and in each rem ch.

Fasten off and weave in ends.

Rep for 2nd Tie on opposite Front.

FINISHING
Sew Flowers randomly to Jacket.

PURSE
Row 1: With B, ch 26; hdc in 3rd ch from hook and in each rem ch, turn. *(24 hdc)*

Row 2: Ch 2, hdc in each hdc, turn.

Rep row 2 until piece measures 12 inches from beg.

FLAP
Row 1: Ch 2, **hdc dec** *(see Stitch Guide)* in first 2 hdc; hdc in each hdc to last 2 hdc; hdc dec in last 2 hdc, turn. *(22 hdc)*

Row 2: Ch 2, hdc dec in first 2 hdc; hdc in each hdc to last 2 hdc; hdc dec in last 2 hdc, turn. *(20 hdc)*

Rows 3 & 4: Rep row 2.

Fasten off and weave in ends.

STRAP
Row 1: With B, ch 110; sc in 2nd ch from hook and in each rem ch, turn.

Row 2: Ch 1, working in **back lps** *(see Stitch Guide)* only, sc in each sc, turn.

Row 3: Rep row 2.

EDGING
Rnd 1: Ch 1, working in back lps only, 3 sc in first sc; sc in each sc to last sc; 3 sc in last sc; working across next side in ends of rows, sc in each row; working across next side in unused lps of beg ch, 3 sc in first lp; sc in each lp to last lp; 3 sc in last lp; working across next side in ends of rows, sc in each row; join with sl st in first sc. Fasten off.

Rnd 2: Hold piece with WS facing you; join A in **front lp** *(see Stitch Guide)* of any sc; ch 1, sc in same lp; working in front lps only, *sc in next sc, sl st in next sc; rep from * around; join with sl st in first sc.

ASSEMBLY
Hold piece with WS facing you; match 5 inches of Purse front to 5 inches of Strap. With Strap edging on top, sew Purse body to Strap on front, across bottom of Strap, and to 5 inches of Purse back.

EDGING
With A, sc evenly across front edge and around Purse flap. With WS facing you, join B with sl st in front lp of any sc; working in front lps only, *sc in next sc, sl st in next sc; rep from * across.

LARGE FLOWER
MAKE 2.
With A, ch 4; join to form ring; [ch 2, hdc in ring, ch 2, sl st in ring] 6 times.

Fasten off and weave in ends.

SMALL FLOWER
MAKE 3.
With A, ch 4; join to form ring; [ch 2, hdc in ring, ch 2, sl st in ring] 5 times.

Fasten off and weave in ends.

FINISHING
Sew Flowers randomly to Purse and Strap.

Color-Play Sweater & Beanie

BEANIE

Rnd 1 (RS): With A, ch 4; join with sl st to form ring; ch 3 *(counts as a dc)*, 15 dc in ring; join with sl st in 3rd ch of beg ch-3. *(16 dc)* Fasten off.

Rnd 2: With B make slip knot on hook and join with sc in same ch as joining of rnd 1; **fpdc** *(see Special Stitch)* around next dc; [sc in next dc, fpdc around next dc] 7 times; join with sl st in joining sc. *(16 sts)* Fasten off.

Rnd 3: With C make slip knot on hook and join with sc in same sc as joining of rnd 2; dc in same sc; in each rem st work (sc, dc); join with sl st in joining sc. *(32 sts)* Fasten off.

Rnd 4: With F make slip knot on hook and join with sc in same sc as joining of previous rnd; fpdc around next fpdc, [sc in next sc, fpdc around next fpdc] 15 times; join with sl st in joining sc. Fasten off.

Rnd 5: With D, rep rnd 4.

Rnd 6: With G, rep rnd 3. *(64 sts)*

Rnd 7: With E, rep rnd 4.

Rnds 8–15 [8–18, 8–21]: Working in same color sequence as Sweater, rep rnd 4.

FOR SIZE 2 ONLY

Rnd 16: With next color in sequence make slip knot on hook and join with sc in any st; sc in next st, [**sc dec** *(see Stitch Guide)* in next 2 sts] 31 times; join with sl st in joining sc. *(33 sc)*

Do not fasten off.

Continue with For All Sizes.

FOR SIZE 4 ONLY

Rnd 19: With next color in sequence make slip knot on hook and join with sc in any st; sc in next st, [**sc dec** *(see Stitch Guide)* in next 2 sts] 3 times; *sc in next 2 sts, [sc dec in next 2 sts] twice; sc in next 2 sts, [sc dec in next 2 sts] 3 times; rep from * 3 times; join with sl st in joining sc. *(41 sc)*

Do not fasten off.

Continue with For All Sizes.

FOR SIZE 6 ONLY

Rnd 22: With next color in sequence make slip knot on hook and join with sc in any st; sc in next st, **sc dec** *(see Stitch Guide)* in next 2 sts; [sc in next 2 sts, sc dec in next 2 sts] 15 times; join with sl st in joining sc. *(48 sc)*

Do not fasten off.

Continue with For All Sizes.

FOR ALL SIZES

Rnd 17 [20, 23]: Ch 2 *(counts as a hdc)*, hdc in each rem st; join with sl st in 2nd ch of beg ch-2. *(33 [41, 48] hdc)*

Rnd 18 [21, 24]: Ch 1, sc in same ch as joining and in each rem hdc; join with sl st in first sc.

Fasten off and weave in all ends.

I'm So Beautiful Jacket

Row 5: Ch 1, working in back lps only of sc of row 3, sc in each sc. Do not turn.

Row 6: Ch 7, working left to right in front lps only of row 1, sk first dc, sl st in next dc; *ch 7, sl st in next dc; rep from * to beg 3 sk chs; ch 7, sl st in 3rd ch of beg 3 sk chs.

Fasten off and weave in ends.

TIES

Join yarn with sl st in first unused lp of beg ch at neck edge of right Front; ch 30. Fasten off and weave in ends. Work 2nd Tie in same manner at neck edge of left Front. Work 2 additional Ties on Fronts just above ruffles of Bottom Edging. Work 2 additional pairs of Ties between these Ties.

Standard Abbreviations & Symbols

beg .... beg/beginning
bpdc .... back post double crochet
bpsc .... back post single crochet
bptr .... back post treble crochet
CC .... contrasting color
ch .... chain stitch
ch- .... refers to chain or space previously
made (i.e., ch-1 space)
ch sp .... chain space
cl(s) .... cluster(s)
cm .... centimeter(s)
dc .... double crochet
dec .... decrease/decreases/decreasing
dtr .... double treble crochet
fpdc .... front post double crochet
fpsc .... front post treble crochet
fptr .... front post treble crochet
g .... gram(s)
hdc .... half double crochet
inc .... increase/increases/increasing
lp(s) .... loop(s)
MC .... main color
mm .... millimeter(s)
oz .... ounce(s)
pc .... popcorn
rem .... remain/remaining
rep .... repeat(s)
rnd(s) .... round(s)
RS .... right side
sc .... single crochet
sk .... skip(ped)

sl st .... slip stitch
sp(s) .... space(s)
st(s) .... stitch(es)
tog .... together
tr .... treble crochet
trtr .... triple treble crochet
WS .... wrong side
yd(s) .... yard(s)
yo .... yarn over

* An asterisk is used to mark the beginning of a portion of instructions to be worked more than once; thus, "rep from * twice" means after working the instructions once, repeat the instructions following the asterisk twice more (3 times in all).

[ ] Brackets are used to enclose instructions that are to be worked the number of times indicated after the brackets. For example, "[2 dc in next st, sk next st] 5 times" means to follow the instructions within the brackets a total of 5 times.

( ) Parentheses are used to enclose a group of stitches that are worked in one space or stitch. For example, "(2 dc, ch 2, 2 dc) in next st" means to work all the stitches within the parentheses in the next space or stitch. Parentheses are also used to enclose special instructions or stitch counts.

Skill Levels

BEGINNER
Beginner projects for first-time crocheters using basic stitches. Minimal shaping.

EASY
Easy projects using basic stitches, repetitive stitch patterns, simple color changes and simple shaping and finishing.

INTERMEDIATE
Intermediate projects with a variety of stitches, mid-level shaping and finishing.

EXPERIENCED
Experienced projects using advanced techniques and stitches, detailed shaping and refined finishing.

Standard Yarn Weight System

Yarn Weight Symbol & Category Names	1 SUPER FINE	2 FINE	3 LIGHT	4 MEDIUM	5 BULKY	6 SUPER BULKY
Type of Yarns in Category	Sock, Fingering, Baby	Sport, Baby	DK, Light Worsted	Worsted, Afghan, Aran	Chunky, Craft, Rug	Super Chunky, Roving
Crochet Gauge* Ranges in Single Crochet to 4 inch	21–32 sts	16–20 sts	12–17 sts	11–14 sts	8–11 sts	5–9 sts
Recommended Hook in Metric Size Range	2.25–3.5 mm	3.5–4.5 mm	4.5–5.5 mm	5.5–6.5 mm	6.5–9 mm	9 mm and larger
Recommended Hook U.S. Size Range	B-1–E-4	E-4–7	7–I-9	I-9–K-10½	K-10½–M-13	M-13 and larger

* GUIDELINES ONLY: The above reflect the most commonly used gauges and hook sizes for specific yarn categories.

Crochet Stitch Guide

CROCHET HOOKS

Metric	US	Metric	US
.60mm	14	3.00mm	D/3
.75mm	12	3.50mm	E/4
1.00mm	10	4.00mm	F/5
1.50mm	6	4.50mm	G/6
1.75mm	5	5.00mm	H/8
2.00mm	B/1	5.50mm	I/9
2.50mm	C/2	6.00mm	J/10

Chain—ch: Yo, pull through lp on hook.

Slip stitch—sl st: Insert hook in st, yo, pull through both lps on hook.

Front loop—front lp
Back loop—back lp

Front Loop   Back Loop

Single crochet—sc: Insert hook in st, yo, pull through st, yo, pull through both lps on hook.

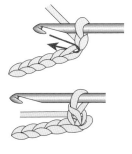

Reverse single crochet—reverse sc: Working from left to right, insert hook in next st, complete as sc.

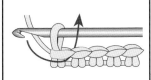

Front post stitch—fp: Back post stitch—bp: When working post st, insert hook from right to left around post st on previous row.

Back   Front

Post of Stitch

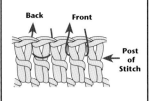

Half double crochet—hdc: Yo, insert hook in st, yo, pull through st, yo, pull through all 3 lps on hook.

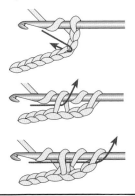

Double crochet—dc: Yo, insert hook in st, yo, pull through st, [yo, pull through 2 lps] twice.

Change colors: Drop first color; with second color, pull through last 2 lps of st.

Treble crochet—tr: Yo twice, insert hook in st, yo, pull through st, [yo, pull through 2 lps] 3 times.

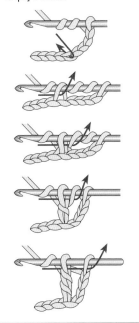

Double treble crochet—dtr: Yo 3 times, insert hook in st, yo, pull through st, [yo, pull through 2 lps] 4 times.

Single crochet decrease (sc dec): (Insert hook, yo, draw up a lp) in each of the sts indicated, yo, draw through all lps on hook.

Example of 2-sc dec

Half double crochet decrease (hdc dec): (Yo, insert hook, yo, draw lp through) in each of the sts indicated, yo, draw through all lps on hook.

Example of 2-hdc dec

Double crochet decrease (dc dec): (Yo, insert hook, yo, draw lp through, yo, draw through 2 lps on hook) in each of the sts indicated, yo, draw through all lps on hook.

Example of 2-dc dec

US		UK
sl st (slip stitch)	=	sc (single crochet)
sc (single crochet)	=	dc (double crochet)
hdc (half double crochet)	=	htr (half treble crochet)
dc (double crochet)	=	tr (treble crochet)
tr (treble crochet)	=	dtr (double treble crochet)
dtr (double treble crochet)	=	ttr (triple treble crochet)
skip	=	miss

Special Thanks

We would like to thank the talented crochet designers whose work is featured in this collection.

Cindy Adams
Baby Burrito Blanket, 66
Mint Smoothie Jumper, 88
Out-With-Baby Bag, 25

Svetlana Avrakh
Blessed Darling Christening Set, 138
Car Toy, 43
Daisy Toy, 46
Ladybug Toy, 45
Sailor Baby, 112
School Bus Toy, 40

Elaine Bartlett
Grandma's Double Delight, 56

Anita Closic
Pleasant Dreams, 7

Nazanin S. Fard
Cute-as-a-Bug Footies, 162
Floral Mary Janes, 160
Heirloom Aran Afghan, 49

Laura Gebhardt
Little Boy Blue, 126
Little Princess, 79

Tamara Gonzales
Pretty Floral Overalls, 16

Karen Hay
Bright Times Romper, 93
Swirly-Fringed Blanket, 64

Cassandra Hennen
Cozy Sacque for Preemie, 38
Play-Date Dress & Hat, 90

Tammy Hildebrand
Color-Play Sweater & Beanie, 157
Sassy-Style Sweater, 154

Sheila Leslie
Daisy Baby Booties, 30
Flower Child Cardigan, 144
Mary Jane Booties, 34
Rose Baby Booties, 33
Running Shoes, 36

Peggy Longshore
Ruffled Dress-Up Set, 19

Melanie Mays
I'm So Beautiful Jacket, 163

Marti Miller
Surround Him With Stripes, 62

Joyce Nordstrom
Day in the Sun Dress & Bag, 151
Gift from Heaven Christening
Ensemble, 132

Get-Up 'n Go Shirt , 169
Out 'n About Jacket & Purse, 148
Sweet Posies, 59

Bonnie Pierce
Visiting Granny Hat, 28

Nanette Seale
Seaside Cardigan, 118

Darla Sims
Lil' Lamb Cardigan & Hat, 70
Prince Charming, 107

Mary Ann Sipes
Beach Baby Ensemble, 74
Warm & Cuddly, 54

Ann E. Smith
Let's Go Play Romper & Jacket, 97
Pink Marshmallow Hoodie, 166

Debbie Tabor
Lullaby Lamb, 52

Karen Whooley
Soft Shells Layette, 10